Presented to:

_____

By:

_____

On:

_____

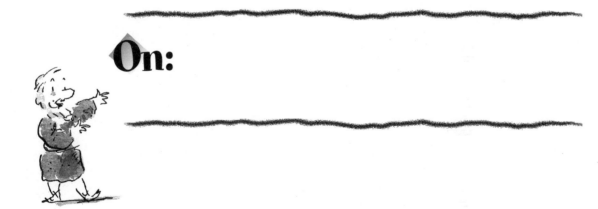

The One-Minute Bible™ for Kids

From the **N**ew **I**nternational **V**ersion of the Bible

Edited by **J**oyce **K**. **E**llis
Illustrated by **S**teve **B**jörkman

GARBORG**S** Inc.
Bloomington, MN 55431

The One-Minute Bible™ for Kids

Contents

A NOTE TO PARENTS:

Do you want your kids to get excited about the Bible?

Then give them bite-size nuggets of Scripture, add some fun illustrations, define words they don't understand, and help them to interact in some way with what they're reading. That's what *The One-Minute Bible™ for Kids* does. In a way, it's teaching them the basic elements of a personal quiet time, which we hope will quickly become a profitable and enjoyable habit.

The Bible is the most amazing book ever written. It is God's personal communication to His creation—us. And He wants young and old alike to be able to read and understand His words. Every day we get thousands of messages from the world around us about how we should live. God wants us to hear every day about living His way.

The 366 daily Scripture readings have been designed so that they can be read by a second- to fifth-grade reader in one minute or less. Each reading has one main focus, which is summed up in the **REMEMBER** statement at the bottom of the page. We look at this as the take-away value—something the kids can remind themselves of throughout the day.

Definitions right on the page allow kids to better understand what they're reading. A glossary in back provides additional help.

The **READ MORE ABOUT IT** references are an expansion of the portion being excerpted or a related Scripture portion that also addresses the focus topic—sometimes from a slightly different angle.

Each day kids can interact with God's Word through one of seven activities—**WRITE ABOUT IT**, **TALK ABOUT IT**, **MEMORIZE IT**, **IMAGINE IT**, **PRAY ABOUT IT**, **TRY IT**, and **DRAW IT**. Your encouragement is important as your children learn how to personalize Scripture in their thoughts, actions, and relationships.

The order of the readings doesn't always follow the order in a complete Bible, but it generally follows a chronological order with breaks for holiday or topical material.

The One-Minute Bible™ for Kids can be used by a child independently, with parents, or as a family devotional tool. But you will undoubtedly want each child to have his or her own copy in order to do the write and draw activities.

Above all, we hope that *The One-Minute Bible™ for Kids* will develop in your kids the life-long habit of reading God's Word every day.

Joyce K. Ellis
August 1993

Hi, Kids!

You're about to start an exciting journey through the greatest book ever written—the Bible. My friend the Raven and I will be your guides through *The One-Minute Bible ™ for Kids*. You can just call me The Prophet.

In the Bible God tells us what He wants us to know about how to live. As you can see, this book isn't a full Bible. But there's a page for every day of the year—even February 29 (for Leap Year)—with a bite-size chunk of God's Word for you to read.

Look for little scrolls or stone tablets on the page for definitions of some words you may not know. You will find other definitions in the glossary in back.

If you can, use a complete Bible to look up the verses given in the **READ MORE ABOUT IT** sections, too.

Then enjoy the **TALK**, **IMAGINE**, **DRAW**, **MEMORIZE**, **PRAY**, **WRITE**, or **TRY** activity for that day. We hope these will help you think about and put into practice what you've learned.

The **REMEMBER** line at the bottom of each page is something you can take with you to think about throughout the day.

Meet the Raven and me here every day and travel with us through the pages of God's Word. We hope *The One-Minute Bible ™ for Kids* will help you get into the habit of reading something from the Bible each day. It's your spiritual food.

May the Bible, God's Word, become your #1 favorite book!

Your friend,
The Prophet

In the beginning God created the heavens and the earth. Now the earth was formless and empty, darkness was over the surface of the deep, and the Spirit of God was hovering over the waters.

And God said, "Let there be light," and there was light. God saw that the light was good, and he separated the light from the darkness. God called the light "day," and the darkness he called "night." And there was evening, and there was morning—the first day. Genesis 1:1-5

READ MORE ABOUT IT: John 1:1-3; Hebrews 11:3

TRY IT!

Have you ever tried to imagine what it was like before God created the world? Go into a closet and close the door. Or wait until it's dark, turn off all the lights, and pull down the shades so you can't see any light. That's what it might have been like before creation. God made the whole world out of nothing. When we believe that God is the great Creator, we know who to thank for all the beautiful things around us.

REMEMBER: The world didn't just happen. God is the great Creator.

Creation—The Second Day

And God said, "Let there be an expanse between the waters to separate water from water." So God made the expanse and separated the water under the expanse from the water above it. And it was so. God called the expanse "sky." And there was evening, and there was morning—the second day.

expanse: wide open space

The heavens declare the glory of God;
　the skies proclaim the work of his hands.
Day after day they pour forth speech;
　night after night they display knowledge.
There is no speech or language
　where their voice is not heard.
Genesis 1:6-8; Psalm 19:1-3

READ MORE ABOUT IT: Psalm 33:1-11

Have you ever seen or heard about a robot that obeys voice commands? Wouldn't it be nice to watch while the robot did your work? What work would you have it do? On the second day of Creation our powerful Creator gave a voice command, and the sky above separated from the waters below. Planet earth was taking shape.

2

REMEMBER: When God says something, it happens.

And God said, "Let the water under the sky be gathered to one place, and let dry ground appear." And it was so. God called the dry ground "land," and the gathered waters he called "seas." And God saw that it was good.

Then God said, "Let the land produce vegetation: seed-bearing plants and trees on the land that bear fruit with seed in it, according to their various kinds." And it was so. The land produced vegetation: plants bearing seed according to their kinds and trees bearing fruit with seed in it according to their kinds. And God saw that it was good. And there was evening, and there was morning—the third day.
Genesis 1:9-13

READ MORE ABOUT IT: Psalm 148

DRAW A FLOWER AT THE TOP OF THIS PLANT.

TRY IT!

Ask your mom or dad if you can cut open an apple, pear, or orange. Look at the seeds inside. Compare them with the whole fruit. Think about the tree the fruit grew on. Isn't it amazing that God can grow such a big tree from such a little seed? All of creation shows us how wonderful God is.

REMEMBER: God planned His creation well.

Creation—The Fourth Day

And God said, "Let there be lights in the expanse of the sky to separate the day from the night, and let them serve as signs to mark seasons and days and years, and let them be lights in the expanse of the sky to give light on the earth." And it was so.

God made two great lights—the greater light to govern the day and the lesser light to govern the night. He also made the stars. God set them in the expanse of the sky to give light on the earth, to govern the day and the night, and to separate light from darkness. And God saw that it was good. And there was evening, and there was morning—the fourth day.
Genesis 1:14-19

READ MORE ABOUT IT: Psalm 104:19-23

PRAY ABOUT IT: Have you ever thanked God for the sun and moon that give us light both day and night? Thank Him today.

REMEMBER: God created an orderly world so we could tell day from day and season from season.

Ａnd God said, "Let the water teem with living creatures, and let birds fly above the earth across the expanse of the sky." So God created the great creatures of the sea and every living and moving thing with which the water teems, according to their kinds, and every winged bird according to its kind. And God saw that it was good. God blessed them and said, "Be fruitful and increase in number and fill the water in the seas, and let the birds increase on the earth." And there was evening, and there was morning—the fifth day. Genesis 1:20-23

READ MORE ABOUT IT: Psalm 104:23-26

Draw the sky full of birds and the sea full of fish.

REMEMBER: God made a great variety of creatures, and everything that God does is good.

5

Creation—The Sixth Day

Then God said, "Let us make man in our image, in our likeness, and let them rule over the fish of the sea and the birds of the air, over the livestock, over all the earth, and over all the creatures that move along the ground."

So God created man in his own image,
in the image of God he created him;
male and female he created them.

God blessed them and said to them, "Be fruitful and increase in number; fill the earth and subdue it. Rule over the fish of the sea and the birds of the air and over every living creature that moves on the ground."

God saw all that he had made, and it was very good. And there was evening, and there was morning—the sixth day.
Genesis 1:26-28, 31

READ MORE ABOUT IT: Psalm 139:13-16

MEMORIZE IT!

> So God created man in his own image, in the image of God he created him; male and female he created them.
> **Genesis 1:27**

REMEMBER: People are like God in some ways. Like God we think and feel and make choices.

Creation Is Finished—The Seventh Day

Thus the heavens and the earth were completed in all their vast array.

By the seventh day God had finished the work he had been doing; so on the seventh day he rested from all his work. And God blessed the seventh day and made it holy, because on it he rested from all the work of creating that he had done.

For in six days the LORD made the heavens and the earth, the sea, and all that is in them, but he rested on the seventh day. Therefore the LORD blessed the Sabbath day and made it holy.

Genesis 2:1-3, Exodus 20:11

READ MORE ABOUT IT: Philippians 1:6, 9-11

When God rests, He is not making any new things. Draw the place where you think God goes when He rests.

REMEMBER: God always finishes what He begins.

7

The First Man on Planet Earth

The LORD God formed the man from the dust of the ground and breathed into his nostrils the breath of life, and the man became a living being.

The LORD God took the man and put him in the Garden of Eden to work it and take care of it. And the LORD God commanded the man, "You are free to eat from any tree in the garden; but you must not eat from the tree of the knowledge of good and evil, for when you eat of it you will surely die."
Genesis 2:7, 15-17

READ MORE ABOUT IT: Job 12:7-10

Adam was the first person to swim in a lake, run through the grass, or climb a tree. He was the only person on earth! Imagine what it might have felt like when Adam took his first breath and looked around at the beautiful world God had created for him to enjoy.

REMEMBER: God has given people a special place in the world.

The LORD God said, "It is not good for the man to be alone. I will make a helper suitable for him."

Now the LORD God had formed out of the ground all the beasts of the field and all the birds of the air. He brought them to the man to see what he would name them; and whatever the man called each living creature, that was its name. So the man gave names to all the livestock, the birds of the air and all the beasts of the field.

But for Adam no suitable helper was found. Genesis 2:18-20

READ MORE ABOUT IT: Genesis 2:8-18

Imagine that God had made an animal that looks like the one above. If God let you name this animal, what would you call it?

REMEMBER: God put Adam in charge of His creation, and He wants us to take care of our world, too.

9

The First Woman on Planet Earth

So the LORD God caused the man to fall into a deep sleep; and while he was sleeping, he took one of the man's ribs and closed up the place with flesh. Then the LORD God made a woman from the rib he had taken out of the man, and he brought her to the man.
The man said,

"This is now bone of my bones
and flesh of my flesh;
she shall be called 'woman,'
for she was taken out of man.""

For this reason a man will leave his father and mother and be united to his wife, and they will become one flesh. Genesis 2:21-24

READ MORE ABOUT IT: Proverbs 31:10-12

WRITE ABOUT IT: Can you think of a reason why the Creator took a bone from Adam's side to make a wife for him? Write one reason here.

_____

_____

10

REMEMBER: God created marriage so that people wouldn't have to be lonely.

Now the serpent was more crafty than any of the wild animals the LORD God had made. He said to the woman, "Did God really say, 'You must not eat from any tree in the garden'?"

The woman said to the serpent, "We may eat fruit from the trees in the garden, but God did say, 'You must not eat fruit from the tree that is in the middle of the garden, and you must not touch it, or you will die.'"

"You will not surely die," the serpent said to the woman. "For God knows that when you eat of it your eyes will be opened, and you will be like God, knowing good and evil."
Genesis 3:1-5

READ MORE ABOUT IT: 1 Corinthians 10:12-13

MEMORIZE IT!

God is faithful; he will not let you be tempted beyond what you can bear. But when you are tempted, he will also provide a way out so that you can stand up under it.
1 Corinthians 10:13b

TRUST ME!

REMEMBER: Ask God to help you be strong when you're tempted to do wrong.

A Terrible Choice

When the woman saw that the fruit of the tree was good for food and pleasing to the eye, and also desirable for gaining wisdom, she took some and ate it. She also gave some to her husband, who was with her, and he ate it. Then the eyes of both of them were opened, and they realized they were naked; so they sewed fig leaves together and made coverings for themselves.

Then the man and his wife heard the sound of the LORD God as he was walking in the garden in the cool of the day, and they hid from the LORD God among the trees of the garden.

Genesis 3:6-8

READ MORE ABOUT IT: 1 John 1:8-10

PRAY ABOUT IT: Sometimes we choose to do the wrong thing. Can you think of something wrong you have done that you haven't asked God to forgive you for? You can ask His forgiveness right now.

REMEMBER: We can't hide from God, but we can ask God to forgive us.

But the LORD God called to the man, "Where are you?" He answered, "I heard you in the garden, and I was afraid because I was naked; so I hid."

And he said, "Who told you that you were naked? Have you eaten from the tree that I commanded you not to eat from?"

The man said, "The woman you put here with me—she gave me some fruit from the tree, and I ate it."

Then the LORD God said to the woman, "What is this you have done?"

The woman said, "The serpent deceived me, and I ate."
Genesis 3:9-13

READ MORE ABOUT IT: Romans 5:12-13, 17

Imagine what this world might be like if no one had ever sinned or blamed others for their wrong choices. No one would lie. No one would hurt anyone else. No one would get in trouble for something he or she didn't do.

REMEMBER: We need to admit when we're wrong and not blame others.

The Serpent Bites the Dust

So the LORD God said to the serpent, "Because you have done this,

"Cursed are you above all the livestock
   and all the wild animals!
You will crawl on your belly
   and you will eat dust
   all the days of your life.
And I will put enmity
   between you and the woman,
   and between your offspring and hers;
he will crush your head,
   and you will strike his heel."   Genesis 3:14-15

enmity: extreme hatred

READ MORE ABOUT IT: Romans 6:12-14, James 4:7

Some people think that at one time the serpent might have been a beautiful creature with legs, and Satan took the form of this beautiful creature to tempt Eve. Then God punished the serpent. From then on it had to crawl on its belly. Draw what you think the serpent might have looked like before God punished it.

REMEMBER: Satan still tempts us today, but we don't have to give in.

14

Bad News for Adam and His Wife

The LORD God said, "Because you listened to your wife and ate from the tree about which I commanded you, 'You must not eat of it,'

"Cursed is the ground because of you;
    through painful toil you will eat of it
    all the days of your life.
It will produce thorns and thistles for you,
    and you will eat the plants of the field.
By the sweat of your brow
    you will eat your food
until you return to the ground,
    since from it you were taken;
for dust you are
    and to dust you
    will return."
Genesis 3:17-19

READ MORE ABOUT IT: Job 34:10-15

REMEMBER: Sin can spoil God's plans for us.

Imagine what it would be like to have a garden without any weeds or to work without sweat. Work is good, and work can be fun. But the painful part of work was God's punishment for sin.

15

Goodbye, Garden of Eden!

Adam named his wife Eve, because she would become the mother of all the living.

The LORD God made garments of skin for Adam and his wife and clothed them. And the LORD God said, "The man has now become like one of us, knowing good and evil. He must not be allowed to reach out his hand and take also from the tree of life and eat, and live forever." So the LORD God banished him from the Garden of Eden to work the ground from which he had been taken. After he drove the man out, he placed on the east side of the Garden of Eden cherubim and a flaming sword flashing back and forth to guard the way to the tree of life.

Genesis 3:20-24

READ MORE ABOUT IT:
Revelation 2:7; 22:1-2

Cherubim are angels. God sometimes sends these special servants into the world to do unusual things for him. The cherubim in today's reading guarded the entrance to the Garden of Eden so Adam and Eve couldn't go back after they sinned. (When we do wrong things, we often lose privileges, too.) Imagine what it would be like to be one of God's cherubim. What special assignment would you like God to give you?

REMEMBER: Even when we do the wrong thing God still loves us and takes care of us.

Adam lay with his wife Eve, and she became pregnant and gave birth to Cain. She said, "With the help of the LORD I have brought forth a man." Later she gave birth to his brother Abel.

Now Abel kept flocks, and Cain worked the soil. In the course of time Cain brought some of the fruits of the soil as an offering to the LORD. But Abel brought fat portions from some of the firstborn of his flock. The LORD looked with favor on Abel and his offering, but on Cain and his offering he did not look with favor. So Cain was very angry, and his face was downcast.
Genesis 4:1-5

READ MORE ABOUT IT: 1 Samuel 15:22-23

WRITE ABOUT IT: Cain and Abel gave gifts to God. Abel's gift pleased God because he did what God asked. Today, what can you give God to show Him you love Him?

_____

_____

REMEMBER: The gift that pleases God most is obedience.

Getting Away with Murder?

Then the Lord said to Cain, "Why are you angry? Why is your face downcast? If you do what is right, will you not be accepted? But if you do not do what is right, sin is crouching at your door; it desires to have you, but you must master it."

Now Cain said to his brother Abel, "Let's go out to the field." And while they were in the field, Cain attacked his brother Abel and killed him.

Then the Lord said to Cain, "Where is your brother Abel?"

"I don't know," he replied. "Am I my brother's keeper?"

The Lord said, "What have you done? Listen! Your brother's blood cries out to me from the ground. Now you are under a curse and driven from the ground, which opened its mouth to receive your brother's blood from your hand. When you work the ground, it will no longer yield its crops for you. You will be a restless wanderer on the earth."

Genesis 4:6-12

READ MORE ABOUT IT: Psalm 33:13-22

TALK ABOUT IT!

Talk about a time you were jealous or angry and did something you were sorry for later. Is it ever okay to be angry? What's the best way to handle your anger?

REMEMBER: God can help us control our anger. Ask Him to help you.

After [Enoch] became the father of Methuselah, Enoch walked with God 300 years and had other sons and daughters. Altogether Enoch lived 365 years. Enoch walked with God; then he was no more, because God took him away.

By faith Enoch was taken from this life, so that he did not experience death; he could not be found, because God had taken him away. For before he was taken, he was commended as one who pleased God. And without faith it is impossible to please God, because anyone who comes to him must believe that he exists and that he rewards those who earnestly seek him.
Genesis 5:22-24; Hebrews 11:5-6

READ MORE ABOUT IT: Hebrews 11:1-3

MEMORIZE IT!

And without faith it is impossible to please God.
Hebrews 11:6a

Methuselah: the oldest man who ever lived. He died at age 969!

REMEMBER: If you want to please God, the first step is to believe in Him.

Trouble on Planet Earth

Noah was a righteous man, blameless among the people of his time, and he walked with God. God saw how corrupt the earth had become, for all the people on earth had corrupted their ways. So God said to Noah, "I am going to put an end to all people, for the earth is filled with violence because of them. I am surely going to destroy both them and the earth. So make yourself an ark of cypress wood; make rooms in it and coat it with pitch inside and out. This is how you are to build it: The ark is to be 450 feet long, 75 feet wide and 45 feet high. Put a door in the side of the ark and make lower, middle, and upper decks."

Noah did everything just as God commanded him. Genesis 6:9b, 12-15, 16b, 22

READ MORE ABOUT IT: Genesis 6:5-10

What if God told Noah to build something instead of a boat to save Noah's family and the animals from the flood? Just for fun, imagine what it might have been and draw a picture of it here.

REMEMBER: When God says something, He expects us to obey. Make wise choices today.

clean animals:
animals that could be eaten and sacrificed.

unclean animals:
animals that could not be eaten or sacrificed.

The LORD then said to Noah, "Go into the ark, you and your whole family, because I have found you righteous in this generation. Take with you seven of every kind of clean animal, a male and its mate, and two of every kind of unclean animal, a male and its mate, and also seven of every kind of bird, male and female, to keep their various kinds alive throughout the earth. Seven days from now I will send rain on the earth for forty days and forty nights, and I will wipe from the face of the earth every living creature I have made."

Pairs of clean and unclean animals, of birds and of all creatures that move along the ground, male and female, came to Noah and entered the ark, as God had commanded Noah. And after the seven days the floodwaters came on the earth.   Genesis 7:1-4; 8-10

READ MORE ABOUT IT: Titus 3:3-7

WRITE ABOUT IT: The ark was about three football fields long, and it was three stories high! Can you imagine something that big filled with all kinds of animals? If you were Noah, which animals would you keep closest to the room you slept in?

REMEMBER: Obey God—even if you feel that you're the only one doing what's right.

Page 1

In the beginning it was dark over the deep sea. Then God spoke and made light. He spoke again and made the sky. Once more God spoke. Water filled the seas, and dry ground appeared. (See January 1.)

Page 2

God filled the sky with all kinds of birds. He filled the seas with living animals—big and small. He filled the land with tame animals, wild animals, and creeping, crawling animals. God looked around at what He had made. Everything was good! (See January 5.)

Page 3

If you could create an animal, what would it look like? Draw it here.

Page 4

The earth was full of birds in the sky and fish in the seas. Then God made a man out of dust. One day He asked the man to be creative—to name all things. The man named the animals that filled the sky and seas and land. (See January 8 and 9.)

Page 5

God made a woman from a rib of the man. One day they both disobeyed God. In the Garden of Eden they tried to hide from God. But He found them. God had to punish sin, but He took care of Adam and Eve's needs. (See January 10-16.)

Pages 6 and 7

Hey kids! Why don't you draw in some fish under the ark?

Page 8

Noah thanked God for saving his family and the animals from the terrible flood. God promised Noah He would never again destroy the whole earth with water. The rainbow is a symbol of that promise. (See January 24-25.)

After Adam and Eve sinned, they hid from God. Do you ever feel like hiding after you do something wrong? What do you think you should do?

The Worst Storm in History

For forty days the flood kept coming on the earth, and as the waters increased they lifted the ark high above the earth. The waters rose and increased greatly on the earth, and the ark floated on the surface of the water. The waters rose and covered the mountains to a depth of more than twenty feet. Every living thing that moved on the earth perished—birds, livestock, wild animals, all the creatures that swarm over the earth, and all mankind. Everything on dry land that had the breath of life in its nostrils died. Every living thing on the face of the earth was wiped out; men and animals and the creatures that move along the ground and the birds of the air were wiped from the earth. Only Noah was left, and those with him in the ark.
Genesis 7:17-18, 20-23

READ MORE ABOUT IT: 2 Peter 3:3-13

MEMORIZE IT!

> For the wages of sin is death, but the gift of God is eternal life in Christ Jesus our Lord.
> **Romans 6:23**

REMEMBER: We, like the people in Noah's time, deserve death for our sin. But we can trust Jesus to save us from our sins like Noah trusted the ark to save him from the flood.

The Earth Dries Up!

By the first day of the first month of Noah's six hundred and first year, the water had dried up from the earth. Noah then removed the covering from the ark and saw that the surface of the ground was dry.

Then God said to Noah, "Come out of the ark, you and your wife and your sons and their wives. Bring out every kind of living creature that is with you...so they can multiply on the earth and be fruitful and increase in number upon it."

So Noah came out, together with his sons and his wife and his sons' wives. All the animals and all the creatures that move along the ground and all the birds—everything that moves on the earth—came out of the ark, one kind after another. Genesis 8:13, 15-19

READ MORE ABOUT IT: Psalm 104:1-9

Imagine being cooped up in an ark for over a year. What's the first thing you would do when you got out? Draw it.

24

REMEMBER: Trust God to help you with your problems.

Then Noah built an altar to the LORD and, taking some of all the clean animals and clean birds, he sacrificed burnt offerings on it. The LORD smelled the pleasing aroma and said in his heart: "Never again will I curse the ground because of man, even though every inclination of his heart is evil from childhood. And never again will I destroy all living creatures, as I have done.

"As long as the earth endures,
seedtime and harvest,
cold and heat,
summer and winter,
day and night
will never cease."
Genesis 8:20-22

READ MORE ABOUT IT: Psalm 118:27-29

PRAY ABOUT IT: Talk to God and thank Him for a problem He has helped you solve, a tough time He has helped you through, or something good He has given you.

REMEMBER: God is pleased when we worship Him.

The Rainbow Promise

Then God blessed Noah and his sons, saying to them, "Be fruitful and increase in number and fill the earth.

"This is the sign of the covenant I am making between me and you and every living creature with you, a covenant for all generations to come: I have set my rainbow in the clouds, and it will be the sign of the covenant between me and the earth. Whenever I bring clouds over the earth and the rainbow appears in the clouds, I will remember my covenant between me and you and all living creatures of every kind. Never again will the waters become a flood to destroy all life."
Genesis 9:1, 12-15

READ MORE ABOUT IT:
Genesis 9:2-1
Hebrews 11:7

TRY IT!

Ask your mom or dad if you can blow soap bubbles outside the house or in the shower. Watch the rainbows that swirl around on the bubbles.

REMEMBER: A rainbow is our reminder that God keeps His promises.

"What's That You Say?"

The nations spread out over the earth after the flood. Now the whole world had one language and a common speech. As men moved eastward, they found a plain in Shinar and settled there. They said to each other, "Come let us build ourselves a city, with a tower that reaches to the heavens, so that we may make a name for ourselves and not be scattered over the face of the whole earth."

But the LORD came down to see the city and the tower that the men had begun building. The LORD said, "...Come, let us go down and confuse their language so they will not understand each other." So the LORD scattered them from there over all the earth, and they stopped building the city. That is why it was called Babel—because there the LORD confused the language of the whole world. From there the LORD scattered them over the face of the whole earth. Genesis 10:32b; 11:1-3a, 4b-6a, 7-9

READ MORE ABOUT IT: Proverbs 16:18-19

REMEMBER: Don't forget who gives you the strength and abilities to do everything you do.

Imagine that you live at this time, and sometimes you get to walk over to the construction site to watch the men build this fantastic new city with its towering skyscraper. Your neighbor is one of the brick layers. Every day, he comes home with stories about how great everything is going. But one day, he comes home and you can't understand a word he's saying. Why did this happen?

27

God Chooses Abraham

The LORD had said to Abraham, "Leave your country, your people and your father's household and go to the land I will show you.

"I will make you into a great nation
    and I will bless you;
I will make your name great,
    and you will be a blessing."

So Abraham left, as the LORD had told him; and Lot went with him.

Abraham traveled through the land as far as the site of the great tree of Moreh at Shechem. At that time the Canaanites were in the land. The LORD appeared to Abraham and said, "To your offspring I will give this land." So he built an altar there to the LORD who had appeared to him. Genesis 12:1-2, 4a, 6-7

READ MORE ABOUT IT: Hebrews 11:8-10

TALK ABOUT IT!

It was not easy for Abraham to leave his father and the country where he had grown up to move to a place he knew nothing about. But Abraham obeyed. Talk about a time when it was not easy for you to obey. Does your mom or dad remember a time like that?

REMEMBER: God is pleased when we obey Him and our parents even if we don't understand why they ask us to do certain things.

After this, the word of the LORD came to Abraham in a vision:

"Do not be afraid, Abraham.
I am your shield,
your very great reward."

But Abraham said, "O Sovereign LORD, what can you give me since I remain childless?"

The LORD took him outside and said, "Look up at the heavens and count the stars—if indeed you can count them." Then he said to him, "So shall your offspring be."

Abraham believed the LORD, and he credited it to him as righteousness.
Genesis 15:1-2a, 5-6

READ MORE ABOUT IT: Romans 4:18-25

TRY IT!

Go outside tonight and see how many stars you can count in the sky.
Can you guess how many people have been in Abraham's family—his children, grandchildren, great-grandchildren, great-great grandchildren, and so on?
Do you think it might be the same number as the stars in the sky?

REMEMBER: We can believe God. When God promises something, He will do it.

The Oldest New Parents in History

Now the LORD was gracious to Sarah as he had said, and the LORD did for Sarah what he had promised. Sarah became pregnant and bore a son to Abraham in his old age, at the very time God had promised him.

Abraham gave the name Isaac to the son Sarah bore him. Abraham was a hundred years old when his son Isaac was born to him. Sarah said, "God has brought me laughter, and everyone who hears about this will laugh with me." And she added, "Who would have said to Abraham that Sarah would nurse children? Yet I have borne him a son in his old age." Genesis 21:1-7

READ MORE ABOUT IT: Hebrews 11:11-12

TALK ABOUT IT!

Abraham and Sarah had to wait a long time, but they never gave up. And God did keep His promise. Finally they had a son—Isaac. Have you ever had to wait a long time for something someone has promised you? Is there something you have prayed for, and it seems that God will never answer?

REMEMBER: God always keeps His promises, but sometimes we must wait.

Some time later God tested Abraham. God said, "Take your son, your only son, Isaac, whom you love, and go to the region of Moriah. Sacrifice him there as a burnt offering on one of the mountains I will tell you about."

Early the next morning Abraham got up and saddled his donkey. He took with him two of his servants and his son Isaac. When he had cut enough wood for the burnt offering, he set out for the place God had told him about. On the third day Abraham looked up and saw the place in the distance. He said to his servants, "Stay here with the donkey while I and the boy go over there. We will worship and then we will come back to you."
Genesis 22:1a, 2-5

READ MORE ABOUT IT: Hebrews 11:17-19

WRITE ABOUT IT: If Abraham was going to sacrifice his son to God, why do you think he told his servants **"We** will worship and then **we** will come back to you"? (Hint: What was God's promise to Abraham?)

_____

_____

REMEMBER: God wants us to obey His Word even if we don't always understand it.

Does Abraham Pass the Test?

When they reached the place God had told him about, Abraham built an altar there and arranged the wood on it. He bound his son Isaac and laid him on the altar, on top of the wood. Then he reached out his hand and took the knife to slay his son. But the angel of the LORD called out to him from heaven, "Abraham! Abraham! Do not lay a hand on the boy," he said. "Do not do anything to him. Now I know that you fear God, because you have not withheld from me your son, your only son."

Abraham looked up and there in a thicket he saw a ram caught by its horns. He went over and took the ram and sacrificed it as a burnt offering instead of his son. So Abraham called that place The LORD Will Provide.
Genesis 22:9-11a, 12-14a

READ MORE ABOUT IT: James 2:21-23

MEMORIZE IT!

To obey is better than sacrifice.
1 Samuel 15:22b

REMEMBER: We can trust God because He wants only what is best for us.

No Baby, Two Babies...

Abraham became the father of Isaac, and Isaac was forty years old when he married Rebekah.

Isaac prayed to the LORD on behalf of his wife, because she was barren. The LORD answered his prayer, and his wife Rebekah became pregnant. The babies jostled each other within her, and she said, "Why is this happening to me?"...

The LORD said to her,

> "Two nations are in your womb,
>   and two peoples from within you will be separated;
> one people will be stronger than the other,
>   and the older will serve the younger."

When the time came for her to give birth, there were twin boys in her womb.
Genesis 25:19b-20a, 21-24

READ MORE ABOUT IT: Psalm 34:15-20

WRITE ABOUT IT: Isaac's prayer wasn't for a fancy house or lots of money or a new whatcha-macallit. He asked God to give his wife something she wanted more than anything in all the world—a baby she could love. Write down something you would like to ask God for today.

REMEMBER: God answers our prayers.

33

A Bad Trade

Once when Jacob was cooking some stew, Esau came in from the open country, famished. He said to Jacob, "Quick, let me have some of that red stew! I'm famished!"...

Jacob replied, "First sell me your birthright."

"Look, I am about to die," Esau said. "What good is the birthright to me?"

But Jacob said, "Swear to me first." So he swore an oath to him, selling his birthright to Jacob.

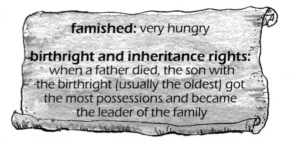

famished: very hungry

birthright and inheritance rights: when a father died, the son with the birthright (usually the oldest) got the most possessions and became the leader of the family

Then Jacob gave Esau some bread and some lentil stew. He ate and drank, and then got up and left.

Esau...for a single meal sold his inheritance rights as the oldest son.
Genesis 25:29-34; Hebrews 12:16b

READ MORE ABOUT IT: Hebrews 12:15-17

TALK ABOUT IT!

Some kids want to be popular so much that they'll do whatever the other kids do—swearing, lying, stealing, even trying drugs. Have you ever wanted something so much that you would do anything to get it? How can you be strong against this temptation?

34

REMEMBER: Never let something you want keep you from doing things God's way.

Dad Always Liked Joseph Best

Joseph, a young man of seventeen, was tending the flocks with his brothers, the sons of Bilhah and the sons of Zilpah, his father's wives, and he brought their father a bad report about them.

Now Jacob loved Joseph more than any of his other sons, because he had been born to him in his old age; and he made a richly ornamented robe for him. When his brothers saw that their father loved him more than any of them, they hated him and could not speak a kind word to him.
Genesis 37:2-4

READ MORE ABOUT IT: Ephesians 4:32

PRAY ABOUT IT: Sometimes, for various reasons, families have trouble getting along. Is there something you need to ask your brother or sister or parent to forgive you for? Do you need to forgive another family member for something? Ask God to help you. Then make it right.

REMEMBER: We can forgive others because God has forgiven us for all our sins.

35

Joseph the Dreamer

Joseph had a dream, and when he told it to his brothers, they hated him all the more. He said to them, "Listen to this dream I had: We were binding sheaves of grain out in the field when suddenly my sheaf rose and stood upright, while your sheaves gathered around mine and bowed down to it."

Then he had another dream, and he told it to his brothers. "Listen," he said, "I had another dream, and this time the sun and moon and eleven stars were bowing down to me."

When he told his father as well as his brothers, his father rebuked him and said, "What is this dream you had? Will your mother and I and your brothers actually come and bow down to the ground before you?" His brothers were jealous of him, but his father kept the matter in mind. Genesis 37:5-7, 9-11

READ MORE ABOUT IT: Genesis 42:1-3, 6-7; 45:1-8

WRITE ABOUT IT: God gave Joseph a special ability with dreams. Write down one or two abilities God has given you.

_____

_____

REMEMBER: God has given you special abilities. Use them to serve God.

Joseph's Brothers Get Rid of Him

Because the patriarchs were jealous of Joseph, they sold him as a slave into Egypt. But God was with him and rescued him from all his troubles. He gave Joseph wisdom and enabled him to gain the goodwill of Pharaoh king of Egypt; so he made him ruler over Egypt and all his palace.

Then a famine struck all Egypt and Canaan, bringing great suffering, and our fathers could not find food. When Jacob heard that there was grain in Egypt, he sent our fathers on their first visit. On their second visit, Joseph told his brothers who he was, and Pharaoh learned about Joseph's family. After this, Joseph sent for his father Jacob and his whole family, seventy-five in all. Then Jacob went down to Egypt. Acts 7:9-15a

READ MORE ABOUT IT: Psalm 46

MEMORIZE IT!

And we know that in all things God works for the good of those who love him, who have been called according to his purpose.
Romans 8:28

I HOPE THERE'S FOOD FOR US HERE IN EGYPT.

REMEMBER: Even in a bad situation, God is with us. He works everything out for our good.

37

Does Joseph Hold a Grudge?

Jacob lived in Egypt seventeen years, and the years of his life were a hundred and forty-seven.

When Joseph's brothers saw that their father was dead, they said, "What if Joseph holds a grudge against us and pays us back for all the wrongs we did to him?" So they sent word to Joseph, saying, "Your father left these instructions before he died: 'This is what you are to say to Joseph: I ask you to forgive your brothers the sins and the wrongs they committed in treating you so badly.' Now please forgive the sins of the servants of the God of your father." When their message came to him, Joseph wept.

Genesis 47:28; 50:15-17

READ MORE ABOUT IT: Matthew 6:9-14

PRAY ABOUT IT: Is there someone you've been holding a grudge against—someone who has done something mean or unkind to you? Thank God for never holding a grudge against you. Then ask Him to help you forgive that person today.

REMEMBER: God has forgiven us for all our sins. He can help us forgive others for the wrong things they have done to us.

God Intended It for Good

His brothers then came and threw themselves down before him. "We are your slaves," they said.

But Joseph said to them, "Don't be afraid. Am I in the place of God? You intended to harm me, but God intended it for good to accomplish what is now being done, the saving of many lives. So then, don't be afraid. I will provide for you and your children."

Joseph stayed in Egypt, along with all his father's family. He lived a hundred and ten years.

Then Joseph said to his brothers, "I am about to die. But God will surely come to your aid and take you up out of this land to the land he promised on oath to Abraham, Isaac and Jacob."
Genesis 50:18-20, 21b-22, 24

READ MORE ABOUT IT: Psalm 34:6-8, 17-19

Joseph was 110 years old when he died. That's old! Draw a picture of someone really old.

REMEMBER: God works everything out for our good. The good may not happen right away, but it will happen someday.

39

The Bible—God's Word

Oh, how I love your law!
I meditate on it all day long.
Your commands make me wiser
than my enemies,
for they are ever with me.

How sweet are your words to my taste,
sweeter than honey to my mouth!
I gain understanding from
your precepts;
therefore I hate every wrong path.
Your word is a lamp to my feet
and a light for my path.

My heart is set on keeping your decrees
to the very end.
The ordinances of the LORD...
are more precious than gold.
By them is your servant warned;
in keeping them there is great reward.
Psalms 119:97-98, 103-105, 112; 19:9b-11

READ MORE ABOUT IT: *Psalm 19*

GOD'S WORD IS LIKE THIS FLASHLIGHT!

TRY IT!

Psalm 119 is the longest chapter in the Bible, and it's all about the Bible. All the verses in that chapter (NIV) except four contain at least one word that refers to God's Word or His law—words such as ways, precepts, and decrees. Can you find which four verses don't have words like that in them?

REMEMBER: Take time to learn something from God's Word every day.

Job—The Greatest Man in the East

In the land of Uz there lived a man whose name was Job. One day the angels came to present themselves before the LORD, and Satan also came with them.

The LORD said to Satan, "Have you considered my servant Job? There is no one like him; he is blameless and upright, a man who fears God and shuns evil."

shun: avoid

"Does Job fear God for nothing?" Satan replied…"You have blessed the work of his hands… But stretch out your hand and strike everything he has, and he will surely curse you to your face."

The LORD said to Satan, "Very well, then, everything he has is in your hands, but on the man himself do not lay a finger."
Job 1:1a, 6, 8-12

READ MORE ABOUT IT: Job 1:1-12

WRITE ABOUT IT: Job was a wealthy man. Read Job 1:1-3 in a full Bible and find out how many sheep he had. Camels? Oxen? Donkeys? If you like to add, find out how many animals he had altogether. How many children did he have?

REMEMBER: Satan could not do anything to test Job without God's permission. God is more powerful than Satan.

41

Job–One Disaster After Another

A messenger came to Job and said, "The oxen were plowing and the donkeys were grazing nearby, and the Sabeans attacked and carried them off."

While he was still speaking, another messenger came and said, "The fire of God fell from the sky and burned up the sheep and the servants."

While he was still speaking, another messenger came and said, "The Chaldeans...swept down on your camels and carried them off."

While he was still speaking, yet another messenger came and said, "Your sons and daughters were feasting and drinking wine at the oldest brother's house, when suddenly a mighty wind swept in from the desert and struck the four corners of the house. It collapsed on them and they are dead!"

At this, Job...fell to the ground in worship and said:

"The LORD gave and the LORD has
taken away;
may the name of the LORD
be praised."
Job 1:14-15a, 16a, 17a, 18-19a, 21

READ MORE ABOUT IT: Psalm 18:30-32

Imagine that you are the first of the servants who came in to deliver bad news to Job. How would you feel as you hear the news get worse and worse? Do you think you would be surprised at Job's reaction to all this bad news?

REMEMBER: God knows what He's doing. We can trust Him to work out everything for our good.

Job–Can It Get Any Worse?

Then the Lord said to Satan, "Have you considered my servant Job? There is no one on earth like him; he is blameless and upright, a man who fears God and shuns evil."

"Skin for skin!" Satan replied. "A man will give all he has for his own life. But stretch out your hand and strike his flesh and bones, and he will surely curse you to your face."

The Lord said to Satan, "Very well, then, he is in your hands; but you must spare his life."

So Satan went out from the presence of the Lord and afflicted Job with painful sores from the soles of his feet to the top of his head. Then Job took a piece of broken pottery and scraped himself with it as he sat among the ashes.

His wife said to him, "Are you still holding on to your integrity? Curse God and die!"

He replied, "...Shall we accept good from God, and not trouble?" Job 2:3a, 4-10a

READ MORE ABOUT IT: James 5:11

integrity: determination to do what's right

TALK ABOUT IT!

How would you feel if almost everything you owned was taken away, including your family? Do you think you would wonder if God still cared about you? Ask your parents if they have ever felt that way. Look up today's READ MORE ABOUT IT verse. What does this verse tell us about God?

REMEMBER: We may not know why bad things happen to us, but we can trust God through the good and bad.

Job Just Keeps Trusting

FEBRUARY 12

Have pity on me, my friends, have pity,
for the hand of God has struck me.
Oh, that my words were recorded,
that they were written on a scroll,
that they were inscribed with an iron tool on lead,
or engraved in rock forever!
I know that my Redeemer lives,
and that in the end he will stand upon the earth.
And after my skin has been destroyed,
yet in my flesh I will see God;
I myself will see him
with my own eyes—I, and not another.
How my heart yearns within me!
Job 19:21, 23-27

READ MORE ABOUT IT: Proverbs 3:5-6

MEMORIZE IT!

I know that my Redeemer lives, and that in the end he will stand upon the earth.
Job 19:25

How my heart yearns: I can't wait!

Redeemer: the Lord who saves us

REMEMBER: Don't give up on God. He'll never give up on you.

Then Job replied to the LORD: "I know that you can do all things; no plan of yours can be thwarted."

thwarted: stopped

The LORD made [Job] prosperous again and gave him twice as much as he had before. All his brothers and sisters and everyone who had known him before came and ate with him in his house. They comforted and consoled him over all the trouble the LORD had brought upon him, and each one gave him a piece of silver and a gold ring.

The LORD blessed the latter part of Job's life more than the first. He had fourteen thousand sheep, six thousand camels, a thousand yoke of oxen and a thousand donkeys. And he also had seven sons and three daughters. Job 42:1-2, 12-13

READ MORE ABOUT IT: Job 42:10

WOW! LOTS OF STUFF!

PRAY ABOUT IT:

Ask God to help you trust Him today, no matter what happens—good or bad. If there's something you're worried about, tell God, and let Him work it out.

REMEMBER: Even if we don't get back double what we've lost, as Job did, God will reward us for trusting Him.

What Is Real Love?

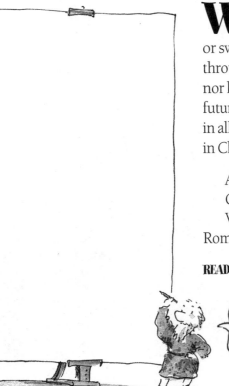

Who shall separate us from the love of Christ? Shall trouble or hardship or persecution or famine or nakedness or danger or sword? No, in all these things we are more than conquerors through him who loved us. For I am convinced that neither death nor life, neither angels nor demons, neither the present nor the future, nor any powers, neither height nor depth, nor anything else in all creation, will be able to separate us from the love of God that is in Christ Jesus our Lord.

And so we know and rely on the love God has for us.
God is love. Whoever lives in love lives in God, and God in him.
We love because he first loved us.
Romans 8:35, 37-39; 1 John 4:16, 19

READ MORE ABOUT IT: Ephesians 3:14-19

Imagine yourself connected with God's love. Draw a picture of the strongest connection you can think of. Perhaps it is a rope, a chain, a bridge, or a steel ladder.

REMEMBER: God loved us enough to send His Son to earth to die for us. His love will never, never let us go.

If I speak in the tongues of men and of angels, but have not love, I am only a resounding gong or a clanging cymbal. If I have the gift of prophecy and can fathom all mysteries and all knowledge, and if I have a faith that can move mountains, but have not love, I am nothing. If I give all I possess to the poor and surrender my body to the flames, but have not love, I gain nothing.

Love is patient, love is kind. It does not envy, it does not boast, it is not proud. It is not rude, it is not self-seeking, it is not easily angered, it keeps no record of wrongs. Love does not delight in evil but rejoices with the truth. It always protects, always trusts, always hopes, always perseveres.

Love never fails.

And now these three remain: faith, hope and love. But the greatest of these is love.
1 Corinthians 13:1-8a, 13

READ MORE ABOUT IT: John 15:12-13

REMEMBER: Love is doing what is best for another person.

MEMORIZE IT!

> We love because he first loved us. And he has given us this command: Whoever loves God must love his brother.
> **1 John 4:19, 21**

HOW DOES IT SOUND?

WITHOUT LOVE IT'S ALL JUST A LOT OF NOISE!

Blessings–For the Poor in Spirit

FEBRUARY 16

[Jesus'] disciples came to him, and he began to teach them, saying: "Blessed are the poor in spirit, for theirs is the kingdom of heaven."

My brothers, as believers in our glorious Lord Jesus Christ, don't show favoritism. Suppose a man comes into your meeting wearing a gold ring and fine clothes, and a poor man in shabby clothes also comes in. If you show special attention to the man wearing fine clothes and say, "Here's a good seat for you," but say to the poor man, "You stand there" or "Sit on the floor by my feet," have you not discriminated among yourselves...?

Listen, my dear brothers: Has not God chosen those who are poor in the eyes of the world to be rich in faith and to inherit the kingdom he promised those who love him?
Matthew 5:1-3; James 2:1-5

WRITE ABOUT IT: Make a list of everything you own that you got all by yourself and everything you can do without God's help. Can't think of anything? Good. Write the word nothing.

READ MORE ABOUT IT:
1 Chronicles 29:11-14

48

REMEMBER: All that we are and have is from God.

"Blessed are those who mourn,
for they will be comforted,"
[Jesus said.]

The Spirit of the Sovereign LORD is on me,
    because the LORD has anointed me
    to preach good news to the poor...
to comfort all who mourn,
    and provide for those who grieve in Zion—
to bestow on them a crown of beauty
    instead of ashes,
the oil of gladness
    instead of mourning,
and a garment of praise
    instead of a spirit of despair.
Matthew 5:4; Isaiah 61:1-3a

READ MORE ABOUT IT: Romans 12:15

MEMORIZE IT!

Praise be to the God and Father of our Lord Jesus Christ, the Father of compassion and the God of all comfort, who comforts us in all our troubles, so that we can comfort those in any trouble with the comfort we ourselves have received from God.
2 Corinthians 1:3-4

REMEMBER: God wants us to comfort those around us who are sad or in trouble.

49

Blessings—For the Meek

FEBRUARY **18**

"**B**lessed are the meek,
for they will inherit the earth,"
[Jesus said.]

Do not fret because of evil men
or be envious of those who
do wrong;
for like the grass they will soon wither,
like green plants they will soon
die away.

Trust in the LORD and do good;
dwell in the land and enjoy
safe pasture.

Delight yourself in the LORD
and he will give you the desires of
your heart.

A little while, and the wicked will
be no more;
though you look for them,
they will not be found.
But the meek will inherit the land
and enjoy great peace.
Matthew 5:5; Psalm 37:1-4, 10-11

READ MORE ABOUT IT: Zephaniah 3:12-13

TRY IT!

Did you ever notice that when you lose your temper, you seldom get what you want? Next time you become angry, try slowly counting to ten out loud before you say anything else. While you're counting, ask God to help you think of a way to work out your problem or disagreement.

REMEMBER: The meek are not weak. They trust God to help them control their emotions.

Blessings—For Those Hungry for Righteousness

"**B**lessed are those who hunger and thirst for righteousness, for they will be filled," [Jesus said.]

Jesus answered, "Everyone who drinks this water will be thirsty again, but whoever drinks the water I give him will never thirst. Indeed, the water I give him will become in him a spring of water welling up to eternal life."

Then Jesus declared, "I am the bread of life. He who comes to me will never go hungry, and he who believes in me will never be thirsty."
Matthew 5:6; John 4:13-14; 6:35

READ MORE ABOUT IT:
John 7:37-38

IT'S LIVING WATER!

Imagine yourself shipwrecked alone on a deserted island. The temperature is 110 degrees. You have been unconscious for several days. When you wake up, you discover that your legs are injured. You can't walk. You are extremely hungry and thirsty, but you don't know where to find food or water. What would you be willing to do to get some food and water? Do you think you would be easily sidetracked? In the same way, God wants us to be willing to do anything to stay close to Him.

REMEMBER: Look to God, not earthly things, to satisfy you.

51

Blessings—For the Merciful

"Blessed are the merciful,
for they will be shown mercy,"
[Jesus said.]

For I desire mercy, not sacrifice,
and acknowledgment of God
rather than burnt offerings.

He has showed you, O man, what
is good.
And what does the LORD require
of you?
To act justly and to love mercy
and to walk humbly with your
God.

Speak and act as those who are going to
be judged by the law that gives freedom,
because judgment without mercy will
be shown to anyone who has not been
merciful. Mercy triumphs over
judgment!
Matthew 5:7; Hosea 6:6; Micah 6:8;
James 2:12-13

READ MORE ABOUT IT: Luke 6:35-36

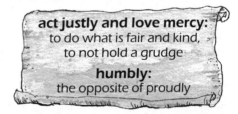

act justly and love mercy:
to do what is fair and kind,
to not hold a grudge

humbly:
the opposite of proudly

TALK ABOUT IT!

Do you know someone that everybody picks on? Maybe it's someone you don't like very
much. How do you think that person feels? Would you like to be in that person's shoes?
How would Jesus treat that person? What will your plan of action be to show kindness
and mercy to that person today?

REMEMBER: God is merciful to us and He wants us to be merciful to others.

"**B**lessed are the pure in heart,
for they will see God,"
[Jesus said.]

Who may ascend the hill of the LORD?
Who may stand in his holy place?
He who has clean hands and a pure heart,
who does not lift up his soul to an idol
or swear by what is false.
He will receive blessing from the LORD.

Create in me a pure heart, O God,
and renew a steadfast spirit within me.

Flee the evil desires of youth, and pursue righteousness, faith, love and peace, along with those who call on the Lord out of a pure heart.
Matthew 5:8; Psalm 24:3-5a; 51:10;
2 Timothy 2:22

READ MORE ABOUT IT: Psalm 139:23-24

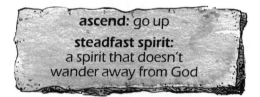

ascend: go up

steadfast spirit:
a spirit that doesn't
wander away from God

TRY IT!

Take a pure white piece of paper with no writing or marks on it. Make a small pencil mark on the paper. Now can you say you have a pure white piece of paper? Of course not. In the same way, even what we call "little sins" can make our lives impure. We need to say no to temptation. But when we do slip up, we can confess our sins right away and keep our lives pure for God.

REMEMBER: There are no "little sins." Confess every sin as soon as you are aware of it.

Blessings—For Peacemakers

"Blessed are the peacemakers,
    for they will be called sons of
    God," [Jesus said.]

Come, my children, listen to me;
    I will teach you the fear of the LORD.
Whoever of you loves life
    and desires to see many good days,
keep your tongue from evil
    and your lips from speaking lies.
Turn from evil and do good;
    seek peace and pursue it.

Consider the blameless,
    observe the upright;
    there is a future for the man of peace.
But all sinners will be destroyed;
    the future of the wicked will be cut off.

If it is possible, as far as it depends on you,
live at peace with everyone.
Matthew 5:9; Psalms 34:11-14; 37:37-38;
Romans 12:18

READ MORE ABOUT IT: Hebrews 12:14;
                          James 3:17-18

I'M MAD AT YOU!

WRITE ABOUT IT: If you find yourself in an argument or fight—regardless of who started it—what can you do to stop it? List two actions you can take that would please God by ending the fight. Remind yourself of these ideas once in a while.

_____

_____

REMEMBER: It takes two to fight. Be the one who chooses not to fight.

Blessings—For Those Who Suffer for Doing Good

"Blessed are those who are persecuted because of righteousness,
> for theirs is the kingdom of heaven," [Jesus said.]

Blessed are you when people insult you, persecute you and falsely say all kinds of evil against you because of me. Rejoice and be glad, because great is your reward in heaven, for in the same way they persecuted the prophets who were before you.

But the LORD is with me like a mighty warrior;
> so my persecutors will stumble and not prevail.

They will fail and be thoroughly disgraced;
> their dishonor will never be forgotten.

For Christ's sake, I delight in weaknesses, in insults, in hardships, in persecutions, in difficulties. For when I am weak, then I am strong.
Matthew 5:10-12; Jeremiah 20:11;
2 Corinthians 12:10

READ MORE ABOUT IT: Matthew 5:43-46

PRAY ABOUT IT: Does anyone make fun of you because you read the Bible, go to church, or believe in God? Take a moment today to pray for that person. That's what Jesus tells us to do. Ask God to help that person come to believe in Him. Pray, too, for Christians in some countries who face torture, prison, or death for their faith.

REMEMBER: Others may treat us badly for living God's way, but He will reward us.

The Israelites Become Slaves

generation: people about the same age. Your parents belong to a different generation than you do.

shrewdly: cleverly

oppress: treat cruelly

Now Joseph and all his brothers and all that generation died, but the Israelites were fruitful and multiplied greatly and became exceedingly numerous, so that the land was filled with them.

Then a new king, who did not know about Joseph, came to power in Egypt. "Look," he said to his people, "the Israelites have become much too numerous for us. Come, we must deal shrewdly with them or they will become even more numerous and, if war breaks out, will join our enemies, fight against us and leave the country."

So they put slave masters over them to oppress them with forced labor. But the more they were oppressed, the more they multiplied and spread; so the Egyptians came to dread the Israelites and worked them ruthlessly.

Exodus 1:6-11a, 12-13

READ MORE ABOUT IT: Psalm 9:7-10

TALK ABOUT IT!

Have you ever been threatened by a bully? Or has anyone ever been mean to you for no reason? How did you handle it? Did you ask God for help? What can you do if that happens again?

REMEMBER: Things are not always easy for God's children. But God helps us do what we must do.

Throw a Baby in the River?

Then Pharaoh gave this order to all his people:
"Every boy that is born you must throw into the Nile,
but let every girl live."

Now a man of the house of Levi married a Levite
woman, and she became pregnant and gave birth to a
son. When she saw that he was a fine child, she hid him
for three months. But when she could hide him no
longer, she got a papyrus basket for him and coated it
with tar and pitch. Then she placed the child in it and put
it among the reeds along the bank of the Nile. His sister
stood at a distance to see what would happen to him.
Exodus 1:22; 2:1-4

READ MORE ABOUT IT: Hebrews 11:23

Draw some of the dangers baby Moses faced
as he floated in the river in his tiny basket boat.

REMEMBER: God loves us, and we can trust Him to care for
those we love even if everything seems hopeless.

57

A Princess for a Stepmother

Then Pharaoh's daughter went down to the Nile to bathe, and her attendants were walking along the river bank. She saw the basket among the reeds and sent her slave girl to get it. She opened it and saw the baby. He was crying, and she felt sorry for him. "This is one of the Hebrew babies," she said.

Then his sister asked Pharaoh's daughter, "Shall I go and get one of the Hebrew women to nurse the baby for you?"

"Yes, go," she answered. And the girl went and got the baby's mother. Pharaoh's daughter said to her, "Take this baby and nurse him for me, and I will pay you." So the woman took the baby and nursed him. When the child grew older, she took him to Pharaoh's daughter and he became her son. She named him Moses, saying, "I drew him out of the water."
Exodus 2:5-10

READ MORE ABOUT IT: Hebrews 11:24-26

TRY IT!

Sometimes brothers and sisters don't get along very well. But Miriam watched over her baby brother to make sure nothing bad happened to him. Think of something kind you could do today for your brother, sister, mom, or dad—for no reason. Make it a surprise if you can, but do it.

58

REMEMBER: Love is kind.

One day, after Moses had grown up, he went out to where his own people were and watched them at their hard labor. He saw an Egyptian beating a Hebrew, one of his own people. Glancing this way and that and seeing no one, he killed the Egyptian and hid him in the sand. The next day he went out and saw two Hebrews fighting. He asked the one in the wrong, "Why are you hitting your fellow Hebrew?"

The man said, "Who made you ruler and judge over us? Are you thinking of killing me as you killed the Egyptian?" Then Moses was afraid and thought, "What I did must have become known."

When Pharaoh heard of this, he tried to kill Moses, but Moses fled from Pharaoh and went to live in Midian.

Exodus 2:11-15a

READ MORE ABOUT IT: Acts 7:23-29

TALK ABOUT IT!

Have you ever messed up when you were trying to do something good? What happened? Did you feel as if you didn't want to try to do anything like that again? What is the best way to get over that feeling? Can God help you forget about it and move on?

REMEMBER: Even if we think we are doing something right, we must be sure we're doing it God's way and in God's time.

God Cares About His People

During that long period, the king of Egypt died.
The Israelites groaned in their slavery and cried out,
and their cry for help because of their slavery went up to God.
God heard their groaning and he remembered his covenant
with Abraham, with Isaac and with Jacob. So God
looked on the Israelites and was concerned
about them.

The LORD provided redemption for his people;
he ordained his covenant forever—
holy and awesome is his name.
Exodus 2:23-25; Psalm 111:9

READ MORE ABOUT IT: 1 Kings 8:23

Imagine you are one
of the Israelites—a slave in Egypt making
bricks for buildings in some of Egypt's
greatest cities. The slave masters probably
made you work long days and whipped
you if you didn't make enough bricks each
day. You would be tired and sweaty and
sore. And imagine how scared you would
be. Wouldn't you wonder when God was
going to come to your rescue?
It must have taken a lot of faith to keep
believing in God.

REMEMBER: Sometimes we need to learn to wait for what God has promised.

Now Moses was tending the flock of Jethro his father-in-law, the priest of Midian, and he led the flock to the far side of the desert and came to Horeb, the mountain of God. There the angel of the LORD appeared to him in flames of fire from within a bush. Moses saw that though the bush was on fire it did not burn up. So Moses thought, "I will go over and see this strange sight—why the bush does not burn up."

When the LORD saw that he had gone over to look, God called to him from within the bush, "Moses! Moses!"

"Do not come any closer," God said. "Take off your sandals, for the place where you are standing is holy ground." Then he said, "I am the God of your father, the God of Abraham, the God of Isaac and the God of Jacob." At this, Moses hid his face, because he was afraid to look at God. Exodus 3:1-4a, 5-6

READ MORE ABOUT IT: Hebrews 12:28-29

Draw what the bush may have looked like as it was burning but not burning up.

REMEMBER: God is our friend, but He is also a holy, perfect God.

God's Rescue Plan

MARCH 1

The LORD said, "I have indeed seen the misery of my people in Egypt. I have heard them crying out because of their slave drivers, and I am concerned about their suffering. So I have come down to rescue them from the hand of the Egyptians and to bring them up out of that land into a good and spacious land, a land flowing with milk and honey.... And now the cry of the Israelites has reached me, and I have seen the way the Egyptians are oppressing them. So now, go. I am sending you to Pharaoh to bring my people the Israelites out of Egypt."
Exodus 3:7-10

READ MORE ABOUT IT: Isaiah 6:8; John 12:26

WRITE ABOUT IT: God chose Moses to lead the Israelites out of Egypt—to take them away from the land where they had suffered so much as slaves. God gives each of us interests and abilities that help us in our life's work. Think about the things you are interested in and write down what you would like to do when you get older.

_____

_____

REMEMBER: God will use you to help others if you'll let Him.

But Moses said to God, "Who am I, that I should go to Pharaoh and bring the Israelites out of Egypt?"

And God said, "I will be with you."

Moses said to God, "Suppose I go to the Israelites and say to them, 'The God of your fathers has sent me to you,' and they ask me, 'What is his name?' Then what shall I tell them?"

God said to Moses, "I AM WHO I AM. This is what you are to say to the Israelites: 'I AM has sent me to you.'"

God also said to Moses, "Say to the Israelites, 'The LORD, the God of your fathers—the God of Abraham, the God of Isaac and the God of Jacob—has sent me to you.' This is my name forever, the name by which I am to be remembered from generation to generation."

Exodus 3:11-12a, 13-15

READ MORE ABOUT IT: Isaiah 41:10

MEMORIZE IT!

I can do everything through him who gives me strength.
Philippians 4:13

IT'S AWESOME TO HAVE THE GOD OF THE UNIVERSE PROMISE TO BE WITH YOU!

REMEMBER: With God's help you can do anything He wants you to do.

The God with Many Names—The LORD

MARCH 3

The LORD is a refuge for the oppressed, a stronghold in times of trouble. Those who know your name will trust in you, for you, LORD, have never forsaken those who seek you.

The name of the LORD is a strong tower; the righteous run to it and are safe.

No one is like you, O LORD; you are great, and your name is mighty in power.

You shall not misuse the name of the LORD your God, for the LORD will not hold anyone guiltless who misuses his name. Psalm 9:9-10; Proverbs 18:10; Jeremiah 10:6; Exodus 20:7

READ MORE ABOUT IT: Psalm 113:2-3

TALK ABOUT IT!

Does it bother you when you hear swearing on television or when people around you are swearing? Do you ever find yourself thinking swear words because you hear them so often? How do you handle it? What could you do if you are with someone and they swear, using God's name?

REMEMBER: Although those around us may swear, we must always be careful to talk respectfully when using the Lord's name.

The God with Many Names—The Almighty

So listen to me, you men of understanding.
Far be it from God to do evil,
 from the Almighty to do wrong.
He repays a man for what he has done;
 he brings upon him what his
 conduct deserves.
It is unthinkable that God would do wrong.

He who dwells in the shelter of the Most High
 will rest in the shadow of the Almighty.
 I will say of the LORD, "He is my refuge
 and my fortress,

my God, in whom I trust."
Surely he will save you from the...
 deadly pestilence.
He will cover you with his feathers,
 and under his wings you will find
 refuge;
 his faithfulness will be your shield.
Job 34:10-12a; Psalm 91:1-4b

READ MORE ABOUT IT: Revelation 1:8

PRAY ABOUT IT: Talk to God today and thank Him for being so holy that He can never do anything wrong, so powerful that He can never be beaten, and so just that He can never be unfair.

REMEMBER: We are safe in God's hands. No one is more powerful than God.

65

The God with Many Names—Lord God Almighty

MARCH 5

And I saw what looked like a sea of glass mixed with fire and, standing beside the sea, those who had been victorious over the beast and his image and over the number of his name. They held harps given them by God and sang the song of Moses the servant of God and the song of the Lamb:

"Great and marvelous are your deeds,
Lord God Almighty.
Just and true are your ways,
King of the ages.

Who will not fear you, O LORD,
and bring glory to your name?
For you alone are holy.
All nations will come
and worship before you,
for your righteous acts have
been revealed."
Revelation 15:2-4

READ MORE ABOUT IT: Psalm 89:5-8

TRY IT!

God has done so many fantastic things! He created all the beautiful things around us. He watches over His people constantly. He offers salvation to all who believe Jesus died on the cross to save them from their sins. Tell someone today about how Jesus can save us from our sins if we believe in Him.

REMEMBER: Someday people from every nation on earth will worship the God of the Bible.

The God with Many Names—The LORD of Lords

For the LORD your God is God of gods and LORD of Lords, the great God, mighty and awesome, who shows no partiality and accepts no bribes. He defends the cause of the fatherless and the widow, and loves the alien, giving him food and clothing.

O LORD, our LORD,
how majestic is your name in all the earth!

LORD, you have been our dwelling place
throughout all generations.
Before the mountains were born
or you brought forth the earth and the world,
from everlasting to everlasting you are God.
Deuteronomy 10:17-18; Psalms 8:9; 90:1-2

READ MORE ABOUT IT: 1 Timothy 6:15b-16

MEMORIZE IT!

That if you confess with your mouth, "Jesus is Lord," and believe in your heart that God raised him from the dead, you will be saved.
Romans 10:9

alien:
someone from
a different country

REMEMBER: God is Lord and Master over everything and everyone. We take our orders from Him.

The God with Many Names—The Most High

My shield is God Most High,
who saves the upright in heart.

God is our refuge and strength,
an ever-present help in trouble.
Therefore we will not fear, though the earth give way
and the mountains fall into the heart of the sea,
though its waters roar and foam
and the mountains quake with their surging.

Clap your hands, all you nations;
shout to God with cries of joy.
How awesome is the LORD Most High,
the great King over all the earth!
Psalms 7:10; 46:1-3; 47:1-2

READ MORE ABOUT IT: Psalms 9:1-2; 21:1-2, 7

Draw a picture of the highest thing you've ever seen (such as a building, mountain, waterfall, hot air balloon, or whatever else you can think of). When the Bible calls God the Most High, it doesn't mean He's taller than all these things, it means no one is greater than God. It means no one gives Him orders because He's at the top.

68

REMEMBER: There is no one stronger or greater than our God.

Remember your Creator
in the days of your youth,
before the days of trouble come
and the years approach when you
will say,
"I find no pleasure in them."

Do you not know?
Have you not heard?
The LORD is the everlasting God,
the Creator of the ends of the earth.
He will not grow tired or weary,
and his understanding no one
can fathom.

I am the LORD, your Holy One,
Israel's Creator, your King.
Ecclesiastes 12:1; Isaiah 40:28; 43:15

READ MORE ABOUT IT: Psalm 8

PRAY ABOUT IT: Thank God for creating you and for creating a beautiful world for you to enjoy. Name specific things that you particularly like—horses? daisies? lakes? other planets? rocks with quartz in them?

REMEMBER: God is our Creator. He doesn't want us to get too busy to think about Him and follow His ways.

The God with Many Names—The Holy One

MARCH 9

Yet you are enthroned as the Holy One;
you are the praise of Israel.
In you our fathers put their trust;
they trusted and you delivered them.
They cried to you and were saved;
in you they trusted and were not
disappointed.

The fear of the LORD is the beginning
of wisdom,
and knowledge of the Holy One
is understanding.

For through me your days will be many,
and years will be added to your life.

Our Redeemer...is the Holy One of Israel.
Psalm 22:3-5; Proverbs 9:10-11;
Isaiah. 47:4

READ MORE ABOUT IT: Psalm 71:22

WRITE ABOUT IT: We can become wise by letting our Holy God become our teacher. Write down two ways we can learn about and from Him.

_____

_____

REMEMBER: True wisdom comes from God, the Holy One, who never makes mistakes.

For the LORD is our judge,
the LORD is our lawgiver,
the LORD is our king;
it is he who will save us.

The Spirit of the LORD will rest on him—
the Spirit of wisdom and of understanding,
the Spirit of counsel and of power,
the Spirit of knowledge and of the fear of the LORD—
and he will delight in the fear of the LORD.

He will not judge by what he sees with his eyes,
or decide by what he hears with his ears;
but with righteousness he will judge the needy,
with justice he will give decisions
for the poor of the earth.
Isaiah 33:22; 11:2-5

READ MORE ABOUT IT: Psalms 58:11; 96:13

GOD'S ALWAYS FAIR!

Imagine that today you were elected as a judge, and you had to begin trying court cases right away. In your first case two men told completely different stories about a crime. There were no eyewitnesses and no other evidence. Whose story would you believe? God is so wise that He always knows who is telling the truth, and He never makes a wrong judgment. Isn't that incredible!

REMEMBER: God will make everything right in the end.

71

The God with Many Names–King

The LORD sits enthroned over the flood;
the LORD is enthroned as King forever.
The LORD gives strength to his people;
the LORD blesses his people with peace.

I am the LORD, your Holy One,
Israel's Creator, your King.

I saw heaven standing open and there before me was a white horse, whose rider is called Faithful and True. With justice he judges and makes war. On his robe and on his thigh he has this name written:
KING OF KINGS AND LORD OF LORDS.
Psalm 29:10-11; Isaiah 43:15; Revelation 19:11, 16

READ MORE ABOUT IT: Psalm 47

TALK ABOUT IT!

God is King of the whole universe, so He could make everyone do only what's right. Why do you think He doesn't? (Hint: What would happen to our choices?)

REMEMBER: God is the great King of the universe. Shouldn't we do what He asks?

72

The God with Many Names–The Mighty One

The Mighty One, God, the LORD,
　speaks and summons the earth
　　from the rising of the sun to the place
　　　where it sets.
Call upon me in the day of trouble;
　I will deliver you, and you will
　　honor me.

Who is this King of glory?
　The LORD strong and mighty,
　the LORD mighty in battle.

I, the LORD, am your Savior,
　your Redeemer, the Mighty One
　　of Jacob.

O great and powerful God,...great are
your purposes and mighty are your
deeds.
Psalm 50:1, 15; Psalm 24:8; Isaiah 49:26c;
Jeremiah 32:18b-19a

READ MORE ABOUT IT: Psalm 132:1-5

WRITE ABOUT IT: Write down the biggest problem you've struggled with lately. Is God strong enough to help you with that problem? Write down what you would like the Lord to do to help you. But don't forget, He doesn't always work the way we expect.

_____

_____

REMEMBER: There is nothing that God cannot do.

73

The God with Many Names—Redeemer

I know that my Redeemer lives,
  and that in the end he will stand upon the earth.
And after my skin has been destroyed,
  yet in my flesh I will see God;
I myself will see him
  with my own eyes—I and not another.
  How my heart yearns within me!

May the words of my mouth and the meditation
  of my heart be pleasing in your sight,
  O LORD, my Rock and my Redeemer.

This is what the LORD says—
  Israel's King and Redeemer,
    the LORD Almighty:
I am the first and I am the last;
  apart from me there is no God.
Job 19:25-27; Psalm 19:14; Isaiah 44:6

READ MORE ABOUT IT: Jeremiah 50:34

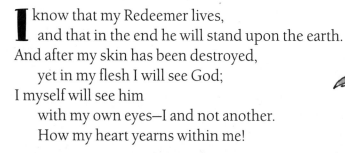

Imagine designing an award-winning kite and spending many hours putting it together. You enjoy watching it follow you high above in the sky as you run through a big field. But one day someone steals your kite. You think you'll never see it again. Weeks later you notice your kite in a second-hand store. Imagine how excited you would be! It's very expensive, but you pay the price and take the kite home. Your kite would be even more special now, wouldn't it?

REMEMBER: It cost God a lot—His very own Son—to buy us back from our sinfulness. We are precious to Him.

The God with Many Names–Refuge

God is our refuge and strength,
an ever-present help in trouble.
Therefore we will not fear, though the earth give way
and the mountains fall into the heart of the sea,
though its waters roar and foam
and the mountains quake with their surging.

"Be still, and know that I am God;
I will be exalted among the nations,
I will be exalted in the earth."

The LORD Almighty is with us;
the God of Jacob is our fortress.
Psalm 46:1-3, 10-11

READ MORE ABOUT IT: Psalm 9:9-10; Jeremiah 16:19-20

Draw a mighty fort or a safe castle.

REMEMBER: God is there whenever we need Him, and He will keep us safe forever.

75

The God with Many Names—Rock

I will proclaim the name of the LORD.
Oh, praise the greatness of our God!
He is the Rock, his works are perfect,
and all his ways are just.
A faithful God who does no wrong,
upright and just is he.

There is no one holy like the LORD;
there is no one besides you;
there is no Rock like our God.

I love you, O LORD, my strength.

The LORD is my rock, my fortress and
my deliverer;
my God is my rock, in whom
I take refuge.
I call to the LORD, who is worthy of praise,
and I am saved from my enemies.
Deuteronomy 32:3-4; 1 Samuel 2:2;
Psalms 18:1-3

READ MORE ABOUT IT: 2 Samuel 22:32-34;
Psalm 62:5-8

PRAY ABOUT IT: Talk to God and thank Him for being a solid rock that you can count on to be there all the time. Ask Him to help you remember to come to Him whenever you're scared or need help of any kind.

REMEMBER: God is strong, and He keeps us safe.

"You are my witnesses," declares the LORD,
"and my servant whom I have chosen,
so that you may know and believe me
and understand that I am he.
Before me no god was formed,
nor will there be one after me.
I, even I, am the LORD,
and apart from me there is no savior.
I have revealed and saved and proclaimed—
I, and not some foreign god among you.
You are my witnesses," declares the LORD,
"that I am God.
Yes, and from ancient days I am he.
No one can deliver out of my hand.
When I act, who can reverse it?"
Isaiah 43:10-13

READ MORE ABOUT IT: Psalm 68:19-20;
Isaiah 45:20-22

MEMORIZE IT!

> I, even I, am the LORD,
> and apart from me
> there is no savior.
> **Isaiah 43:11**

REMEMBER: God loved us so much that He sent Jesus to earth to live and die
to save us from our sin.

77

The God with Many Names–Shepherd

MARCH 17

The LORD is my shepherd, I shall not be in want.
He leads me beside quiet waters,
    he restores my soul.

Restore us, O God;
    make your face shine upon us,
    that we may be saved.

Hear us, O Shepherd of Israel,
    you who lead Joseph like a flock;
Awaken your might;
    come and save us.

He tends his flock like a shepherd;
    He gathers the lambs in his arms
and carries them close to his heart;
    he gently leads those that have young.
Psalms 23:1a, 2b-3a; 80:3, 1a, 2b; Isaiah 40:11.

READ MORE ABOUT IT: Hebrews 13:20-21; 1 Peter 2:25

Draw a picture of God, the Shepherd, carrying you close to His heart.

REMEMBER: God, our Shepherd, takes care of everything we need.

The fruit of the Spirit is love, joy, peace, patience, kindness, goodness, faithfulness, gentleness and self-control. Against such things there is no law.

No good tree bears bad fruit, nor does a bad tree bear good fruit. Each tree is recognized by its own fruit.

Live as children of light (for the fruit of the light consists in all goodness, righteousness and truth) and find out what pleases the Lord.

I am the vine; you are the branches. If a man remains in me and I in him, he will bear much fruit; apart from me you can do nothing.
Galatians 5:22-23; Luke 6:43-44a; Ephesians 5:8b-10; John 15:5

READ MORE ABOUT IT: John 15:16-17

TRY IT!

Ask your mom or dad if you can have a piece of fruit to eat, and while you're eating it, think about the good "fruit" God wants you to show in your life. You might want to write down in a secret place the types of fruit listed above that you want the Spirit to develop in you.

REMEMBER: When we let God's Spirit do what He wants in our lives and don't try to have our own way, we will be like trees growing the fruit of love, joy, peace, and self-control.

The Fruit of the Spirit–Love

I love you, O LORD, my strength.

"The most important [commandment]," answered Jesus, "is this: 'Hear, O Israel, the Lord our God, the Lord is one. Love the Lord your God with all your heart and with all your soul and with all your mind and with all your strength.' The second is this: 'Love your neighbor as yourself.' There is no commandment greater than these."

"A new command I give you: Love one another. As I have loved you, so you must love one another. By this all men will know that you are my disciples, if you love one another."
Psalm 18:1; Mark 12:29-3; John 13:34-35

READ MORE ABOUT IT: Deuteronomy 6:5

MEMORIZE IT!

> As I have loved you, so you must love one another. By this all men will know that you are my disciples, if you love one another.
> **John 13:34b-35**

REMEMBER: Show your love to God and those around you today.

Then the LORD came down in the cloud and stood there with him and proclaimed his name, the LORD. And he passed in front of Moses, proclaiming, "The LORD, the LORD, the compassionate and gracious God, slow to anger, abounding in love and faithfulness, maintaining love to thousands, and forgiving wickedness, rebellion and sin. Yet he does not leave the guilty unpunished."

For God so loved the world that he gave his one and only Son, that whoever believes in him shall not perish but have eternal life.

God is love. Whoever lives in love lives in God, and God in him.
Exodus 34:5-7; John 3:16; 1 John 4:16b

READ MORE ABOUT IT: 1 John 4:7-12; Song of Songs 2:4

PRAY ABOUT IT: Is there someone you have trouble being nice to? Who is it? Ask God to help you love that person today. Don't wait until you feel loving feelings for the person. As you do thoughtful things, the feelings will come.

REMEMBER: Only God can help you love someone you have trouble loving.

The Fruit of the Spirit—Joy

MARCH 21

Sing joyfully to the LORD, you righteous;
    it is fitting for the upright to
        praise him.
Praise the LORD with the harp;
    make music to him on the
        ten-stringed lyre.
Sing to him a new song;
    play skillfully, and shout for joy.

For the word of the LORD is right and true;
    he is faithful in all he does.

Though the fig tree does not bud
    and there are no grapes on the vines,

though the olive crop fails
    and the fields produce no food,
though there are no sheep in the pen
    and no cattle in the stalls,
yet I will rejoice in the LORD,
    I will be joyful in God my Savior.

Rejoice in the LORD always. I will
say it again: Rejoice!
Psalm 33:1-4; Habakkuk 3:17-18;
Philippians 4:4

READ MORE ABOUT IT: Romans 15:13;
                        1 Peter 1:8

TRY IT!

Do you know a hymn or a song with the word joy in it? Sing it joyfully to God as a song of praise to the God who gives us joy. Or try making up your own joyful song to God. Teach it to your family or to a friend.

REMEMBER: Happiness comes from what's happening around us. Joy comes from inside, from knowing God.

82

May the glory of the LORD endure forever;
   may the LORD rejoice in his works.

The LORD your God is with you,
   he is mighty to save.
He will take great delight in you,
   he will quiet you with his love,
   he will rejoice over you with singing.

Let us fix our eyes on Jesus, the author and perfecter of our faith, who for the joy set before him endured the cross, scorning its shame, and sat down at the right hand of the throne of God. Consider him who endured such opposition from sinful men, so that you will not grow weary and lose heart.
Psalm 104:31; Zephaniah 3:17; Hebrews 12:2-3

READ MORE ABOUT IT:
1 Chronicles 16:23-27

You don't look very joyful today, my friend.

TALK ABOUT IT!

What do you do on days when you don't feel joyful—just decide it's one of those days and mope around? Paste a smile on your face and pretend to be happy even if you don't feel like it? Ask God to help you be more joyful? Talk to your dad or mom and ask what he or she does to be more joyful.

REMEMBER: We can be joyful because we worship the God who gives joy.

The Fruit of the Spirit—Peace

MARCH 23

steadfast: settled on God

You [God] will keep in perfect peace him whose mind is steadfast, because he trusts in you.
Trust in the LORD forever, for the LORD, the LORD, is the Rock eternal.

Peace I leave with you; my peace I give you. I do not give to you as the world gives. Do not let your hearts be troubled and do not be afraid.

Do not be anxious about anything, but in everything, by prayer and petition, with thanksgiving, present your requests to God. And the peace of God, which transcends all understanding, will guard your hearts and your minds in Christ Jesus.
Isaiah 26:3-4; John 14:27; Philippians 4:6-7

READ MORE ABOUT IT: Psalm 119:165

WRITE ABOUT IT: Do you ever feel worried about things? Write down one or two things that you've been worrying about lately. Then copy the first three lines of today's Scripture reading underneath. You may even want to make a sign for your room with that verse on it.

_____

_____

REMEMBER: Don't worry. Trust God.

The LORD bless you
and keep you;
the LORD make his face shine upon you
and be gracious to you;
the LORD turn his face toward you
and give you peace.

I will listen to what God the LORD will say;
he promises peace to his people.

Now may the LORD of peace himself give you peace at
all times and in every way. The LORD be with all of you.
Numbers 6:24-26; Psalm 85:8a; 2 Thessalonians 3:16

READ MORE ABOUT IT: Romans 15:33

When are you most peaceful? Draw a
picture of yourself in that situation.

REMEMBER: The God of peace can calm us inside.

Page 1

Wicked Pharaoh ordered all Israelite babies thrown into the Nile River. But God used a tiny basket boat to save baby Moses from the dangerous Nile. His sister, Miriam, stood nearby, watching. And when the Egyptian princess found the baby, Miriam offered to get someone to care for him—his own mother. (See February 25-26.)

Page 2

Once when Moses was tending his sheep, God got Moses' attention with a bush that was on fire but didn't burn up. God spoke to Moses from the bush and told him to lead the Israelites out of Egypt. (See February 29 and March 1.)

Page 3

Day after day Moses and Aaron stood before Pharaoh. Each day they said, "Let God's people go so that we may worship the LORD." But Pharaoh was stubborn. Every day he said no. (See April 7.)

Page 4

Pharaoh refused to obey God. So God punished him for treating the Israelites, God's people, so badly. God sent ten horrible plagues, including gnats, flies, and frogs everywhere, the river turning to blood, hail so big that it killed the animals, and a death angel that killed the oldest child in each family. (See April 9.)

Page 5

Pharaoh finally let the Israelites leave, but the Egyptian army chased them. God miraculously pushed the water back to let the Israelites cross the sea on dry ground. But when the Egyptians tried to follow, the walls of water crashed down on them. They all drowned. (See April 25-28.)

Pages 6 and 7

The Bible says 600,000 Israelite men, besides women and children, left Egypt. God led them with a pillar of cloud every day and a pillar of fire every night. (See April 25 and 29.) How many people in all do you think left Egypt? How long do you think the line of Israelites stretched?

Page 8

When Moses came down from the mountain, His face was shining because he had spoken to God. In his hands Moses held the Lord's commands written by God's own hand. (See April 30.)

I waited patiently for the LORD;
    he turned to me and heard my cry.
He lifted me out of the slimy pit,
    out of the mud and mire;
he set my feet on a rock
    and gave me a firm place to stand.

yield: give

Love is patient.

Be patient, then, brothers, until the Lord's coming.
See how the farmer waits for the land to yield its
valuable crop and how patient he is for the
autumn and spring rains. You too, be
patient and stand firm, because
the Lord's coming is near.
Psalm 40:1-2; 1 Corinthians 13:4a;
  James 5:7-8

READ MORE ABOUT IT: Proverbs 14:29

Sometimes, when things aren't going well in our world, we may get impatient to go to heaven. While you're waiting, imagine what you would like to do first when you get to heaven. If you could talk to any of the people in the Bible, who would you want to talk to first?

REMEMBER: Be patient with God. He always does everything at just the right time.

87

God Is Patient

Here is a trustworthy saying that deserves full acceptance: Christ Jesus came into the world to save sinners—of whom I am the worst. But for that very reason I was shown mercy so that in me, the worst of sinners, Christ Jesus might display his unlimited patience as an example for those who would believe on him and receive eternal life.

The Lord is not slow in keeping his promise, as some understand slowness. He is patient with you, not wanting anyone to perish, but everyone to come to repentance.
1 Timothy 1:15-16; 2 Peter 3:9

READ MORE ABOUT IT: Numbers 14:18

PRAY ABOUT IT: Do you ever get impatient with people who can't do things as well as you? If God did that, He'd be impatient with everyone all the time, wouldn't He? Thank God today for His patience with you, and ask Him to give you patience with others.

REMEMBER: Patience comes from God.

A kind man benefits himself,
but a cruel man brings trouble on himself.

He who despises his neighbor sins,
but blessed is he who is kind to the needy.

Be kind and compassionate to one another, forgiving each other, just as in Christ God forgave you.

Therefore, as God's chosen people, holy and dearly loved, clothe yourselves with compassion, kindness, humility, gentleness and patience. Bear with each other and forgive whatever grievances you may have against one another. Forgive as the Lord forgave you. And over all these virtues put on love, which binds them all together in perfect unity.
Proverbs 11:17; 14:21; Ephesians 4:32; Colossians 3:12-14

READ MORE ABOUT IT: Romans 12:10

MEMORIZE IT!

> Be kind and compassionate to one another, forgiving each other, just as in Christ God forgave you.
> **Ephesians 4:32**

despises his neighbor:
hates or is mean to someone

bear with each other:
be patient, not getting angry if people don't do things your way

grievances:
things people do that bother you or make you angry

REMEMBER: Because God is kind to us, we know how to be kind to others.

God Is Kind

I will tell of the kindnesses of the LORD
the deeds for which he is to be
praised, according to all the LORD has
done for us—
yes, the many good things he has done
for the house of Israel,
according to his compassion and
many kindnesses.

"I am the LORD, who exercises kindness,
justice and righteousness on earth,
for in these I delight,"
declares the LORD.

When the kindness and love of God our
Savior appeared, he saved us, not because
of righteous things we had done, but
because of his mercy.
Isaiah 63:7; Jeremiah 9:24b; Titus 3:3-5a

READ MORE ABOUT IT: Isaiah 54:8-10

TRY IT!

Do you know an older person in your neighborhood who needs some help around the house or someone to talk to? Or is there something kind you could do for a teacher, classmate, brother, sister, or parent today? Do you know a missionary kid you could write an encouraging letter to? Decide now who you want to show God's kindness to today—then do it!

REMEMBER: God does good things for us because He is a kind God.

People do not pick figs from thornbushes, or grapes from briers. The good man brings good things out of the good stored up in his heart, and the evil man brings evil things out of the evil stored up in his heart. For out of the overflow of his heart his mouth speaks.

For we are God's workmanship, created in Christ Jesus to do good works, which God prepared in advance for us to do.

Dear friend, do not imitate what is evil but what is good. Anyone who does what is good is from God. Anyone who does what is evil has not seen God.
Luke 6:44b-45; Ephesians 2:10; 3 John 11

READ MORE ABOUT IT: Hebrews 13:16

Draw a picture of yourself doing something good to help someone else. If possible, actually do that good thing sometime this week.

REMEMBER: We were created to do good things for God and others.

God Is Good

Taste and see that the LORD is good;
blessed is the man who takes refuge
in him.

I will praise you forever for what you
have done;
in your name I will hope, for your
name is good.
I will praise you in the presence of
your saints.

Surely God is good to Israel,
to those who are pure in heart.

For the LORD is good and his love
endures forever;
his faithfulness continues through
all generations.

You are good, and what you do is good;
teach me your decrees.

The LORD is good to all;
he has compassion on all he has made.
Psalms 34:8; 52:9; 73:1; 100:5; 119:68; 145:9

READ MORE ABOUT IT: Nahum 1:7

TALK ABOUT IT!

What is the difference between being kind and being good? Can you think of a time when you thought your mom or dad was not being very kind to you, but you later found out that what they did was somehow good? Does that ever happen with God and us?

92

REMEMBER: We can trust God completely because He can only do what is good.

But be sure to fear the LORD and serve him faithfully with all your heart; consider what great things he has done for you.

Love the LORD, all his saints!
    The LORD preserves the faithful,
    but the proud he pays back in full.
Be strong and take heart,
    all you who hope in the LORD.

Let love and faithfulness never leave you;
bind them around your neck,
write them on the tablet of your heart.
Then you will win favor and a good name
in the sight of God and man.
1 Samuel 12:24; Psalm 31:23-24;
Proverbs 3:3-4

READ MORE ABOUT IT: 2 Samuel 22:26

WRITE ABOUT IT: To be faithful to God means that we don't let anyone or anything else take His place in our lives. Write down two things you might be tempted to think or do that would be unfaithful to God. Then ask God to help you be faithful.

_____

_____

REMEMBER: God wants us to be people He can count on.

God Is Faithful

I will sing of the LORD's great love forever;
  with my mouth I will make your faithfulness known
    through all generations.
I will declare that your love stands firm forever,
    that you established your faithfulness in heaven itself.

Yet this I call to mind
    and therefore I have hope:
Because of the LORD's great love
    we are not consumed,
for his compassions never fail.
They are new every morning;
    great is your faithfulness.

If we confess our sins, he is faithful
and just and will forgive us our sins and
purify us from all unrighteousness.
Psalm 89:1-2; Lamentations 3:21-23; 1 John 1:9

READ MORE ABOUT IT: Deuteronomy 7:9

REMEMBER: We can trust our faithful God.

consumed: destroyed

Imagine what it would be like if we couldn't count on God. Would the planets stay where they are? Would the sun come up every morning? Would we be sure that God had forgiven us if we confessed our sins? Would we be sure that God wouldn't let anything happen to us that wasn't for our good? What other problems might come up?

Agentle answer turns away wrath, but a harsh word stirs up anger.

Be completely humble and gentle; be patient, bearing with one another in love. Make every effort to keep the unity of the Spirit through the bond of peace.

Let your gentleness be evident to all. The Lord is near.

But in your hearts set apart Christ as Lord. Always be prepared to give an answer to everyone who asks you to give the reason for the hope that you have. But do this with gentleness and respect, keeping a clear conscience, so that those who speak maliciously against your good behavior in Christ may be ashamed of their slander. Proverbs 15:1; Ephesians 4:2-3; Philippians 4:5; 1 Peter 3:15-16

READ MORE ABOUT IT: 2 Timothy 2:24

PRAY ABOUT IT: Gentleness is not easy for most of us. We want our own way, and we're willing to fight for it. Ask God to help you be gentle today in the way you act and talk with your friends, teachers, and parents.

REMEMBER: It's easy to quarrel, but God wants us to be gentle with others.

God Is Gentle

APRIL 3

See, the Sovereign LORD comes with power,
and his arm rules for him.
See, his reward is with him,
   and his recompense accompanies him.
He tends his flock like a shepherd:
   He gathers the lambs in his arms
and carries them close to his heart;
   he gently leads those that have young.

[Jesus said,] "Come to me, all you who are weary and burdened, and I will give you rest. Take my yoke upon you and learn from me, for I am gentle and humble in heart, and you will find rest for your souls. For my yoke is easy and my burden is light."
Isaiah 40:10-11; Matthew 11:28-30

READ MORE ABOUT IT: Zechariah 9:9;
                    Matthew 21:1-12

sovereign:
a ruler who doesn't have to take orders from anyone else

96

REMEMBER: Even though God is very powerful, He treats us gently.

Like a city whose walls are broken down
is a man who lacks self-control.

The grace of God that brings salvation has appeared to all men. It teaches us to say "No" to ungodliness and worldly passions, and to live self-controlled, upright and godly lives in this present age, while we wait for the blessed hope—the glorious appearing of our great God and Savior, Jesus Christ, who gave himself for us to redeem us from all wickedness and to purify for himself a people that are his very own, eager to do what is good.
Proverbs 25:28; Titus 2:11-14

READ MORE ABOUT IT: 2 Peter 1:5-8

TALK ABOUT IT!

When we are self-controlled, we don't let ourselves do things we shouldn't do. And we do what's right whether we feel like it or not. Talk about a time when you weren't self-controlled. What happened? How did it affect those around you? Was God pleased? Talk about a time when you were self-controlled. What can you do when you think you're losing control?

REMEMBER: If you need help with self-control, ask God.

God Is Slow to Anger

APRIL 5

The LORD is compassionate
        and gracious,
    slow to anger, abounding in love.
He will not always accuse,
    nor will he harbor his anger forever;
he does not treat us as our sins deserve
    or repay us according to our iniquities.
For as high as the heavens are above
        the earth,
    so great is his love for those who
        fear him;
as far as the east is from the west,

so far has he removed our
    transgressions from us.

The LORD is slow to anger and
    great in power;
    the LORD will not leave
        the guilty unpunished.
His way is in the whirlwind and the storm,
    and clouds are the dust of his feet.
Psalm 103:8-12; Nahum 1:3

READ MORE ABOUT IT: Psalm 145:8-9

abounding: overflowing
iniquities: sins
transgressions: sins

WRITE ABOUT IT: Aren't you glad that God doesn't get angry quickly? Write God a thank-you note of a sentence or two, thanking Him that He is slow to get angry and always ready to forgive.

_____

_____

98   **REMEMBER:** God gives us time to change our minds and do things His way.

Moses' Not-So-Secret Mission

God also said to Moses, "Say to the Israelites, 'The LORD, the God of your fathers—the God of Abraham, the God of Isaac and the God of Jacob—has sent me to you.' This is my name forever, the name by which I am to be remembered from generation to generation.

"The elders of Israel will listen to you. Then you and the elders are to go to the king of Egypt and say to him, 'The LORD, the God of the Hebrews, has met with us. Let us take a three-day journey into the desert to offer sacrifices to the LORD our God.' But I know that the king of Egypt will not let you go unless a mighty hand compels him. So I will stretch out my hand and strike the Egyptians with all the wonders that I will perform among them. After that, he will let you go." Exodus 3:15, 18-20

READ MORE ABOUT IT: Acts 7:30-36

> The king of Egypt was stubborn. Think of a stubborn animal and draw it.

REMEMBER: God will do everything in His power to help His people.

99

Moses and Aaron Stand Up to Pharaoh

The LORD said to Aaron, "Go into the desert to meet Moses." So he met Moses at the mountain of God and kissed him. Then Moses told Aaron everything the LORD had sent him to say, and also about all the miraculous signs he had commanded him to perform.

Moses and Aaron brought together all the elders of the Israelites, and Aaron told them everything the LORD had said to Moses. He also performed the signs before the people, and they believed. And when they heard that the LORD was concerned about them and had seen their misery, they bowed down and worshiped.

Afterward Moses and Aaron went to Pharaoh and said, "This is what the LORD, the God of Israel, says: 'Let my people go, so that they may hold a festival to me in the desert.'"

Pharaoh said, "Who is the LORD, that I should obey him and let Israel go?...I will not let Israel go."
Exodus 4:27–5:2

READ MORE ABOUT IT: Proverbs 29:1-2

TRY IT!

Sometimes we don't realize our own abilities. Moses didn't think he was a leader, but God knew he would become one of the greatest leaders this world has ever known. Are you willing to be a leader in your school and among your friends? Will you stand up for God and what's right? Give it a try. God may have great adventures ahead for you.

REMEMBER: God doesn't ask you to do anything that He won't help you do.

Pharaoh Gets Stubborn

T he LORD said to Moses and Aaron, "When Pharaoh says to you, 'Perform a miracle,' then say to Aaron, 'Take your staff and throw it down before Pharaoh,' and it will become a snake."

So Moses and Aaron went to Pharaoh and did just as the LORD commanded, Aaron threw his staff down in front of Pharaoh and his officials, and it became a snake. Pharaoh then summoned wise men and sorcerers, and the Egyptian magicians also did the same things by their secret arts: Each one threw down his staff and it became a snake. But Aaron's staff swallowed up their staffs. Yet Pharaoh's heart became hard and he would not listen to them, just as the LORD had said.
Exodus 7:8-13

READ MORE ABOUT IT: Exodus 7:1-5

MEMORIZE IT!

The Holy Spirit says: "Today, if you hear his voice, do not harden your hearts."
Hebrews 3:7-8b

REMEMBER: People who don't love God can always find an excuse to not believe what He says.

101

Ten Terrible, Horrible Plagues

The day the LORD displayed his
miraculous signs in Egypt...
He turned their rivers to blood;
they could not drink from
their streams.
He sent swarms of flies that
devoured them,
and frogs that devastated them.
He gave their crops to the grasshopper,
their produce to the locust.
He destroyed their vines with hail
and their sycamore-figs with sleet.
He gave over their cattle to the hail,
their livestock to bolts of lightning.
He unleashed against them his hot anger,
his wrath, indignation and hostility—
a band of destroying angels.

He prepared a path for his anger;
he did not spare them from death
but gave them over to the plague.
He struck down all the firstborn of Egypt,
the firstfruits of manhood.
Psalm 78:43-51a

READ MORE ABOUT IT: Exodus 12:31-32

Imagine that you were
an Egyptian child at the time God sent
the ten plagues. Which of the plagues
do you think would be the worst—slimy
frogs covering your bed? painful sores
called boils all over your body? no water
to drink because the river had turned to
blood? Do you think you might
have wished you believed in the
powerful God of Moses?

REMEMBER: God sometimes takes drastic steps to get people's attention. Be sure you listen to Him.

The LORD said to Moses, "When you return from Egypt, see that you perform before Pharaoh all the wonders I have given you the power to do. But I will harden his heart so that he will not let the people go. Then say to Pharaoh, "This is what the LORD says: Israel is my firstborn son, and I told you, 'Let my son go, so he may worship me.' But you refused to let him go; so I will kill your firstborn son."

So Moses said, "This is what the LORD says: 'About midnight I will go throughout Egypt. Every firstborn son in Egypt will die, from the firstborn son of Pharaoh, who sits on the throne, to the firstborn son of the slave girl, who is at her hand mill, and all the firstborn of the cattle as well.'"
Exodus 4:21-23; 11:4-5

READ MORE ABOUT IT: Exodus 12:29-30; 13:1-3

TALK ABOUT IT!

God was punishing the Egyptians because they were cruel to the Israelites and wouldn't let them go free. Do you think that today God might still punish whole nations for cruel things they do to people? Why or why not?

REMEMBER: God is so powerful that He has the power of life and death in His hands.

A Night They'd Never Forget!

Then Moses summoned all the elders of Israel and said to them, "Go at once and select the animals for your families and slaughter the Passover lamb. Take a bunch of hyssop, dip it into the blood in the basin and put some of the blood on the top and on both sides of the doorframe. Not one of you shall go out the door of his house until morning. When the LORD goes through the land to strike down the Egyptians, he will see the blood on the top and sides of the doorframe and will pass over that doorway, and he will not permit the destroyer to enter your houses and strike you down."

Then the people bowed down and worshiped. The Israelites did just what the LORD commanded Moses and Aaron.
Exodus 12:21-23, 27b-28

READ MORE ABOUT IT: Exodus 12:1-14

Imagine that you are in an Israelite family at this time. Your father asks you to pick some of the pleasant-smelling hyssop plant. Imagine yourself watching as your father paints the top and sides of the doorframe of your house with the blood of the Passover lamb. Do you think you would want to be sure your father put enough blood on the doorframe so it could be seen easily? How do you think you would feel every time you smelled the fragrance of a hyssop bush after that?

REMEMBER: God helps us through difficult situations, but He expects us to do what He asks.

See, my servant will act wisely;
he will be raised and lifted up and highly exalted.

He was despised and rejected by men,
    a man of sorrows, and familiar with suffering.
Like one from whom men hide their faces
    he was despised, and we esteemed him not.

Surely he took up our infirmities
    and carried our sorrows,
yet we considered him stricken by God,
    smitten by him, and afflicted.
But he was pierced for our transgressions,
    he was crushed for our iniquities;
the punishment that brought us peace
        was upon him,
    and by his wounds we are healed.
Isaiah 52:13; 53:3-5

READ MORE ABOUT IT: John 19:1-6, 17-18

MEMORIZE IT!

We all, like sheep, have gone astray, each of us has turned to his own way; and the Lord has laid on him the iniquity of us all.
Isaiah 53:6

esteem: think highly of
infirmities: weaknesses or flaws
stricken, smitten, afflicted: bruised, beaten, badly hurt

REMEMBER: Isaiah wrote these words 800 years before Jesus lived, but they perfectly describe how Jesus suffered, died, and came back to life for us.

Jesus—The Lamb of God

The next day John saw Jesus coming toward him and said, "Look, the Lamb of God, who takes away the sin of the world! I have seen and I testify that this is the Son of God."

Then I looked and heard the voice of many angels, numbering thousands upon thousands, and ten thousand times ten thousand. They encircled the throne and the living creatures and the elders. In a loud voice they sang:

"Worthy is the Lamb, who was slain,
to receive power and wealth and wisdom and strength
and honor and glory and praise!"
John 1:29, 34; Revelation 5:11-12

READ MORE ABOUT IT: Isaiah 53:7-8

What do you think an angel looks like?
Draw an angel singing by God's throne.

REMEMBER: Jesus is called the Lamb because He was sacrificed for our sins. But He did not remain dead. He came back to life.

Jesus Predicts His Resurrection

Once when Jesus was praying in private and his disciples were with him, he asked them, "Who do the crowds say I am?"

They replied, "Some say John the Baptist; others say Elijah; and still others, that one of the prophets of long ago has come back to life."

"But what about you?" he asked. "Who do you say I am?"

Peter answered, "The Christ of God."

Jesus...said, "The Son of Man must suffer many things and be rejected by the elders, chief priests and teachers of the law, and he must be killed and on the third day be raised to life."

Luke 9:18-22

READ MORE ABOUT IT: Mark 10:32-34, 45

WRITE ABOUT IT: Jesus asked His disciples who they thought He was. Write here in your own words what you would say if He asked you the same question.

_____

_____

REMEMBER: Jesus said He would come back to life, and He did!

It Looks Like a Parade!

As they approached Jerusalem and came to Bethphage on the Mount of Olives, Jesus sent two disciples, saying to them, "Go to the village ahead of you, and at once you will find a donkey tied there, with her colt by her. Untie them and bring them to me. If anyone says anything to you, tell him that the Lord needs them, and he will send them right away."

The disciples went and did as Jesus had instructed them. The crowds that went ahead of him and those that followed shouted,

"Hosanna to the Son of David!"

"Blessed is he who comes in the name of the Lord!"
Matthew 21:1-3, 6, 9a

READ MORE ABOUT IT: Mark 11:1-11

Draw a donkey like the one Jesus may have ridden that day.

REMEMBER: Jesus came as a gentle Savior, just as the prophet Zechariah predicted.

The blind and the lame came to him at the temple, and he healed them. But when the chief priests and the teachers of the law saw the wonderful things he did and the children shouting in the temple area, "Hosanna to the Son of David," they were indignant.

"Do you hear what these children are saying?" they asked him.

"Yes," replied Jesus, "have you never read,

"'From the lips of children and infants
you have ordained praise'?"

Matthew 21:14-16

READ MORE ABOUT IT: Psalm 8:1-2

> **the lame:** people who can't use their arms or legs
>
> **indignant:** angry (because they didn't think shouting was proper behavior)

WRITE ABOUT IT: Imagine you are one of the children who watched Jesus give blind people their sight and heal people who couldn't walk. Wouldn't you feel like shouting, "Hooray for Jesus!"? Below, write a cheer of your own for Jesus, the miracle worker.

_____

_____

REMEMBER: Jesus loves to hear us praise Him.

Jesus' Riddle

While the Pharisees were gathered together, Jesus asked them, "What do you think about the Christ? Whose son is he?"

"The son of David," they replied.

He said to them, "How is it then that David, speaking by the Spirit, calls him 'Lord'? For he says,

"'The Lord said to my Lord:
"Sit at my right hand
until I put your enemies
under your feet.'"

"If then David calls him 'Lord,' how can he be his son?" No one could say a word in reply, and from that day on no one dared to ask him any more questions.

Matthew 22:41-46

READ MORE ABOUT IT: *Psalm 110:1;*
1 Corinthians 8:6

I don't get it!

TRY IT!

Do you like riddles? What is the toughest riddle you ever figured out? Jesus gives the people in today's reading a riddle. Can you solve it? How could Jesus be David's Lord if Jesus was born after David? (If you need a hint, read John 1:1-3. "The Word" is another name for Jesus.)

REMEMBER: Although Jesus had an earthly stepfather when He came to earth, Jesus' real father is God. Jesus is the Son of God.

When the hour came, Jesus and his apostles reclined at the table. And he said to them, "I have eagerly desired to eat this Passover with you before I suffer. For I tell you, I will not eat it again until it finds fulfillment in the kingdom of God."

And he took bread, gave thanks and broke it, and gave it to them, saying, "This is my body given for you; do this in remembrance of me."

In the same way, after the supper he took the cup, saying, "This cup is the new covenant in my blood, which is poured out for you." Luke 22:14-16, 19-20

READ MORE ABOUT IT: 1 Corinthians 11:23-26

TALK ABOUT IT!

When we have a communion service at church, we are doing what Jesus asked His disciples to do—remembering that Jesus died to save us from our sin. If your mom or dad attends these services, ask what he or she likes to think about during the quiet moments. Ask family members if they have a favorite hymn that talks about Jesus' death for us.

REMEMBER: Jesus wants us to think often about what He suffered for us.

Judas Betrays Jesus

APRIL 19

When he had finished praying, Jesus left with his disciples and crossed the Kidron Valley. On the other side there was an olive grove, and he and his disciples went into it.

Judas came to the grove, guiding a detachment of soldiers and some officials from the chief priests and Pharisees. They were carrying torches, lanterns and weapons.

Jesus, knowing all that was going to happen to him, went out and asked them, "Who is it you want?"

"Jesus of Nazareth," they replied.

"I am he," Jesus said. When Jesus said, "I am he," they drew back and fell to the ground.   John 18:1, 3-5a, 6

READ MORE ABOUT IT: Mark 14:43-50; Matthew 26:52-54

If you were a soldier on that dark night what would you have done after Jesus' words knocked you over? Draw it here.

REMEMBER: Jesus was so powerful that with a simple "I am He" He knocked the soldiers over. But Jesus chose to let them arrest Him so He could give His life to save us.

The high priest said to Jesus, "I charge you under oath by the living God: Tell us if you are the Christ, the Son of God."

"Yes, it is as you say," Jesus replied. "But I say to all of you: In the future you will see the Son of Man sitting at the right hand of the Mighty One and coming on the clouds of heaven."

Then the high priest tore his clothes and said, "He has spoken blasphemy! Why do we need any more witnesses? Look, now you have heard the blasphemy. What do you think?"

"He is worthy of death," they answered.
Matthew 26:63b-66

READ MORE ABOUT IT: Colossians 2:9

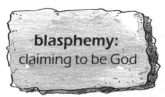

blasphemy:
claiming to be God

Imagine that you were one of the children Jesus healed. Before Jesus' touch, you couldn't walk, but now you can run and jump and play. While you are playing near the building where trials are held, you hear the crowd shout, "Jesus must die!" How would you feel? Would you be sad? scared? Would you rush into the crowd and try to stop what was happening? Later you might realize that Jesus had to die so that we all could be saved from our sins.

REMEMBER: Jesus agreed that He was the Christ, the Son of God. Yet He also called himself the Son of Man. Our Savior is both God and man.

113

Jesus Is Crucified

It was the third hour when they crucified Jesus. The written notice of the charge against him read: THE KING OF THE JEWS. They crucified two robbers with him, one on his right and one on his left. Those who passed by hurled insults at him, shaking their heads and saying, "So! You who are going to destroy the temple and build it in three days, come down from the cross and save yourself!"

With a loud cry, Jesus breathed his last.

The curtain of the temple was torn in two from top to bottom. And when the centurion, who stood there in front of Jesus, heard his cry and saw how he died, he said, "Surely this man was the Son of God!"
Mark 15:25-30, 37-39

READ MORE ABOUT IT: Matthew 27:41-43

WRITE ABOUT IT: When you think about Jesus suffering so that we could have our sins forgiven, how does it make you feel? Does it make you want to act any differently? How?

_____

_____

114

REMEMBER: Jesus could have saved himself, but He chose to suffer and die for us. He took the punishment we deserved for our sin.

After the Sabbath, at dawn on the first day of the week, Mary Magdalene and the other Mary went to look at the tomb.

There was a violent earthquake, for an angel of the Lord came down from heaven and, going to the tomb, rolled back the stone and sat on it. His appearance was like lightning, and his clothes were white as snow. The guards were so afraid of him that they shook and became like dead men.

The angel said to the women, "Do not be afraid, for I know that you are looking for Jesus, who was crucified. He is not here; he has risen, just as he said. Come and see the place where he lay."
Matthew 28:1-6

READ MORE ABOUT IT: Mark 16:1-8

PRAY ABOUT IT: If Jesus hadn't come back to life, He couldn't offer us eternal life. Talk to God and thank Him that Jesus not only died for us but He also came back to life for us. Now all who believe in Him can spend forever with Jesus in heaven.

REMEMBER: Jesus is alive today!

The Resurrection—Why It's So Important

But if it is preached that Christ has been raised from the dead, how can some of you say that there is no resurrection of the dead? If there is no resurrection of the dead, then not even Christ has been raised. And if Christ has not been raised, your faith is futile; you are still in your sins.

But Christ has indeed been raised from the dead. For since death came through a man, the resurrection of the dead comes also through a man. For as in Adam all die, so in Christ all will be made alive.

1 Corinthians 15:12-13, 17, 20a, 21-22

READ MORE ABOUT IT: Acts 2:22-24, 32

MEMORIZE IT!

> If Christ has not been raised, your faith is futile; you are still in your sins. But Christ has indeed been raised from the dead.
> **1 Corinthians 15:17, 20a**

futile: useless

He's alive! He's alive!

116

REMEMBER: Our living Savior wants us to live every day for Him.

We Are Very Important to Jesus

For you know that it was not with perishable things such as silver or gold that you were redeemed from the empty way of life handed down to you from your forefathers, but with the precious blood of Christ, a lamb without blemish or defect. He was chosen before the creation of the world, but was revealed in these last times for your sake. Through him you believe in God, who raised him from the dead and glorified him, and so your faith and hope are in God.
1 Peter 1:18-21

READ MORE ABOUT IT: 1 Corinthians 6:19b-20

perishable things: things that don't last

TRY IT!

Do you ever feel "down"? Do you sometimes feel as if you're not worth much? Right now reread today's Scripture passage and think about how important you must be to Jesus. He let people do horribly painful things to Him and even died so that your sins could be forgiven and you could live with Him in heaven someday. Remind yourself often that **you are important to Jesus.**

REMEMBER: To Jesus you are worth everything!

Pharaoh Says, "Go!"

At midnight the LORD struck down all the firstborn in Egypt, from the firstborn of Pharaoh, who sat on the throne, to the firstborn of the prisoner, who was in the dungeon, and the firstborn of all the livestock as well.

During the night Pharaoh summoned Moses and Aaron and said, "Up! Leave my people, you and the Israelites! Go, worship the LORD as you have requested. Take your flocks and herds, as you have said, and go. And also bless me."

By day the LORD went ahead of them in a pillar of cloud to guide them on their way and by night in a pillar of fire to give them light, so that they could travel by day or night.   Exodus 12:29, 31-32; 13:21

READ MORE ABOUT IT: Nehemiah 9:19-20

Imagine that your family has to leave in a hurry. You can take only 5 things. What will you take with you? Draw them here.

REMEMBER: God judges those who ignore Him and leads those who choose to follow Him.

The Egyptians—all Pharaoh's horses and chariots, horsemen and troops—pursued the Israelites and overtook them as they camped by the sea near Pi Hahiroth, opposite Baal Zephon.

As Pharaoh approached, the Israelites looked up, and there were the Egyptians, marching after them. They were terrified and cried out to the LORD.

Moses answered the people, "Do not be afraid. Stand firm and you will see the deliverance the LORD will bring you today. The Egyptians you see today you will never see again. The LORD will fight for you; you need only to be still."

Then the LORD said to Moses, "...Raise your staff and stretch out your hand over the sea to divide the water so that the Israelites can go through the sea on dry ground."
Exodus 14:9-10, 13-16

READ MORE ABOUT IT: Exodus 23:27

I'm running away.

That wont help!

TALK ABOUT IT!

Do you ever feel as though your problems at school or home or in your neighborhood are way too much for you to handle? Do you ever feel like running away? Usually that's not the best solution. Try to talk to your mom or dad about what's bothering you. And talk to God about your problems, too. He loves to help.

REMEMBER: God cares about our troubles, and He will deliver us.

Walls of Water?

hen Moses stretched out his hand over the sea, and all that night the LORD drove the sea back with a strong east wind and turned it into dry land. The waters were divided, and the Israelites went through the sea on dry ground, with a wall of water on their right and on their left.

The Egyptians pursued them, and all Pharaoh's horses and chariots and horsemen followed them into the sea.

Moses stretched out his hand over the sea, and at daybreak the sea went back to its place. The Egyptians were fleeing toward it, and the LORD swept them into the sea. The water flowed back and covered the chariots and horsemen—the entire army of Pharaoh that had followed the Israelites into the sea. Not one of them survived. Exodus 14:21-23, 27-28

READ MORE ABOUT IT: Exodus 14:24-26, 29

TRY IT!

Run some cool water into the tub or kitchen sink until there's about an inch of water in it. Put your hands together in the middle of the sink and see if you can push the water back from the center as God did for the Israelites. If you can't do it with your hands, try two plates or two pieces of thick cardboard or Styrofoam. Can you think of any other way it might work? Do you think God is the only one who could do it?

 REMEMBER: God will do whatever it takes to protect His people.

Songs for Israel's Great God

That day the Lord saved Israel from the hands of the Egyptians, and Israel saw the Egyptians lying dead on the shore. And when the Israelites saw the great power the Lord displayed against the Egyptians, the people feared the Lord and put their trust in him and in Moses his servant.

Then Moses and the Israelites sang this song to the Lord:

"I will sing to the Lord,
for he is highly exalted.
The horse and its rider
he has hurled into the sea.
The Lord is my strength and my song;
he has become my salvation.
He is my God, and I will praise him,
my father's God, and I will exalt him.
The Lord is a warrior;
the Lord is his name.

Exodus 14:30–15:3

READ MORE ABOUT IT: Psalm 136:1, 13-15

WRITE ABOUT IT: The Israelites made up a song about their great God, who delivered them from trouble. Think about a time the Lord helped you out of a difficult situation and write a short song about it here. Make up a tune, too, if you'd like. Or just write a few words that describe how you felt after God helped you.

REMEMBER: God loves to hear us praise Him, whether it's in a song or prayer or writing thoughts.

Everything They Needed

The LORD brought out Israel, laden
   with silver and gold,
   and from among their tribes no
      one faltered.
He spread out a cloud as a covering,
   and fire to give light at night.
They asked, and he brought
      them quail
   and satisfied them with the bread
      of heaven.
He opened the rock, and water
      gushed out;
like a river it flowed in the desert.
For he remembered his holy promise...
He brought out his people with
      rejoicing,
   his chosen ones with shouts of joy;
he gave them the lands of the nations,
   and they fell heir to what others
      had toiled for—
that they might keep his precepts
   and observe his laws.
Praise the LORD.
Psalm 105:37, 39-48

READ MORE ABOUT IT: Acts 7:36

PRAY ABOUT IT: Today, instead of a hurried prayer before your meals, take time to honestly thank God that you have food to eat, a place to live, and clothes to wear. And let Him know that you're trusting Him for anything you need.

122

REMEMBER: God takes care of His people.

In the third month after the Israelites left Egypt—on the very day—they came to the Desert of Sinai...and Israel camped there in the desert in front of the mountain.

Then Moses went up to God, and the LORD called to him from the mountain and said, "This is what you are to say to the house of Jacob and what you are to tell the people of Israel: 'You yourselves have seen what I did to Egypt, and how I carried you on eagles' wings and brought you to myself. Now if you obey me fully and keep my covenant, then out of all nations you will be my treasured possession. Although the whole earth is mine, you will be for me a kingdom of priests and a holy nation.'"
Exodus 19:1-6a

READ MORE ABOUT IT: Exodus 19:7-9

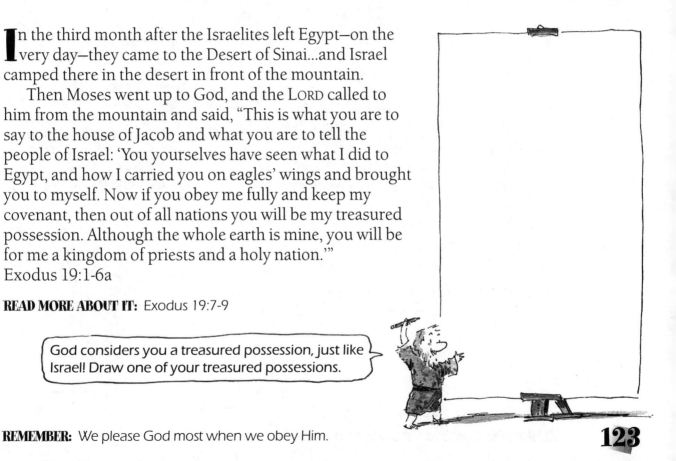

God considers you a treasured possession, just like Israel! Draw one of your treasured possessions.

REMEMBER: We please God most when we obey Him.

The Ten Commandments–No Other Gods

MAY 1

I am the LORD your God, who brought you out of Egypt out of the land of slavery. You shall have no other gods before me.

Sing to the LORD, all the earth;
   proclaim his salvation day after day.
Declare his glory among the nations,
   his marvelous deeds among all peoples.
For great is the LORD and most worthy of praise;
   he is to be feared above all gods.
For all the gods of the nations are idols,
   but the LORD made the heavens.
Exodus 20:2-3; 1 Chronicles 16:23-26

READ MORE ABOUT IT: Deuteronomy 4:35;
                          2 Samuel 7:22

124

REMEMBER: Give God first place in your heart.

King Solomon...loved many foreign women besides Pharaoh's daughter—Moabites, Ammonites, Edomites, Sidonians and Hittites. They were from nations about which the LORD had told the Israelites, "You must not intermarry with them, because they will surely turn your hearts after their gods." Nevertheless, Solomon held fast to them in love. As Solomon grew old, his wives turned his heart after other gods, and his heart was not fully devoted to the LORD his God, as the heart of David his father had been.

The LORD became angry with Solomon because his heart had turned away from the LORD, the God of Israel, who had appeared to him twice. Although he had forbidden Solomon to follow other gods, Solomon did not keep the LORD's command.

1 Kings 11:1-2, 4, 9-10

READ MORE ABOUT IT: 1 Kings 11:11-13

PRAY ABOUT IT: Ask the Lord to show you today if there is anything that you love more than you love Him. Then ask His help in putting that thing in its proper place and keeping Him first.

REMEMBER: God is not pleased when we let anything else become more important to us than He is.

125

The Ten Commandments—No Idols

You shall not make for yourself an idol in the form of anything in heaven above or on the earth beneath or in the waters below. You shall not bow down to them or worship them; for I, the LORD your God, am a jealous God.

Not to us, O LORD, not to us
        but to your name be the glory,
        because of your love and faithfulness.

Our God is in heaven;
        he does whatever pleases him.
But their idols are silver and gold,
        made by the hands of men.
Exodus 20:4-5a; Psalm 115:1, 3-4

READ MORE ABOUT IT: Isaiah 42:8;
                                1 John 5:21

Imagine you are one of the Israelites living in Egypt. The Egyptians all around you have statues of the gods they worship. They can see and touch their gods. They ask you about your God, and you say He is invisible. They laugh and ask you how you can worship something you can't see. What will you tell them? Do you have any questions you would like to ask them about how they worship their gods? (Think about Psalm 115:4.)

REMEMBER: Anything that means more to us than God does is an idol. Keep Him first.

126

King Nebuchadnezzar made an image of gold. Then the herald loudly proclaimed, "This is what you are commanded to do, O peoples, nations and men of every language: As soon as you hear the...music, you must fall down and worship the image of gold that King Nebuchadnezzar has set up. Whoever does not fall down and worship will immediately be thrown into a blazing furnace."

At this time some astrologers came forward and denounced the Jews. They said to King Nebuchadnezzar, "Shadrach, Meshach and Abednego...neither serve your gods nor worship the image of gold you have set up."

Furious with rage, Nebuchadnezzar summoned Shadrach, Meshach and Abednego. "If you do not worship [the idol], you will be thrown immediately into a blazing furnace. Then what god will be able to rescue you from my hand?"

Shadrach, Meshach and Abednego replied to the king, "If we are thrown into the blazing furnace, the God we serve is able to save us from it.... We will not serve your gods or worship the image of gold you have set up."

Daniel 3:1a, 4-6, 8-9a, 12b-13a, 15b-16a, 17-18

READ MORE ABOUT IT: Daniel 3:19-30

TALK ABOUT IT!

Has anyone ever pressured you to skip church for a sports event or other activity? How did you handle it? How can we show God that we want to keep Him first in our life?

REMEMBER: Don't let anyone pressure you to put something else before God.

The Ten Commandments–Be Careful with God's Name

You shall not misuse the name of the LORD your God, for the LORD will not hold anyone guiltless who misuses his name.

Do not swear falsely by my name and so profane the name of your God. I am the LORD.

If anyone curses his God, he will be held responsible.

The name of the LORD is a strong tower;
    the righteous run to it and are safe.
Exodus 20:7; Leviticus 19:12; 24:15; Proverbs 18:10

READ MORE ABOUT IT: Matthew 6:9

PRAY ABOUT IT: Do you ever find yourself misusing God's name when you're excited, surprised, or angry? Ask God to help you be careful how you use His name. If this isn't a problem for you, ask God to help your friends stop swearing. Sometimes when we're around people who swear a lot, we find ourselves swearing without thinking about it.

REMEMBER: Be careful how you use our great God's name.

Now Balak son of Zippor saw all that Israel had done to the Amorites, and Moab was terrified because there were so many people.

So Balak son of Zippor, who was king of Moab at that time, sent messengers to summon Balaam.... Balak said:

"A people has come out of Egypt; they cover the face of the land and have settled next to me. Now come and put a curse on these people, because they are too powerful for me. Perhaps then I will be able to defeat them and drive them out of the country. For I know that those you bless are blessed, and those you curse are cursed."

But God said to Balaam, "Do not go with them. You must not put a curse on those people, because they are blessed."

[Speaking about Israel, Balaam said,] "May those who bless you be blessed and those who curse you be cursed!"
Numbers 22:2-3a, 4b-5-6, 12; 24:9b
READ MORE ABOUT IT: James 3:9-10

TRY IT!

Balaam tried to curse Israel, but God would only let blessings come out of his mouth. Today, keep track of how many times you hear someone you know or someone on television swear (use God's name with disrespect) or curse (call for something bad to happen to a person). It's all around us, isn't it? But God wants us to be different.

REMEMBER: Cursing does not please God. Use your mouth to honor God and bless others.

The Ten Commandments–Take a Day of Rest

Remember the Sabbath day by keeping it holy. Six days you shall labor and do all your work, but the seventh day is a Sabbath to the LORD your God. On it you shall not do any work, neither you, nor your son or daughter, nor your manservant or maidservant, nor your animals, nor the [foreigner] within your gates. For in six days the LORD made the heavens and the earth, the sea, and all that is in them, but he rested on the seventh day. Therefore the LORD blessed the Sabbath day and made it holy.   Exodus 20:8-11d

READ MORE ABOUT IT: Exodus 34:21;
                                        Isaiah 58:13-14

TALK ABOUT IT: God wanted to make sure we wouldn't wear ourselves out, so He set aside one day of rest every week. Does that mean that if someone's car broke down in front of your house on your day of rest you shouldn't help or make some lemonade for that person? (Hint: Peek at tomorrow's reading.)

REMEMBER: God knows our bodies need rest. We need to learn that, too.

Jesus Heals on the Day of Rest

Jesus went into their synagogue, and a man with a shriveled hand was there. Looking for a reason to accuse Jesus, they asked him, "Is it lawful to heal on the Sabbath?"

He said to them, "If any of you has a sheep and it falls into a pit on the Sabbath, will you not take hold of it and lift it out? How much more valuable is a man than a sheep! Therefore it is lawful to do good on the Sabbath."

Then he said to the man, "Stretch out your hand." So he stretched it out and it was completely restored, just as sound as the other. But the Pharisees went out and plotted how they might kill Jesus.
Matthew 12:9b-14

READ MORE ABOUT IT: Mark 2:27

Imagine that you were one of the young people in the crowd when Jesus healed on the day of rest. Would you be angry with Jesus for breaking the rules about work on that day? Or would you be glad? Why?

REMEMBER: The day of rest is for our good. God knows what is best for us.

The Ten Commandments–Obey Your Parents

Children, obey your parents in the LORD, for this is right. "Honor your father and mother"—which is the first commandment with a promise—"that it may go well with you and that you may enjoy long life on the earth."

Honor your father and your mother, so that you may live long in the land the LORD your God is giving you.

Listen to your father, who gave you life,
and do not despise your mother when she
is old.
Ephesians 6:1-3; Exodus 20:12; Proverbs 23:22

READ MORE ABOUT IT: Proverbs 6:20

MEMORIZE IT!

"Honor your father and mother"—which is the first commandment with a promise—"that it may go well with you and that you may enjoy long life on the earth."
Ephesians 6:2-3

Hi, mom! I'm just calling to say I love you!

132

REMEMBER: God rewards those who honor and obey their parents.

The Sons Who Wouldn't Obey

Hophni and Phineas, the two sons of Eli, were priests of the LORD. Eli's sons were wicked men; they had no regard for the LORD.

[The] sin of the young men was very great in the LORD's sight, for they were treating the LORD's offering with contempt.

Now Eli, who was very old, heard about everything his sons were doing to all Israel. So he said to them, "Why do you do such things? I hear from all the people about these wicked deeds of yours. No, my sons; it is not a good report that I hear spreading among the LORD's people." His sons, however, did not listen to their father's rebuke, for it was the LORD's will to put them to death.   1 Samuel 1:3b; 2:12, 17, 22a, 23-24, 25b

contempt: extreme disrespect

READ MORE ABOUT IT: 1 Samuel 4:1-11

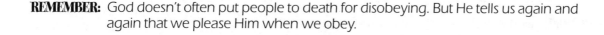

WRITE ABOUT IT: When we obey our parents, we are learning how to obey God. And obeying God is very important. Think of something your mom or dad asks you to do—something you don't like doing but do anyway because you know God is pleased when you obey. Write it here.

_____

_____

REMEMBER: God doesn't often put people to death for disobeying. But He tells us again and again that we please Him when we obey.

The Best Wife and Mom

A wife of noble character...provides
food for her family....
She sets about her work vigorously;
    her arms are strong for her tasks.
She opens her arms to the poor
    and extends her hands to
        the needy.
Her children arise and call her blessed;
    her husband also, and he
        praises her;
Charm is deceptive, and beauty
    is fleeting;
but a woman who fears the LORD is
    to be praised.
Give her the reward she has earned,
    and let her works bring her praise
        at the city gate.

Honor your...mother, as the LORD your
God has commanded you, so that you
may live long and that it may go well
with you.
Proverbs 31:10a, 15, 17, 20, 28, 30-31;
Deuteronomy 5:16a

READ MORE ABOUT IT: Proverbs 31:11:16;
                                            18:22

TRY IT!

Around Mother's Day every year, many of us buy or make our moms a card. Sometimes the card has a funny saying, and sometimes it's a serious card. But we often forget to tell our moms how much we appreciate them the rest of the year. Today make plans to do something special for your mom three weeks or three months from now. What will you do? Write yourself a note and put it where you'll see it once in a while, so you won't forget.

134

REMEMBER: God wants us to show our moms how much we appreciate them.

Listen, my son, to your father's instruction
and do not forsake your mother's teaching.
They will be a garland to grace your head
    and a chain to adorn your neck.

[A good wife and mother] speaks with wisdom,
    and faithful instruction is on her tongue.

garland:
a ring of
flowers
or leaves

But as for you, continue in what you have learned and have become
convinced of, because you know those from whom you learned it, and
how from infancy you have known the holy Scriptures, which are able to
make you wise for salvation through faith in Christ Jesus.
Proverbs 1:8-9; 31:26; 2 Timothy 3:14-15

READ MORE ABOUT IT: Proverbs 7:1

TALK ABOUT IT!

Ask your mom or dad these three questions: What is the funniest saying of your
mom's that you still remember? What is the best advice your mom ever gave
you? Do you remember a time when you ignored what your mom said and
something bad happened? Then talk about one important lesson you, yourself,
have learned from your mom or dad.

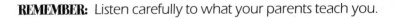

REMEMBER: Listen carefully to what your parents teach you.

135

God's Word–Hide It in Your Heart

How can a young man keep his way pure?
   By living according to your word.
I seek you with all my heart;
   do not let me stray from your commands.
I have hidden your word in my heart
   that I might not sin against you.
Praise be to you, O LORD;
   teach me your decrees.
With my lips I recount
   all the laws that come from your mouth.
I meditate on your precepts
   and consider your ways.
I delight in your decrees;
   I will not neglect your word.
Psalm 119:9-13, 15-16

MEMORIZE IT!

> How can a young man keep his way pure? By living according to your word. I have hidden your word in my heart that I might not sin against you.
> **Psalm 119:9, 11**

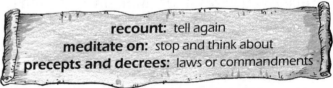

recount: tell again
meditate on: stop and think about
precepts and decrees: laws or commandments

READ MORE ABOUT IT: Psalm 119:47, 97, 140

136

REMEMBER: When we memorize God's Word, we are storing God's truths in our mind. Then He can remind us of them at just the right moment.

The Ten Commandments–Don't Commit Adultery

You shall not commit adultery.

Do you not know that the wicked will not inherit the kingdom of God? Do not be deceived: Neither the sexually immoral nor...adulterers...nor homosexual offenders...will inherit the kingdom of God.

Do you not know that your body is a temple of the Holy Spirit, who is in you, whom you have received from God? You are not your own; you were bought at a price. Therefore honor God with your body.

How can a young man keep his way pure?
By living according to your word.

Exodus 20:14; 1 Corinthians 6:9-10, 19-20; Psalm 119:9

READ MORE ABOUT IT: Philippians 4:8

PRAY ABOUT IT: God wants us to keep ourselves pure for the person we will someday marry. Pray that God will help you keep yourself pure in both body and mind. Jesus told us to even be careful about our thoughts. So ask God to help you make wise choices in what you read and what you watch on TV.

REMEMBER: Keep yourself pure in both body and mind.

I n the spring, at the time when kings go off to war, David sent Joab out with the king's men and the whole Israelite army.... But David remained in Jerusalem.

One evening David got up from his bed and walked around on the roof of the palace. From the roof he saw a woman bathing. The woman was very beautiful, and David sent someone to find out about her. The man said, "Isn't this Bathsheba, the daughter of Eliam and the wife of Uriah the Hittite?" Then David sent messengers to get her. She came to him, and he slept with her.... Then she went back home. The woman...sent word to David, saying, "I am pregnant."

The thing David had done displeased the LORD.

2 Samuel 11:1-5, 27b

READ MORE ABOUT IT: 2 Samuel 11:6-17

WRITE ABOUT IT: Kids around you may joke about sex, but it's not a joke. God gave the gift of sex to married couples to enjoy. When people have sex without being married, it only causes problems. This would be a good time to promise God that you will keep yourself pure for the person you will someday marry. Write your promise to God here. And don't let anyone pressure you to break your promise.

_____

_____

REMEMBER: God wants us to keep ourselves pure for Him.

You shall not murder.

> Whoever sheds the blood of man,
>   by man shall his blood be shed;
> for in the image of God
>   has God made man.

[Jesus said,] "You have heard that it was said to the people long ago, 'Do not murder, and anyone who murders will be subject to judgment.' But I tell you that anyone who is angry with his brother will be subject to judgment."

This is the message you heard from the beginning: We should love one another. Do not be like Cain, who belonged to the evil one and murdered his brother.
Exodus 20:13; Genesis 9:6; Matthew 5:21-22a; 1 John 3:11-12a

READ MORE ABOUT IT: 1 John 3:15-16

WHO SAYS I'M ANGRY?

TALK ABOUT IT!

Why do you think Jesus said there would be judgment for anger? Why did He connect anger with murder? Can anger get out of control? Have you ever heard anyone say, "I'm so angry I could kill you"? Do you need help controlling your anger sometimes? Don't forget that God is always there to help.

REMEMBER: It is wrong to kill another human being, but it is also wrong to get angry enough to kill someone.

David Panics

In the morning David wrote a letter to Joab and sent it with Uriah. In it he wrote, "Put Uriah in the front line where the fighting is fiercest. Then withdraw from him so he will be struck down and die."

So while Joab had the city under siege, he put Uriah at a place where he knew the strongest defenders were. When the men of the city came out and fought against Joab...Uriah the Hittite died.

When Uriah's wife heard that her husband was dead, she mourned for him. After the time of mourning was over, David had her brought to his house, and she became his wife and bore him a son. But the thing David had done displeased the LORD. 2 Samuel 11:14-17, 26-27

READ MORE ABOUT IT: Romans 6:23

David tried to cover up one sin with another. Design a poster to remind yourself that two wrongs don't make a right.

REMEMBER: God sees everything. We can't fool Him by trying to cover up our sin.

The Ten Commandments–Don't Covet

You shall not covet your neighbor's house. You shall not covet your neighbor's wife, or his manservant or maidservant, his ox or donkey, or anything that belongs to your neighbor.

Love one another, for he who loves his fellowman has fulfilled the law. The commandments, "Do not commit adultery," "Do not murder," "Do not steal," "Do not covet," and whatever other commandment there may be, are summed up in this one rule: "Love your neighbor as yourself." Love does no harm to its neighbor. Therefore love is the fulfillment of the law.
Exodus 20:17; Romans 13:8b-10

READ MORE ABOUT IT: 1 Timothy 6:6-8

covet: to want something someone else has

Imagine that coveting isn't wrong—that you can have anything you want—even if it belongs to someone else. What might you do? If your friends have video games that you like, you might decide to take the games home. Your friends would certainly fight to keep their property, and you might hurt them to take it away. Do you see why God makes the rules He does?

REMEMBER: Don't covet anything your friends have. Be happy with what God has given you.

The Prophet Who Knew David's Secret

The LORD sent Nathan to David. When he came to him, he said, "There were two men in a certain town.... The rich man had a very large number of sheep and cattle, but the poor man had nothing except one little ewe lamb he had bought. He raised it and it grew up with him and his children. It shared his food, drank from his cup and even slept in his arms.

"Now a traveler came to the rich man, but the rich man refrained from taking one of his own sheep or cattle to prepare a meal for the traveler.... Instead, he took the ewe lamb that belonged to the poor man and prepared it for the one who had come to him."

David burned with anger.... "The man who did this deserves to die!"

Then Nathan said to David, "You are the man! You struck down Uriah the Hittite with the sword and took his wife to be your own.... Now, therefore, the sword will never depart from your house."   2 Samuel 12:1-4, 5, 7a, 9b-10a

READ MORE ABOUT IT: 2 Samuel 12:13-18

WRITE ABOUT IT: King David's sins of adultery and murder began with coveting. List two or three other sins that we might commit if we covet something.

_____

_____

142   **REMEMBER:** Coveting can often lead to other sins. Be happy with what you have.

Have mercy on me, O God,
according to your unfailing love;
according to your great compassion....
Wash away all my iniquity
   and cleanse me from my sin.
Against you, you only, have I sinned
   and done what is evil in your sight,
so that you are proved right when you speak
   and justified when you judge.
Wash me, and I will be whiter than snow.
Create in me a pure heart, O God,
   and renew a steadfast spirit within me.
Restore to me the joy of your salvation
   and grant me a willing spirit, to sustain me.
Psalm 51:1-2, 4, 7b, 10, 12

READ MORE ABOUT IT: Psalm 51:13-17

sustain: support
iniquity: sin

MEMORIZE IT!

Psalm 51 is the prayer
David prayed after his adultery
with Bathsheba. Memorize
the part below to pray
whenever you have sinned
against God in any way:

Wash me, and I will be
whiter than snow. Create
in me a pure heart, O
God, and renew a
steadfast spirit within me.
Psalm 51:7b, 10

REMEMBER: God hates sin, but He loves to forgive us when we confess our sin to Him.

The Ten Commandments—Don't Steal

You shall not steal.

Ill-gotten gain...takes away the lives of those who get it.

A thief must certainly make restitution.

He who has been stealing must steal no longer, but must work, doing something useful with his own hands, that he may have something to share with those in need.

God...richly provides us with everything for our enjoyment. Command them to do good, to be rich in good deeds, and to be generous and willing to share.
Exodus 20:15; Proverbs 1:19b; Exodus 22:3b; Ephesians 4:28; 1 Timothy 6:17-18

READ MORE ABOUT IT: Ezekiel 33:15-16

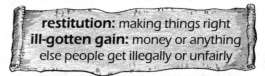

restitution: making things right
ill-gotten gain: money or anything else people get illegally or unfairly

TRY IT!

Have you ever taken anything that didn't belong to you? Even something little? If at all possible, God wants you to give it back or pay for it. It won't be easy, but it will please God. And don't forget to ask for forgiveness—from God and from the person you stole from. Make it your goal to be generous to others.

REMEMBER: Be a giver, not a taker.

Joshua sent men from Jericho to Ai.... When they returned to Joshua, they said, "Not all the people will have to go up against Ai." ...So about three thousand men went up; but they were routed by the men of Ai.

The LORD said to Joshua,..."Israel has sinned.... They have taken some of the devoted things; they have stolen, they have lied, they have put them with their own possessions. That is why the Israelites cannot stand against their enemies."

Joshua said to Achan, "Tell me what you have done."

Achan replied, "It is true! I have sinned against the LORD.... When I saw in the plunder a beautiful robe from Babylonia, two hundred shekels of silver and a wedge of gold weighing fifty shekels, I coveted them and took them."

Then all Israel stoned him.

Joshua 7:2-4, 10-12a, 19a, 19c-21a, 25c

plunder: stolen things

READ MORE ABOUT IT: Joshua 6:18-19; 7:10-26

Draw and label one or all of the items Achan stole from Jericho.

REMEMBER: One person's sin can cause trouble for many people.

145

The Ten Commandments–Don't Lie

Y ou shall not give false testimony
against your neighbor.

The LORD detests lying lips,
but he delights in men who are truthful.

Keep your tongue from evil
and your lips from speaking lies.

Whoever would love life
and see good days
must keep his tongue from evil
and his lips from deceitful speech.

I have chosen the way of truth;
I have set my heart on your laws.
Exodus 20:16; Proverbs 12:22;
Psalm 34:13; 1 Peter 3:10;
Psalm 119:30

READ MORE ABOUT IT: Psalm 15:1-2;
Ephesians 4:25

I'm not really a raven, I'm a white dove with a black suit on!

Imagine what would happen if people came to know you as someone who often told lies. How would you convince them when you were telling the truth?

146

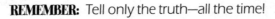

REMEMBER: Tell only the truth—all the time!

Ananias and Sapphira Get Caught

Now a man named Ananias, together with his wife Sapphira, also sold a piece of property. With his wife's full knowledge he kept back part of the money for himself, but brought the rest and put it at the apostles' feet.

Then Peter said, "Ananias, how is it that...you have lied to the Holy Spirit and have kept for yourself some of the money you received for the land?... You have not lied to men but to God."

When Ananias heard this, he fell down and died.

Later his wife came in, not knowing what had happened. Peter asked her, "Tell me, is this the price you and Ananias got for the land?"

"Yes," she said, "that is the price."

Peter said to her, "...The feet of the men who buried your husband are at the door, and they will carry you out also."

At that moment she fell down at his feet and died.
Acts 5:1-5a, 7-10a

READ MORE ABOUT IT: Psalm 119:163; Acts 4:32-37

PRAY ABOUT IT: Sometimes we may think that lying isn't as bad as some other sins. But God takes lying very seriously. Ask Him to help you be completely truthful today.

REMEMBER: God is pleased when we make truthfulness a habit.

147

The Greatest Commandment

Love the LORD your God with all your heart and with all your soul and with all your strength. These commandments that I give you today are to be upon your hearts. Impress them on your children. Talk about them when you sit at home and when you walk along the road, when you lie down and when you get up.... Write them on the doorframes of your houses and on your gates.

"Teacher, which is the greatest commandment in the Law?"

Jesus replied: "'Love the Lord your God with all your heart and with all your soul and with all your mind.' This is the first and greatest commandment. And the second is like it: 'Love your neighbor as yourself.' All the Law and the Prophets hang on these two commandments."
Deuteronomy 6:5-9;
Matthew 22:36-40

READ MORE ABOUT IT: Leviticus 19:18, 33-34; Joshua 22:5

TALK ABOUT IT!

In what ways can you love God with all your heart? What does it mean to love God with all your soul? How can you love God with all your strength? Think of some ways you can show love to those around you today.

REMEMBER: Love God with everything you've got. And love the people around you, too.

If anyone takes the life of a human being, he must be put to death. Anyone who takes the life of someone's animal must make restitution—life for life. If anyone injures his neighbor, whatever he has done must be done to him: fracture for fracture, eye for eye, tooth for tooth. As he has injured the other, so he is to be injured. Whoever kills an animal must make restitution, but whoever kills a man must be put to death. You are to have the same law for the [foreigner] and the native-born. I am the LORD your God.

[Jesus said,] "You have heard that it was said, 'Eye for eye, and tooth for tooth.' But I tell you, Do not resist an evil person. If someone strikes you on the right cheek, turn to him the other also."
Leviticus 24:17-22; Matthew 5:38-39

READ MORE ABOUT IT: Luke 6:27-31

MEMORIZE IT!

In Old Testament times when a person hurt someone else, that person would be punished in the same way. Jesus gave us a better way. Memorize these important words:

"Do to others as you would have them do to you."
Luke 6:31

REMEMBER: Don't get even. Let God show His love through you.

The Law—Helping Others

Do not deprive the [foreigner] or the fatherless of justice, or take the cloak of the widow as a pledge. Remember that you were slaves in Egypt and the LORD your God redeemed you from there. That is why I command you to do this.

When you are harvesting in your field and you overlook a sheaf, do not go back to get it. Leave it for the [foreigner], the fatherless and the widow, so that the LORD your God may bless you in all the work of your hands.

Carry each other's burdens, and in this way you will fulfill the law of Christ.

Let us not become weary in doing good.
Deuteronomy 24:17-19;
Galatians 6:2, 9a

READ MORE ABOUT IT:
Acts 20:35;
James 1:27

TRY IT!

Watch for an opportunity to be helpful to someone today. Do whatever you can to help.

REMEMBER: Be God's helper in helping others today.

150

Now the first covenant had regulations for worship and also an earthly sanctuary. A tabernacle was set up. In its first room were the lampstand, the table and the consecrated bread; this was called the Holy Place. Behind the second curtain was a room called the Most Holy Place, which had the golden altar of incense and the gold-covered ark of the covenant. This ark contained the gold jar of manna, Aaron's staff that had budded, and the stone tablets of the covenant. Above the ark were the cherubim of the Glory, overshadowing the atonement cover.

When Christ came as high priest...he entered the Most Holy Place once for all by his own blood, having obtained eternal redemption.
Hebrews 9:1-5a, 11-12

READ MORE ABOUT IT: Mark 15:37-38

> The Tabernacle was a tent that God used as His home among the Israelites. Read today's scripture again and draw something that was in the ark of the covenant.

REMEMBER: Today God lives in those who believe in Him. If God is living in us, we should be careful how we act.

God Is Compassionate

The LORD is gracious and compassionate,
slow to anger and rich in love.
The LORD is good to all;
he has compassion on all he has made.

compassion: showing deep concern for people who are hurting or needy

Praise be to the God and Father of our Lord Jesus Christ, the Father of compassion and the God of all comfort, who comforts us in all our troubles, so that we can comfort those in any trouble with the comfort we ourselves have received from God. For just as the sufferings of Christ flow over into our lives, so also through Christ our comfort overflows.
Psalm 145:8-9; 2 Corinthians 1:3-5

READ MORE ABOUT IT: Psalm 103:1-14

WRITE ABOUT IT: Write down three things you can do this week to help someone you know who is hurting or needs help. Next to each, put the day you will do what you planned. Then follow through and do it.

_____

_____

REMEMBER: God wants us to show others that He cares and we care.

W ho is a God like you,
who pardons sin and forgives?
You will again have compassion on us;
you will tread our sins underfoot
and hurl all our iniquities into the
depths of the sea.

For as far as the heavens are above
the earth,
so great is his love for those who
fear him;
as far as the east is from the west,

so far has he removed our
transgressions from us.

But if we walk in the light, as he is in
the light, we have fellowship with one
another, and the blood of Jesus, his
Son, purifies us from all sin.
Micah 7:18a, 19; Psalm 103:11-12;
1 John 1:7

READ MORE ABOUT IT:
Psalm 32:5; Isaiah 44:22

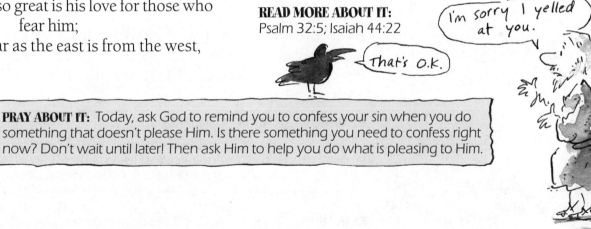

PRAY ABOUT IT: Today, ask God to remind you to confess your sin when you do something that doesn't please Him. Is there something you need to confess right now? Don't wait until later! Then ask Him to help you do what is pleasing to Him.

REMEMBER: God loves to forgive our sin. All we have to do is ask Him.

God Is Holy

MAY 31

I am the LORD who brought you up out of Egypt to be your God; therefore be holy, because I am holy.

Who among the gods is like you, O LORD?
Who is like you—
 majestic in holiness,
 awesome in glory,
 working wonders?

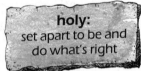

holy:
set apart to be and
do what's right

As for God, his way is perfect;
 the word of the LORD is flawless.

As obedient children...just as he who called you is holy, so be holy in all you do.
Leviticus 11:45; Exodus 15:11; Psalm 18:30a;
1 Peter 1:14-15

READ MORE ABOUT IT: Psalm 99:1-5, 9

When we get to heaven, we will have holy, perfect bodies like Jesus' body after He rose from the dead. What do you think yours will look like? Draw yourself praising our holy God in your holy body.

REMEMBER: God is a holy God. In every choice you make today, do what would please Him.

154

When the people saw that Moses was so long in coming down from the mountain, they gathered around Aaron and said, "Come, make us gods who will go before us. As for this fellow Moses who brought us up out of Egypt, we don't know what has happened to him."

Aaron answered them, "Take off the gold earrings that your wives, your sons and your daughters are wearing, and bring them to me." So all the people took off their earrings and brought them to Aaron. He took what they handed him and made it into an idol cast in the shape of a calf, fashioning it with a tool. Then they said, "These are your gods, O Israel, who brought you up out of Egypt."

"I have seen these people," the LORD said to Moses, "and they are a stiff-necked people. Now leave me alone so that my anger may burn against them and that I may destroy them. Then I will make you into a great nation."

Exodus 32:1-4, 7-8a, 9-10

stiff-necked: stubborn

READ MORE ABOUT IT: Psalm 106:19-22

Imagine how God felt when the Israelites made an idol to worship instead of worshiping Him. God had just delivered them from a terrible life in Egypt. Now they wanted to worship a cow!

REMEMBER: We hurt God, too, when we let other things take His place in our lives. Keep Him first today and always.

155

Moses Pleads with God

But Moses sought the favor of the LORD his God. "O LORD," he said, "why should your anger burn against your people, whom you brought out of Egypt with great power and a mighty hand? Why should the Egyptians say, 'It was with evil intent that he brought them out, to kill them in the mountains and to wipe them off the face of the earth'? Turn from your fierce anger; relent and do not bring disaster on your people. Remember your servants Abraham, Isaac and Israel, to whom you swore by your own self: 'I will make your descendants as numerous as the stars in the sky and I will give your descendants all this land I promised them, and it will be their inheritance forever.'"

Then the LORD relented and did not bring on his people the disaster he had threatened. Exodus 32:11-14

READ MORE ABOUT IT: Exodus 32:19-24

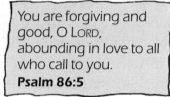

MEMORIZE IT!

You are forgiving and good, O LORD, abounding in love to all who call to you.
Psalm 86:5

Thank you, thank you, oh my Lord.

REMEMBER: We can be glad that God often does not give us what we deserve.

The LORD said to Moses, "Send some men to explore the land of Canaan, which I am giving to the Israelites. From each ancestral tribe send one of its leaders."

They came back to Moses and Aaron and the whole Israelite community at Kadesh in the Desert of Paran. There they reported to them and to the whole assembly and showed them the fruit of the land. They gave Moses this account: "We went into the land to which you sent us, and it does flow with milk and honey! Here is its fruit. But the people who live there are powerful, and the cities are fortified and very large."

Then Caleb silenced the people before Moses and said, "We should go up and take possession of the land, for we can certainly do it."

But the men who had gone up with him said, "We can't attack those people; they are stronger than we are." Numbers 13:1-2, 26-28a, 30-31

READ MORE ABOUT IT: Numbers 14:1-4

TRY IT!

Ask a brother, sister, or friend to go exploring on a pretend spy mission today. Pretend you are the two good spies Moses sent out to explore Canaan. You will find giants and big fruit and lots of milk and honey. Ask your mom and dad if you may have a glass of milk and something sweet like honey when you get back from your spy mission.

REMEMBER: Believe God's promises or you may miss out on something good.

Heat, Sweat, and Sand—40 Years in the Desert

The LORD said to Moses and Aaron: "How long will this wicked community grumble against me? I have heard the complaints of these grumbling Israelites. So tell them, 'As surely as I live, declares the LORD, I will do to you the very things I heard you say: In this desert your bodies will fall—every one of you twenty years old or more who was counted in the census and who has grumbled against me. Not one of you will enter the land I swore with uplifted hand to make your home, except Caleb son of Jephunneh and Joshua son of Nun. As for your children that you said would be taken as plunder, I will bring them in to enjoy the land you have rejected.

"'For forty years—one year for each of the forty days you explored the land—you will suffer for your sins and know what it is like to have me against you.'"
Numbers 14:26-31, 34

READ MORE ABOUT IT: 1 Corinthians 10:1-6

TALK ABOUT IT!

It's easy to grumble when things aren't going our way, isn't it? Ask your mom or dad what she or he does to avoid grumbling during unpleasant times. Are there things you can do to help each other make the best of a bad situation? What are they?

REMEMBER: Even the sin of grumbling has consequences.

So, as the Holy Spirit says:
"Today, if you hear his voice,
  do not harden your hearts
as you did in the rebellion,
  during the time of testing
  in the desert,
where your fathers tested and tried
  me and for forty years saw
  what I did.
That is why I was angry with that
  generation, and I said, 'Their
  hearts are always going astray,
and they have not known
  my ways.'"
  See to it, brothers, that none of you
has a sinful, unbelieving heart that
turns away from the living God. But
encourage one another daily, as long
as it is called Today, so that none of
you may be hardened by sin's
deceitfulness.
Hebrews 3:7-10, 12-13

READ MORE ABOUT IT: Psalm 119:176

do not harden your hearts: don't ignore God

PRAY ABOUT IT: Ask God to help you keep your mind and your heart open to Him so that you don't try to live without Him.

REMEMBER: God has done wonderful things for us. Don't turn away from Him.

Two Strikes Against Moses

Now there was no water for the community, and the people gathered in opposition to Moses and Aaron.

The LORD said to Moses, "Take the staff, and you and your brother Aaron gather the assembly together. Speak to that rock before their eyes and it will pour out its water."

[Moses] and Aaron gathered the assembly together in front of the rock and Moses said to them, "Listen, you rebels, must we bring you water out of this rock?" Then Moses raised his arm and struck the rock twice with his staff. Water gushed out, and the community and their livestock drank.

But the LORD said to Moses and Aaron, "Because you did not trust in me enough to honor me as holy in the sight of the Israelites, you will not bring this community into the land I give them." Numbers 20:2, 7-8a, 10-12

READ MORE ABOUT IT: Numbers 20:13

WRITE ABOUT IT: Moses hit the rock. He didn't speak to it. He did things his own way and took credit for God's miracle. Moses did not treat God as holy. In your own words, write yourself a reminder here to do things God's way. Then make a copy to put in your room or in your school notebook.

_____

_____

REMEMBER: God is holy and perfect and He knows what He's doing. We need to do things His way.

The people grew impatient on the way; they spoke against God and against Moses, and said, "Why have you brought us up out of Egypt to die in the desert? There is no bread! There is no water! And we detest this miserable food!"

Then the LORD sent venomous snakes among them; they bit the people and many Israelites died. So Moses prayed for the people.

The LORD said to Moses, "Make a snake and put it up on a pole; anyone who is bitten can look at it and live." So Moses made a bronze snake and put it up on a pole. Then when anyone was bitten by a snake and looked at the bronze snake, he lived.

Just as Moses lifted up the snake in the desert, so the Son of Man must be lifted up, that everyone who believes in him may have eternal life.

For God so loved the world that he gave his one and only Son, that whoever believes in him shall not perish but have eternal life. Numbers 21:4b-6, 7c-9; John 3:14-16

READ MORE ABOUT IT: John 3:36

REMEMBER: Jesus died to save us from our sins.

MEMORIZE IT!

Just as Moses lifted up the snake in the desert, so the Son of Man must be lifted up, that every-one who believes in him may have eternal life.
John 3:14-15

Have you accepted Him as your personal savior?

God Is All-Powerful

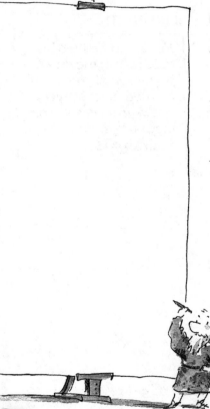

Then Job replied to the LORD:
"I know that you can do all things."

Proclaim the power of God,
    whose majesty is over Israel,
    whose power is in the skies.
You are awesome, O God,
    in your sanctuary;
    the God of Israel gives
        power and strength
        to his people.
Praise be to God!

Ah, Sovereign LORD, you have made the heavens and the earth by your great power and outstretched arm. Nothing is too hard for you.

You are worthy, our LORD
        and God,
    to receive glory and honor
        and power,
for you created all things,
    and by your will they were
        created and have
        their being.
Job 42:1-2a; Psalm 68:34-35;
Jeremiah 32:17; Revelation 4:11

READ MORE ABOUT IT: Luke 1:37

Draw a picture of something God can do but you can't.

162

REMEMBER: We can trust God because there is nothing He cannot do.

Where can I go from your Spirit?
 Where can I flee from your presence?
If I go up to the heavens, you are there;
 if I make my bed in the depths, you are there.
If I rise on the wings of the dawn,
 if I settle on the far side of the sea,
even there your hand will guide me,
 your right hand will hold me fast.

"Am I only a God nearby,"
 declares the LORD,
 "and not a God far away?
Can anyone hide in secret places
 so that I cannot see him?"
 declares the LORD.
"Do not I fill heaven and earth?"
 declares the LORD.
Psalm 139:7-10; Jeremiah 23:23-24

READ MORE ABOUT IT: 1 Kings 8:27

Imagine what it would be like if God couldn't be everywhere at once. What if He could only be at one place at a time? What if He were busy helping someone in Timbuktu at the exact time you needed His help to survive a car crash or to tell a friend about Christ? Thank God that He is everywhere!

REMEMBER: No matter where you go, God is there.

163

God Knows Everything

Oh, the depth of the riches of the
wisdom and knowledge of God!
How unsearchable his judgments,
and his paths beyond tracing out!
"Who has known the mind of the Lord?
Or who has been his counselor?"
"Who has ever given to God,
that God should repay him?"
For from him and through him and
to him are all things.
To him be the glory forever! Amen.

Nothing in all creation is hidden from
God's sight. Everything is uncovered
and laid bare before the eyes of him to
whom we must give account.
Romans 11:33-36; Hebrews 4:13

READ MORE ABOUT IT: *Psalm 139:1-6*

TRY IT!

Get together with your family or some friends and play a little guessing game.
Try guessing what various people are thinking by their conversation and the
expressions on their faces. Sometimes—only sometimes—we can guess what
other people are thinking, but we never know for sure. God knows everything,
including our thoughts, what's going to happen tomorrow, and what choices
would be best for us.

REMEMBER: God knows everything, so we can trust Him to do what is best for us.

And now, O Israel, what does the LORD your God ask of you but to fear the LORD your God, to walk in all his ways, to love him, to serve the LORD your God with all your heart and with all your soul, and to observe the LORD'S commands and decrees that I am giving you today for your own good?

To the LORD your God belong the heavens, even the highest heavens, the earth and everything in it. Yet the LORD set his affection on your forefathers and loved them, and he chose you, their descendants, above all the nations, as it is today.

Love the LORD your God and keep his requirements, his decrees, his laws and his commands always.
Deuteronomy 10:12-15; 11:1

READ MORE ABOUT IT: Deuteronomy 30:15-20

PRAY ABOUT IT: Do you ever feel as if you don't love the Lord "with all your heart"? Most of us feel that way from time to time. But remember that we couldn't love God at all if He didn't help us. Ask God to help you love Him more. Ask Him to help you show your love to Him and those around you today.

REMEMBER: Our God is great in so many ways. We serve Him because we love Him.

And the Next Leader Is...

Then Moses went out and spoke these words to all Israel: "I am now a hundred and twenty years old and I am no longer able to lead you. The LORD has said to me, 'You shall not cross the Jordan.' The LORD your God himself will cross over ahead of you. He will destroy these nations before you, and you will take possession of their land.

"Joshua also will cross over ahead of you, as the LORD said. The LORD will deliver them to you, and you must do to them all that I have commanded you. Be strong and courageous. Do not be afraid or terrified because of them, for the LORD your God goes with you; he will never leave you nor forsake you."

Then Moses summoned Joshua and said to him in the presence of all Israel, "Be strong and courageous, for you must go with this people into the land that the LORD swore to their forefathers to give them, and you must divide it among them as their inheritance. The LORD himself goes before you and will be with you."   Deuteronomy 31:1-3, 5-8a

READ MORE ABOUT IT: Psalm 139:2-3

REMEMBER: God will never leave us nor forsake us.

166

MEMORIZE IT!

Be strong and courageous. Do not be afraid or terrified because of them, for the LORD your God goes with you; he will never leave you nor forsake you.
Deuteronomy 31:6

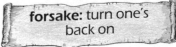

forsake: turn one's back on

After the death of Moses the servant of the LORD, the LORD said to Joshua son of Nun, Moses' aide: "Moses my servant is dead. Now then, you and all these people, get ready to cross the Jordan River into the land I am about to give to them—to the Israelites.

"Be strong and very courageous. Be careful to obey all the law my servant Moses gave you; do not turn from it to the right or to the left, that you may be successful wherever you go. Do not let this Book of the Law depart from your mouth; meditate on it day and night, so that you may be careful to do everything written in it. Then you will be prosperous and successful. Have I not commanded you? Be strong and courageous. Do not be terrified; do not be discouraged, for the LORD your God will be with you wherever you go."   Joshua 1:1-2, 7-9

READ MORE ABOUT IT: Psalm 31:23-24

TALK ABOUT IT!

What if the Israelites had held an election to fill Moses' position as leader? Think about the way the people had rebelled against God so many times and in so many ways. If you had been an Israelite back then, would you have campaigned for the job? Talk about times when you need to be strong and courageous.

REMEMBER: God's Word can help you be strong and courageous. Memorize it and do what it says.

God Is One

Hear, O Israel: The LORD our God, the LORD is one.

The LORD will be king over the whole earth. On that day there will be one LORD, and his name the only name.

Is God the God of Jews only? Is he not the God of Gentiles too? Yes, of Gentiles too, since there is only one God.

There is one one body and one Spirit—just as you were called to one hope when you were called—one Lord, one faith, one baptism; one God and Father of all, who is over all and through all and in all.
Deuteronomy 6:4; Zechariah 14:9; Romans 3:29-30a; Ephesians 4:4-6

READ MORE ABOUT IT: 1 Corinthians 8:4b-6

WRITE ABOUT IT: There is one God, but He shows himself to us in the Bible in three ways. Write down one thing you know about each—God the Father, God the Son (Jesus), and God the Holy Spirit. (If you need help, look at these verses: 1 John 3:1; 1 John 4:14; John 16:13.)

_____

_____

REMEMBER: We don't have to try to please many gods. We love and serve
one God—the God of the Bible.

168

My shield is God Most High,
who saves the upright in heart.
God is a righteous judge.

righteous:
being fair
and doing
what's right

"The days are coming," declares the LORD,
"when I will raise up to David a righteous Branch,
a King who will reign wisely
and do what is just and right in the land.
In his days Judah will be saved
and Israel will live in safety.
This is the name by which he will be called:
The LORD Our Righteousness."

If anybody does sin, we have one who speaks to the
Father in our defense–Jesus Christ, the Righteous One.
Psalm 7:10-11a; Jeremiah 23:5-6; 1 John 2:1b

READ MORE ABOUT IT: Acts 3:12-16

God's righteousness is like a mighty shield to protect us. Draw a shield that could protect you from anything. Draw yourself behind it.

REMEMBER: God is always fair. He always does what is right.

God Is Our Heavenly Father

"**I** will be a Father to you,
and you will be my sons and daughters,"
says the Lord Almighty.

How great is the love the Father has lavished on us, that we should be called children of God! And that is what we are! The reason the world does not know us is that it did not know him. Dear friends, now we are children of God, and what we will be has not yet been made known. But we know that when he appears, we shall be like him, for we shall see him as he is.
2 Corinthians 6:18; 1 John 3:1-2

READ MORE ABOUT IT: Deuteronomy 32:6; Galatians 3:26-29

PRAY ABOUT IT: Talk to God and thank Him that He is your heavenly Father. Thank Him for loving you and taking care of you and giving you what you need.

REMEMBER: God is our Father. Trust Him for what you need today.

The Best Husband and Dad

Husbands, love your wives. He who loves his wife loves himself. After all, no one ever hated his own body, but he feeds and cares for it, just as Christ does the church.

Honor your father...so that you may live long in the land the LORD your God is giving you.

What son is not disciplined by his father? Our fathers disciplined us for a little while as they thought best; but God disciplines us for our good, that we may share in his holiness. No discipline seems pleasant at the time, but painful. Later on, however, it produces a harvest of righteousness and peace for those who have been trained by it.
Ephesians 5:25a, 28b-29; Exodus 20:12; Hebrews 12:7b, 10-11

READ MORE ABOUT IT: Luke 11:11-13

TRY IT!

When was the last time you told your dad how much you appreciate him—not including Father's Day? Today, make plans to do something special about three weeks or three months from today to show your dad how much you appreciate him. Put a reminder somewhere you will see it often so you don't forget. What will you do?

REMEMBER: God wants us to show our fathers how much we appreciate them.

"My Dad Always Told Me..."

Listen, my sons, to a father's instruction;
pay attention and gain understanding.
I give you sound learning,
so do not forsake my teaching.
When I was a boy in my father's house,
still tender, and an only child of my mother,
he taught me and said,
"Lay hold of my words with all your heart;
keep my commands and you will live.
Get wisdom, get understanding;
do not forget my words or swerve from them.
Do not forsake wisdom, and she will protect you;
love her, and she will watch over you.
Wisdom is supreme; therefore get wisdom.
Though it cost all you have,
get understanding."
Proverbs 4:1-7

READ MORE ABOUT IT: Proverbs 2:1-5

MEMORIZE IT!

For the LORD gives
wisdom, and from his
mouth come knowledge
and understanding.
Proverbs 2:6

Wisdom is important

I'm better at wisecracks!

172

REMEMBER: Pay attention to what the Bible and your parents teach you.

Then Joshua son of Nun secretly sent two spies from Shittim. "Go, look over the land," he said, "especially Jericho." So they went and entered the house of...Rahab and stayed there.

The king of Jericho was told, "Look! Some of the Israelites have come here tonight to spy out the land." So the king of Jericho sent this message to Rahab: "Bring out the men who came to you and entered your house, because they have come to spy out the whole land."

But the woman had taken the two men and hidden them. Joshua 2:1-4a

READ MORE ABOUT IT: Hebrews 11:31

Draw where you would hide if you had to hide in your house.

REMEMBER: Don't be afraid to take some risks to do what you know is right.

The Trumpets, the Shout, and the Crumbling Walls

Then the LORD said to Joshua, "See, I have delivered Jericho into your hands, along with its king and its fighting men."

When the trumpets sounded, the people shouted, and at the sound of the trumpet, when the people gave a loud shout, the wall collapsed; so every man charged straight in, and they took the city. They devoted the city to the LORD and destroyed with the sword every living thing in it–men and women, young and old, cattle, sheep and donkeys.

But Joshua spared Rahab...with her family and all who belonged to her, because she hid the men Joshua had sent as spies to Jericho. Joshua 6:2, 20, 25

READ MORE ABOUT IT: Hebrews 11:30

delivered Jericho into your hands: Jericho became part of Israel's land.

Imagine that you are one of the men who is spying out Jericho. Rahab offers to hide you because she's heard about your God and wants to follow Him. You might wonder if you should stay there because she has a bad reputation, but God has provided this place to hide so you can win the battle with Jericho. What other feelings might you have as you wait to hear the trumpets?

174　　**REMEMBER:** God can help us win the toughest battles.

"Now fear the LORD and serve him with all faithfulness," [Joshua said.] "Throw away the gods your forefathers worshiped beyond the River and in Egypt, and serve the LORD. But if serving the LORD seems undesirable to you, then choose for yourselves this day whom you will serve, whether the gods your forefathers served beyond the River, or the gods of the Amorites, in whose land you are living. But as for me and my household, we will serve the LORD."

Then the people answered, "Far be it from us to forsake the LORD to serve other gods! It was the LORD our God himself who brought our fathers up out of Egypt, from that land of slavery, and performed those great signs before our eyes. He protected us on our journey and among all the nations through which we traveled. And the LORD drove out before us all the nations, including the Amorites, who lived in the land. We too will serve the LORD, because he is our God." Joshua 24:14-18

READ MORE ABOUT IT: Colossians 3:23-24

TALK ABOUT IT!

What does it mean to serve the Lord? Do you have to wait to grow up before you can serve Him? Are pastors and missionaries the only ones who can serve the Lord? Can you only serve the Lord on Sundays, or are there ways to serve Him every day? How will you serve Him today?

REMEMBER: Serve the Lord in everything you do today.

The Days of the Judges

JUNE 22

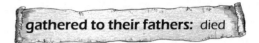

The people served the LORD throughout the lifetime of Joshua and of the elders who outlived him and who had seen all the great things the LORD had done for Israel.

After that whole generation had been gathered to their fathers, another generation grew up, who knew neither the LORD nor what he had done for Israel. Then the Israelites did evil in the eyes of the LORD and served the Baals. They forsook the LORD, the God of their fathers, who had brought them out of Egypt. In his anger against Israel the LORD handed them over to raiders who plundered them.

Then the LORD raised up judges, who saved them out of the hands of these raiders. Whenever the LORD raised up a judge for them, he was with the judge and saved them out of the hands of their enemies as long as the judge lived, for the LORD had compassion on them.
Judges 2:7, 10-12a, 14a, 16, 18a

READ MORE ABOUT IT: Psalm 78:1-7

WRITE ABOUT IT: In the time of the judges, the Israelites got into trouble. The parents didn't pass on what they had learned about the Lord—like how good it is to love and serve Him. Write here what you want to tell your children someday about God.

176

REMEMBER: Sometimes we go our own way instead of God's, but He is always ready to take us back.

Trumpets, Jars, and Torches?

Gideon...returned to the camp of Israel and called out, "Get up! The LORD has given the Midianite camp into your hands." Dividing the three hundred men into three companies, he placed trumpets and empty jars in the hands of all of them, with torches inside.

"Watch me," he told them. "Follow my lead. When I get to the edge of the camp, do exactly as I do."

Gideon and the hundred men with him reached the edge of the camp at the beginning of the middle watch, just after they had changed the guard.

The three companies blew the trumpets and smashed the jars. Grasping the torches in their left hands and holding in the right hands the trumpets they were to blow, they shouted, "A sword for the LORD and for Gideon!"

While each man held his position around the camp, all the Midianites ran, crying out as they fled.
Judges 7:15-17, 19a, 20-21

READ MORE ABOUT IT: Judges 7:1-15

> Imagine that you are one of only 300 soldiers that went with Gideon to fight the Midianites. The Bible says the Midianites' "camels could no more be counted than the sand on the seashore." That's a huge army! And what are your weapons? Would you think you were going to get creamed? What is your battle cry? Does that help you feel more confident?

REMEMBER: God is not impressed with the size of the enemy. God is stronger than any army.

Samson's Super Strength

Samson led Israel for twenty years in the days of the Philistines.

One day Samson went to Gaza. The people of Gaza were told, "Samson is here!" So they surrounded the place and lay in wait for him all night at the city gate. They made no move during the night, saying, "At dawn we'll kill him."

But Samson lay there only until the middle of the night. Then he got up and took hold of the doors of the city gate, together with the two posts, and tore them loose, bar and all. He lifted them to his shoulders and carried them to the top of the hill that faces Hebron. Judges 15:20–16:1a, 2-3

READ MORE ABOUT IT: Judges 14:5-6

Draw Samson lifting something very heavy that only a man with his strength could pick up by himself.

REMEMBER: We may not be super strong like Samson, but God has promised us all the strength we need.

Some time later, [Samson] fell in love with a woman in the Valley of Sorek whose name was Delilah. The rulers of the Philistines went to her and said, "See if you can lure him into showing you the secret of his great strength and how we can overpower him so we may tie him up and subdue him. Each one of us will give you eleven hundred shekels of silver."

So Delilah said to Samson, "Tell me the secret of your great strength and how you can be tied up and subdued."

He said, "If anyone ties me securely with new ropes that have never been used, I'll become as weak as any other man."

So Delilah took new ropes and tied him with them. Then, with men hidden in the room, she called to him, "Samson, the Philistines are upon you!" But he snapped the ropes off his arms as if they were threads.
Judges 16:4-6, 11-12

READ MORE ABOUT IT: 2 Timothy 2:22

PRAY ABOUT IT: Samson got into trouble because he spent too much time with people who were a bad influence on him. Delilah and her friends didn't care about God. Ask God to help you be faithful to Him. Ask Him to help you do what's right no matter what everyone around you is doing.

REMEMBER: When we do what God's enemies want us to do, we aren't serving God.

The Secret Is Out!

Then [Delilah] said to Samson, "How can you say, 'I love you,' when you won't confide in me? This is the third time you have made a fool of me and haven't told me the secret of your great strength." With such nagging she prodded him day after day until he was tired to death.

So he told her everything. "No razor has ever been used on my head," he said, "because I have been a Nazirite set apart to God since birth. If my head were shaved, my strength would leave me, and I would become as weak as any other man."
Judges 16:15-17

READ MORE ABOUT IT: 1 Corinthians 16:13

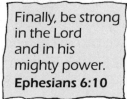

180

REMEMBER: Don't let anyone pressure you into doing something you know is wrong.

When Delilah saw that he had told her everything, she sent word to the rulers of the Philistines, "Come back once more; he has told me everything." So the rulers of the Philistines returned with the silver in their hands. Having put him to sleep on her lap, she called a man to shave off the seven braids of his hair, and so began to subdue him. And his strength left him.

Then she called, "Samson, the Philistines are upon you!"

He awoke from his sleep and thought, "I'll go out as before and shake myself free." But he did not know that the LORD had left him.

Then the Philistines seized him, gouged out his eyes and took him down to Gaza. Binding him with bronze shackles, they set him to grinding in the prison.
Judges 16:18-21

READ MORE ABOUT IT: Numbers 6:1-8

I shouldn't have listened to her.

TRY IT!

Do you know someone who used to follow God but now doesn't seem to care? Try to talk kindly to that person or send a note, gently reminding him or her how good it is to know God is guiding you and helping you each day.

REMEMBER: There are often sad consequences if we decide we don't need to follow the Lord.

Samson's Revenge

JUNE **28**

Now the rulers of the Philistines assembled to offer a great sacrifice to Dagon their god and to celebrate, saying, "Our god has delivered Samson, our enemy, into our hands."

While they were in high spirits, they shouted, "Bring out Samson to entertain us." So they called Samson out of the prison, and he performed for them.

When they stood him in the pillars,...Samson prayed to the LORD, "O Sovereign LORD, remember me. O God, please strengthen me just once more, and let me with one blow get revenge on the Philistines for my two eyes." Then Samson reached toward the two central pillars on which the temple stood. Bracing himself against them, his right hand on the one and his left hand on the other, Samson said, "Let me die with the Philistines!" Then he pushed with all his might, and down came the temple on the rulers and all the people in it. Judges 16:23, 25-30b

READ MORE ABOUT IT: Hebrews 11:32-34

WRITE ABOUT IT: Write a note to God, promising that with His help you will stay close to Him.

_____

_____

REMEMBER: God is always ready to help when we change our minds and come back to Him.

I lift up my eyes to you,
  to you whose throne is in heaven.
As the eyes of slaves look to the hand
    of their master,
  as the eyes of a maid look to the
    hand of her mistress,
so our eyes look to the LORD our God,
  till he shows us his mercy.
Have mercy on us, O LORD,
    have mercy on us,
  for we have endured
    much contempt.

We have endured much ridicule
    from the proud,
  much contempt from the arrogant.

But because of his great love for us,
God, who is rich in mercy, made us
alive with Christ even when we were
dead in transgressions—it is by grace
you have been saved.
Psalm 123:1-4; Ephesians 2:4-5

READ MORE ABOUT IT: Deuteronomy 4:31

TALK ABOUT IT!

Ask your mom or dad if there are some projects your family could do to help the homeless or others who are poor or sick. Make plans to do something sometime this month for those less fortunate than you. Meanwhile, look for ways to show mercy to those you spend time with every day.

REMEMBER: God is merciful, and He wants us to show mercy to others who
    are hurting or in trouble.

God Is Gracious

The LORD is gracious and righteous;
  our God is full of compassion.
The LORD protects the simplehearted;
  when I was in great need,
    he saved me.
Be at rest once more, O my soul,
  for the LORD has been good to you.

The Word became flesh and made his dwelling among us. We have seen his glory, the glory of the One and Only, who came from the Father, full of grace and truth.

From the fullness of his grace we have all received one blessing after another. For the law was given through Moses; grace and truth came through Jesus Christ.
Psalm 116:5-7; John 1:14, 16-17

READ MORE ABOUT IT:
Ephesians 2:8-9

grace: kindness that we don't deserve or work for

PRAY ABOUT IT: There is no way we could ever earn salvation for our sin. Jesus showed us incredible kindness when He, as God, became a human being and died and rose again to take the punishment for our sin and give us new life. Have you accepted His gift of salvation? Have you thanked Him lately for dying for you? Why don't you pray and do that right now?

REMEMBER: We cannot earn our way to heaven. We are saved by God's grace alone.

There was a famine in the land, and a man from Bethlehem in Judah, together with his wife and two sons, went to live for a while in the country of Moab. The man's name was Elimelech, his wife's name Naomi, and the names of his two sons were Mahlon and Kilion.

Now Elimelech, Naomi's husband, died, and she was left with her two sons. They married Moabite women, one named Orpah and the other Ruth.... Both Mahlon and Kilion also died, and Naomi was left without her two sons and her husband.

Then Naomi said to her two daughters-in-law, "Go back, each of you, to your mother's home. May the LORD show kindness to you, as you have shown to your dead and to me. May the LORD grant that each of you will find rest in the home of another husband."   Ruth 1:1-2a, 3-5, 8-9a

READ MORE ABOUT IT: Psalm 119:75-77

First there wasn't enough food to eat. Then Naomi's husband died, and then her two sons died. How do you think she felt? Draw Naomi's face to show how she must have felt.

REMEMBER: God cares about us when sad things happen to us.

185

Naomi and Ruth—Loyal Friends

But Ruth replied, "Don't urge me to leave you or to turn back from you. Where you go I will go, and where you stay I will stay. Your people will be my people and your God my God. Where you die I will die, and there I will be buried. May the LORD deal with me, be it ever so severely, if anything but death separates you and me." When Naomi realized that Ruth was determined to go with her, she stopped urging her.

So Naomi returned from Moab accompanied by Ruth the Moabitess, her daughter-in-law, arriving in Bethlehem as the barley harvest was beginning.
Ruth 1:16-18, 22

READ MORE ABOUT IT: *1 Corinthians 13*

TALK ABOUT IT!

Have you ever had friends who decided they didn't want to be your friends anymore? Did you try to get them back as friends? What happened? Ask your mom or dad if this ever happened to her or him. How should we act toward those who turn their backs on us?

REMEMBER: We please God when we are loyal and don't turn our backs on our friends.

Now Naomi had a relative on her husband's side, from the clan of Elimelech, a man of standing, whose name was Boaz.

And Ruth the Moabitess said to Naomi, "Let me go to the fields and pick up the leftover grain behind anyone in whose eyes I find favor."

Naomi said to her, "Go ahead, my daughter." So she went out and began to glean in the fields behind the harvesters. As it turned out, she found herself working in a field belonging to Boaz.

So Boaz said to Ruth, "My daughter, listen to me. Don't go and glean in another field and don't go away from here. Stay here with my servant girls."

At this, she bowed down with her face to the ground. She exclaimed, "Why have I found such favor in your eyes that you notice me—a foreigner?" Ruth 2:1-3b, 8, 10

READ MORE ABOUT IT: Leviticus 19:9-10

man of standing: a well-respected, important person in the community

TRY IT!

Sometimes we are kind to strangers but forget to do kind things for the people in our family. Look for a way to do something kind for a parent or sister or brother today. If possible, don't let anyone know who did the kind deed.

REMEMBER: God wants us to be kind to others, whether we know them or not.

Wedding Bells and Baby Clothes

So Boaz took Ruth and she became his wife. Then he went to her, and the LORD enabled her to conceive, and she gave birth to a son. The women said to Naomi: "Praise be to the LORD, who this day has not left you without a kinsman-redeemer. May he become famous throughout Israel! He will renew your life and sustain you in your old age. For your daughter-in-law, who loves you and who is better to you than seven sons, has given him birth."

Then Naomi took the child, laid him in her lap and cared for him. The women living there said, "Naomi has a son." And they named him Obed. He was the father of Jesse, the father of David.
Ruth 4:13-17

kinsman-redeemer: a relative who would marry or take care of a widow

READ MORE ABOUT IT: Leviticus 25:25-27

PRAY ABOUT IT: Sometimes we feel jealous when good things happen to others. But Naomi's friends praised God for bringing a new baby into Naomi's family. Did one of your friends just get a new bike or go on a great vacation? One way to keep from being jealous is to pray and thank God that something good is happening to others. Pray for your friends now.

188

REMEMBER: Praise God for the good things He gives to you and those around you.

Clap your hands, all you nations;
shout to God with cries of joy.
How awesome is the LORD Most High,
 the great King over all the earth!

Shout with joy to God, all the earth!
 Sing the glory of his name;
 make his praise glorious!
Say to God, "How awesome are your deeds!
 So great is your power
 that your enemies cringe before you;
All the earth bows down to you;

they sing praise to you,
 they sing praise to your name."

Come and see what God has done,
 how awesome his works in man's behalf!

You are awesome, O God, in your sanctuary;
 the God of Israel gives power and
 strength to his people.
Praise be to God!
Psalms 47:1-2; 66:1-5; 68:35

READ MORE ABOUT IT: Deuteronomy 10:17-21

WRITE ABOUT IT: Write a note to God telling Him three ways you think He is awesome.

_____

_____

REMEMBER: God is greater than anything we can imagine. He's awesome!

God Is the Great I AM

Moses said to God, "Suppose I go to the Israelites and say to them, 'The God of your fathers has sent me to you,' and they ask me, 'What is his name?' Then what shall I tell them?"

God said to Moses, "I AM WHO I AM. This is what you are to say to the Israelites: 'I AM has sent me to you.'"

God also said to Moses, "I am the LORD. I appeared to Abraham, to Isaac and to Jacob as God Almighty, but by my name the LORD I did not make myself known to them.

"Therefore say to the Israelites: 'I am the LORD. I will take you as my own people, and I will be your God. Then you will know that I am the LORD your God.'"

"I tell you the truth," Jesus answered, "before Abraham was born, I am!" Exodus 3:13-14; 6:2-3, 6a, 7a, b; John 8:58

READ MORE ABOUT IT: Hebrews 13:8

TALK ABOUT IT!

Why do you think Jesus said, "Before Abraham was born, **I am,**" instead of "**I was**"? What does that tell us about Him? Look at the titles of the next seven days' readings to see some of the ways Jesus used His I AM name.

REMEMBER: Jesus is God—the Great I AM.

I AM–The Bread of Life

So [the people] asked Jesus, "What miraculous sign then will you give that we may see it and believe you? What will you do? Our forefathers ate the manna in the desert; as it is written: 'He gave them bread from heaven to eat.'"

Jesus said to them, "I tell you the truth, it is not Moses who has given you the bread from heaven, but it is my Father who gives you the true bread from heaven. For the bread of God is he who comes down from heaven and gives life to the world."

"Sir," they said, "from now on give us this bread."

Then Jesus declared, "I am the bread of life. He who comes to me will never go hungry, and he who believes in me will never be thirsty."
John 6:30-35

READ MORE ABOUT IT: John 6:37

I like bread

Imagine that you are a great inventor, and you invent the perfect food—a food that people would only have to eat once and they would never get hungry again. What would you call it? Jesus wasn't talking about bread or food for our physical bodies. He meant that if we accept Him, we won't have to keep looking everywhere else for things to satisfy us. Jesus satisfies us completely.

REMEMBER: Jesus is everything we need.

191

I AM—The Light of the World

As he went along, he saw a man blind from birth. His disciples asked him, "Rabbi, who sinned, this man or his parents, that he was born blind?"

"Neither this man nor his parents sinned," said Jesus, "but this happened so that the work of God might be displayed in his life. As long as it is day, we must do the work of him who sent me. Night is coming, when no one can work. While I am in the world, I am the light of the world."

Having said this, he spit on the ground, made some mud with the saliva, and put it on the man's eyes. "Go," he told him, "wash in the Pool of Siloam" (this word means Sent). So the man went and washed, and came home seeing.
John 9:1-7

READ MORE ABOUT IT: John 8:12

MEMORIZE IT!

[Jesus said,] "I am the light of the world. Whoever follows me will never walk in darkness, but will have the light of life."
John 8:12

I can see! I can see!

REMEMBER: In our dark, sinful world, Jesus is a light to help us know and do what's right.

"I tell you the truth," [Jesus said,] "the man who does not enter the sheep pen by the gate, but climbs in by some other way, is a thief and a robber. The man who enters by the gate is the shepherd of his sheep."

Therefore Jesus said again, "I tell you the truth, I am the gate for the sheep. All who ever came before me were thieves and robbers, but the sheep did not listen to them. I am the gate; whoever enters through me will be saved. He will come in and go out, and find pasture. The thief comes only to steal and kill and destroy; I have come that they may have life, and have it to the full."
John 10:1-2, 7-10

READ MORE ABOUT IT: Hebrews 13:20-21

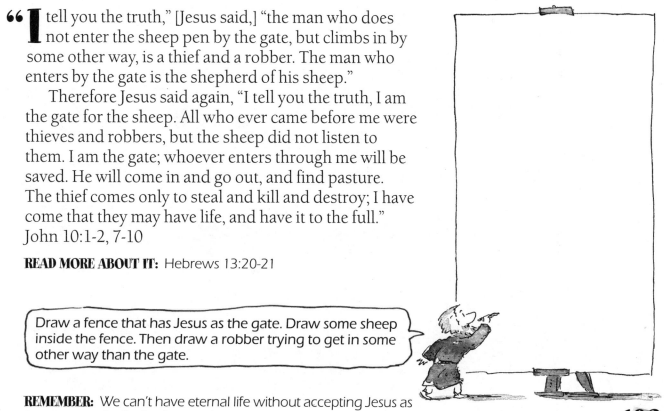

Draw a fence that has Jesus as the gate. Draw some sheep inside the fence. Then draw a robber trying to get in some other way than the gate.

REMEMBER: We can't have eternal life without accepting Jesus as the Savior for our sins.

193

I AM—The Good Shepherd

"I am the good shepherd," [Jesus said.] "The good shepherd lays down his life for the sheep. The hired hand is not the shepherd who owns the sheep. So when he sees the wolf coming, he abandons the sheep and runs away. Then the wolf attacks the flock and scatters it. The man runs away because he is a hired hand and cares nothing for the sheep.

"My sheep listen to my voice; I know them, and they follow me. I give them eternal life, and they shall never perish; no one can snatch them out of my hand. My Father, who has given them to me, is greater than all, no one can snatch them out of my Father's hand. I and the Father are one." John 10:11-13, 27-30.

READ MORE ABOUT IT:
Psalm 23

Get out of here!

TALK ABOUT IT!

What are some things that shepherds do for their sheep? (lead them? provide food and water? take care of their medical needs? rescue them? what else?) How is Jesus like that for us?

194

REMEMBER: Nobody knows how to take care of us better than Jesus.

I AM—The Resurrection and the Life

Now a man named Lazarus was sick. He was from Bethany, the village of Mary and her sister Martha.

On his arrival, Jesus found that Lazarus had already been in the tomb for four days.

"Lord," Martha said to Jesus, "if you had been here, my brother would not have died. But I know that even now God will give you whatever you ask."

Jesus said to her, "Your brother will rise again. I am the resurrection and the life. He who believes in me will live, even though he dies; and whoever lives and believes in me will never die."

Jesus called in a loud voice, "Lazarus, come out!" The dead man came out, his hands and feet wrapped with strips of linen, and a cloth around his face.
John 11:1, 17, 21-23, 25, 43-44

READ MORE ABOUT IT: John 5:19-23

PRAY ABOUT IT: If you have never accepted Jesus as the Savior for your sin and accepted the eternal life He offers, wouldn't today be a good day to do that? If you need help, read through the plan of salvation on pages 372-373 in the back of this book. Then just thank Jesus for dying for your sins and ask Him to come into your life. If you already have done this, pray for a friend who hasn't yet accepted Christ.

REMEMBER: Jesus gives new life. If we believe in Him, we will live with Him forever.

I AM—The Way and the Truth and the Life

"Do not let your hearts be troubled," [Jesus said.] "Trust in God; trust also in me. In my Father's house are many rooms; if it were not so, I would have told you. I am going there to prepare a place for you. And if I go and prepare a place for you, I will come back and take you to be with me that you also may be where I am. You know the way to the place where I am going."

Thomas said to him, "Lord, we don't know where you are going, so how can we know the way?"

Jesus answered, "I am the way and the truth and the life. No one comes to the Father except through me."
John 14:1-6

READ MORE ABOUT IT: John 14:8-12

MEMORIZE IT!

Jesus answered, "I am the way and the truth and the life. No one comes to the Father except through me."
John 14:5-6

REMEMBER: Believe in Jesus. He is the only one who can take away our sins. And that's the only way we can have eternal life.

"**I** am the true vine, and my Father is the gardener," [Jesus said.] "He cuts off every branch in me that bears no fruit, while every branch that does bear fruit he prunes so that it will be even more fruitful. You are already clean because of the word I have spoken to you. Remain in me, and I will remain in you. No branch can bear fruit by itself; it must remain in the vine. Neither can you bear fruit unless you remain in me.

"I am the vine; you are the branches. If a man remains in me and I in him, he will bear much fruit; apart from me you can do nothing."
John 15:1-5

READ MORE ABOUT IT: *John 15:9-11*

TRY IT!

If there are any flowers in your yard, ask your mom or dad if you can pick two of them for an experiment. Even dandelions from a park will do. Set one of the flowers in a nice jar or vase on the table, but don't add water. Put the other flower in a container with water. Keep track of how long each one lives. What happens when flowers are cut off from the plant they were growing on? Do you think we will grow well as Christians if we ignore Jesus, who called himself the True Vine?

REMEMBER: When we love Jesus and do what He says, He helps us do great things for Him.

197

Hannah's Prayer and Promise

There was a certain man...from the hill country of Ephraim, whose name was Elkanah.... He had two wives; one was called Hannah and the other Peninnah. Peninnah had children, but Hannah had none.

Year after year this man went up from his town to worship and sacrifice to the LORD Almighty at Shiloh.

In bitterness of soul Hannah wept much and prayed to the LORD. And she made a vow, saying, "O LORD Almighty, if you will only look upon your servant's misery and remember me, and not forget your servant but give her a son, then I will give him to the LORD for all the days of his life."
1 Samuel 1:1-3a, 10-11b

VOW: a promise. If people make a vow to God, they must keep the promise.

READ MORE ABOUT IT: Psalm 113:9

WRITE ABOUT IT: Write down something that you want very much—not for yourself but for someone else or for God.

_____

_____

198

REMEMBER: God cares about the things that mean the most to us.

Samuel—God's Answer to Prayer

Early the next morning they arose and worshiped before the LORD and then went back to their home at Ramah. Elkanah lay with Hannah his wife, and the LORD remembered her. So in the course of time Hannah conceived and gave birth to a son. She named him Samuel, saying, "Because I asked the LORD for him."

After he was weaned, she took the boy with her, young as he was, and brought him to the house of the LORD at Shiloh. And she said to [Eli], "As surely as you live, my lord, I am the woman who stood here beside you praying to the LORD. I prayed for this child, and the LORD has granted me what I asked of him. So now I give him to the LORD. For his whole life he will be given over to the LORD." And he worshiped the LORD there.
1 Samuel 1:19-22, 24, 26-28

READ MORE ABOUT IT: Psalm 34:4-6, 15

PRAY ABOUT IT: Talk to God today about what you wrote down yesterday. God always answers in one of three ways—yes, no, or wait. When God answers, write on yesterday's page the date He answered and what the answer was.

REMEMBER: Trust God to answer your prayers, and don't forget to keep your promises to Him.

Samuel—The Boy Who Grew Up in the Temple

Samuel was ministering before the LORD. Each year his mother made him a little robe and took it to him when she went up with her husband to offer the annual sacrifice. Eli would bless Elkanah and his wife, saying, "May the LORD give you children by this woman to take the place of the one she prayed for and gave to the LORD." Then they would go home. And the LORD was gracious to Hannah; she conceived and gave birth to three sons and two daughters. Meanwhile, the boy Samuel grew up in the presence of the LORD.
1 Samuel 2:18a, 19-21

READ MORE ABOUT IT: *1 Samuel 2:1-10*

If someone offered to make you a special robe or an outfit of clothes, what would you want it to look like?

REMEMBER: Hannah offered her son to the Lord as a servant, but Samuel also had to be willing to serve. The Lord wants you to be His willing servant, too.

Samuel was lying down in the temple of the LORD, where the ark of God was. Then the LORD called Samuel.

[Samuel] ran to Eli and said, "Here I am; you called me."

But Eli said, "I did not call; go back and lie down." So he went and lay down.

Again the LORD called, "Samuel!"

Now Samuel did not yet know the LORD: The word of the LORD had not yet been revealed to him.

The LORD called Samuel a third time, and Samuel got up and went to Eli and said, "Here I am; you called me."

Then Eli realized that the LORD was calling the boy. So Eli told Samuel, "Go and lie down, and if he calls you, say, 'Speak, LORD, for your servant is listening.'" So Samuel went and lay down in his place.

The LORD came and stood there, calling as at the other times, "Samuel! Samuel!"

Then Samuel said, "Speak, for your servant is listening."
1 Samuel 3:3b, 5-6a, 7-10

MEMORIZE IT!

Speak, for your servant is listening.
1 Samuel 3:10b

Lord, I'm listening

READ MORE ABOUT IT: 1 Samuel 3:11-18

REMEMBER: God speaks to us through the Bible, but we only learn when we listen.

201

Samuel—God's Servant

The LORD was with Samuel as he grew up, and he let none of his words fall to the ground. And all Israel from Dan to Beersheba recognized that Samuel was attested as a prophet of the LORD. The LORD continued to appear at Shiloh, and there he revealed himself to Samuel through his word.

Throughout Samuel's lifetime, the hand of the LORD was against the Philistines.

Samuel continued as judge over Israel all the days of his life. From year to year he went on a circuit from Bethel to Gilgal to Mizpah, judging Israel in all those places. But he always went back to Ramah, where his home was, and there he also judged Israel. And he built an altar there to the LORD.

1 Samuel 3:19-21; 7:13b, 15-17

READ MORE ABOUT IT: Colossians 3:17

Imagine that you are Samuel back in Bible times. As a prophet you preached to the Israelite people. What kinds of things would you want the people to know about the Lord? As a judge you traveled from one place to another to settle legal matters. What kinds of court cases do you think you might have had to settle? Who would you talk to if you didn't know the answers?

REMEMBER: We can serve God in whatever we do—if we do it for Him.

When Samuel grew old, he appointed his sons as judges for Israel. But his sons did not walk in his ways. They turned aside after dishonest gain and accepted bribes and perverted justice.

So all the elders of Israel gathered together and came to Samuel at Ramah. They said to him, "You are old, and your sons do not walk in your ways; now appoint a king to lead us, such as all the other nations have."

But when they said, "Give us a king to lead us," this displeased Samuel; so he prayed to the LORD. And the LORD told him: "Listen to all that the people are saying to you; it is not you they have rejected, but they have rejected me as their king." 1 Samuel 8:1, 3-7

READ MORE ABOUT IT: 1 Samuel 8:10-22

WRITE ABOUT IT: God was supposed to be Israel's king, but they wanted a human king. Who is the king of your life right now—God? yourself? friends? Are you happy about who is king in your life? Write about it here.

_____

_____

REMEMBER: God wants to be King of our lives. Who could do a better job?

Saul—Israel's First King

Samuel summoned the people of Israel to the LORD at Mizpah and said to them, "This is what the LORD, the God of Israel, says: 'I brought Israel up out of Egypt, and I delivered you from the power of Egypt and all the kingdoms that oppressed you.' But you have now rejected your God, who saves you out of all your calamities and distresses. And you have said, 'No, set a king over us.' So now present yourselves before the LORD by your tribes and clans."

Samuel brought all the tribes of Israel near. Finally Saul son of Kish was chosen.

They ran and brought him out, and as he stood among the people he was a head taller than any of the others. Samuel said to all the people, "Do you see the man the LORD has chosen? There is no one like him among all the people."
1 Samuel 10:17-20a, 21b, 23-24a

READ MORE ABOUT IT: 1 Samuel 11:12-14

Draw King Saul the way you think he would have looked—handsome and tall. Draw yourself standing next to him.

REMEMBER: Sometimes when God gives us what we ask for, we're sorry later that we asked for it.

Then the word of the LORD came to Samuel: "I am grieved that I have made Saul king, because he has turned away from me and has not carried out my instructions."

When Samuel reached him, Saul said, "The LORD bless you! I have carried out the LORD'S instructions."

But Samuel replied:

"Does the LORD delight in burnt offerings and sacrifices as much as in obeying the voice of the LORD?
To obey is better than sacrifice,
and to heed is better than the fat of rams.
Because you have rejected the word of the LORD,
he has rejected you as king."
1 Samuel 15:10-11a, 13, 22, 23b

READ MORE ABOUT IT: 1 Samuel 15:1-9

heed:
pay attention (to what God wants)

the fat of rams:
the sheep offered in sacrifice to God

TALK ABOUT IT!

It's easy to get fooled into thinking that if we do good things for others or go to church a lot, we don't have to worry about the sin in our lives. What does God say about this? In what ways do you have trouble obeying God's Word?

REMEMBER: God is more pleased when we obey Him than when we try to do great things for Him by ourselves.

The Lord Looks at the Heart

The LORD said to Samuel, "How long will you mourn for Saul, since I have rejected him as king over Israel? Fill your horn with oil and be on your way; I am sending you to Jesse of Bethlehem. I have chosen one of his sons to be king."

When they arrived, Samuel saw Eliab and thought, "Surely the LORD's anointed stands here before the LORD."

But the LORD said to Samuel, "Do not consider his appearance or his height, for I have rejected him. The LORD does not look at the things man looks at. Man looks at the outward appearance, but the LORD looks at the heart."

1 Samuel 16:1, 6-7

READ MORE ABOUT IT: Psalm 78:70-72

MEMORIZE IT!

The LORD does not look at the things man looks at. Man looks at the outward appearance, but the LORD looks at the heart.
1 Samuel 16:7b

REMEMBER: The kind of person we are inside is more important than the way we look outside.

206

Jesse had seven of his sons pass before Samuel, but Samuel said to him, "The LORD has not chosen these." So he asked Jesse, "Are these all the sons you have?"

"There is still the youngest," Jesse answered, "but he is tending the sheep."

Samuel said, "Send for him; we will not sit down until he arrives."

So he sent and had him brought in. He was ruddy, with a fine appearance and handsome features.

Then the LORD said, "Rise and anoint him; he is the one." So Samuel took the horn of oil and anointed him in the presence of his brothers, and from that day on the Spirit of the LORD came upon David in power.

1 Samuel 16:10-13a

READ MORE ABOUT IT: Acts 13:21-23

ruddy: having a healthy, reddish complexion

anoint: to dedicate someone to God by pouring special oil on the person

Imagine that you are David, Jesse's youngest son, tending your father's sheep in the pasture. You sing praise songs to God while you practice your slingshot in case you have to rescue a lamb from a lion or bear. You have heard the prophet Samuel is looking for a new king for Israel. How would you feel when you hear that he wants to see you?

REMEMBER: If God wants you to do something, He will give you the strength to do it.

Goliath–The Philistine Bully

Now the Philistines gathered their forces for war and assembled at Socoh in Judah. A champion named Goliath, who was from Gath, came out of the Philistine camp. He was over nine feet tall.

Goliath stood and shouted to the ranks of Israel, "Why do you come out and line up for battle? Am I not a Philistine, and are you not the servants of Saul? Choose a man and have him come down to me. If he is able to fight and kill me, we will become your subjects; but if I overcome him and kill him, you will become our subjects and serve us." Then the Philistine said, "This day I defy the ranks of Israel! Give me a man and let us fight each other." On hearing the Philistine's words, Saul and all the Israelites were dismayed and terrified.
1 Samuel 17:1a, 4, 8-11

READ MORE ABOUT IT: 1 Samuel 17:2-3, 5-7; Matthew 19:26

That's a big guy!

TRY IT!

Goliath was nine feet tall. Use a ladder and yardstick to measure nine feet high on a tree or wall. Ask your mom or dad for help if necessary. Put a big piece of masking tape there. Then stand next to the tree or wall and look up at the tape. Imagine a soldier that tall challenging you to fight him! Do you see why the Israelites were afraid to fight someone so big?

REMEMBER: Even though things may look hopeless, nothing is impossible for God.

David said to Saul, "Let no one lose heart on account of this Philistine; your servant will go and fight him."

David said to the Philistine, "You come against me with sword and spear and javelin, but I come against you in the name of the LORD Almighty, the God of the armies of Israel, whom you have defied. All those gathered here will know that it is not by sword or spear that the LORD saves; for the battle is the LORD'S, and he will give all of you into our hands."

As the Philistine moved closer to attack him, David ran quickly toward...him. Reaching into his bag and taking out a stone, he slung it and struck the Philistine on the forehead. The stone sank into his forehead, and he fell facedown on the ground.

So David triumphed over the Philistine with a sling and a stone; without a sword in his hand he struck down the Philistine and killed him. 1 Samuel 17:32, 45, 47-50

READ MORE ABOUT IT: 1 Samuel 17:41-44

PRAY ABOUT IT: Do you know a bully who is always pushing you around? Is there someone at school who is constantly mean to you or others? We don't need to live in fear of others if we have God in our lives. Ask God to help you be strong for Him and not let other people push you around. Pray, too, for the bully. God can change even the hearts of bullies.

REMEMBER: God is stronger than any enemy or bully.

Saul Gets Jealous

After David had finished talking with Saul, Jonathan [Saul's son] became one in spirit with David, and he loved him as himself.

Whatever Saul sent him to do, David did it so successfully that Saul gave him a high rank in the army. This pleased all the people, and Saul's officers as well.

When the men were returning home after David had killed the Philistine, the women came out from all the towns of Israel to meet King Saul with singing and dancing, with joyful songs and with tambourines and lutes. As they danced, they sang:

> "Saul has slain his thousands,
>   and David his tens of thousands."

Saul was very angry; this refrain galled him. "They have credited David with tens of thousands," he thought, "but me with only thousands. What more can he get but the kingdom?" And from that time on Saul kept a jealous eye on David.   1 Samuel 18:1, 5-9

galled him: irritated him

READ MORE ABOUT IT: Proverbs 27:4

WRITE ABOUT IT: What would you do if someone were jealous of you? How would you act toward them? talk to them? pray for them? Write down your ideas here.

_____

_____

210

REMEMBER: All good things come from God. Jealousy does not.

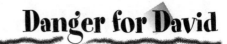

Saul...was prophesying in his house, while David was playing the harp, as he usually did. Saul had a spear in his hand and he hurled it, saying to himself, "I'll pin David to the wall." But David eluded him twice.

Saul was afraid of David, because the LORD was with David but had left Saul. So he sent David away from him and gave him command over a thousand men, and David led the troops in their campaigns. In everything he did he had great success, because the LORD was with him. When Saul saw how successful he was, he was afraid of him. But all Israel and Judah loved David, because he led them in their campaigns.
1 Samuel 18:10b-16

READ MORE ABOUT IT: 1 Samuel 19:1-7, 9-10

TALK ABOUT IT!

Ask your dad or mom about the most dangerous situation he or she has ever been in. How did he or she get out of it? Did God do something miraculous to help? Talk about dangerous situations you've been in, too. Who do we need to turn to when we're in danger?

REMEMBER: Trust God to protect you from danger.

Saul's Terrible Defeat

Now the Philistines fought against Israel; the Israelites fled before them, and many fell slain on Mount Gilboa. The Philistines pressed hard after Saul and his sons, and they killed his sons Jonathan, Abinadab and Malki-Shua. The fighting grew fierce around Saul, and when the archers overtook him, they wounded him.

Saul took his own sword and fell on it. So Saul and his three sons died, and all his house died together.

Saul died because he was unfaithful to the LORD; he did not keep the word of the LORD and even consulted a medium for guidance, and did not inquire of the LORD. So the LORD put him to death and turned the kingdom over to David son of Jesse.
1 Chronicles 10:1-3, 4c, 6, 13-14

READ MORE ABOUT IT: 1 Chronicles 10:5, 7-12

medium: someone who claims to be able to talk to dead people's spirits

PRAY ABOUT IT: Pray that the Lord will keep you faithful to Him even in the little things like what you say and what you think and what you watch on TV. Ask God to help you make wise choices today.

212

REMEMBER: There are consequences when we are not faithful to the Lord.

"Now then, tell my servant David, 'This is what the LORD Almighty says: I took you from the pasture and from following the flock to be ruler over my people Israel. I have been with you wherever you have gone, and I have cut off all your enemies from before you. Now I will make your name great, like the names of the greatest men of the earth.

"'The LORD declares to you that the LORD himself will establish a house for you: When your days are over and you rest with your fathers, I will raise up your offspring to succeed you, who will come from your own body, and I will establish his kingdom. He is the one who will build a house for my Name, and I will establish the throne of his kingdom forever. I will be his father, and he will be my son.'"

2 Samuel 7:8-9, 11b-14a

READ MORE ABOUT IT:
2 Samuel 7:1-7

Imagine that you are David. It seems like only a little while ago that you were playing with your slingshot while you watched your dad's sheep. But since then you have killed a mean giant that threatened your whole nation. You've had to duck twice to keep from getting skewered with King Saul's javelin. How do you think you would feel when God makes this promise to you? Today we know that the son of David who sits on the throne of heaven forever is Jesus.

REMEMBER: God has kept His promise to David, and He keeps His promises to us, too.

Page 1
Joshua marched with the Israelites around and around Jericho as God had commanded. The trumpets blasted, and the people shouted. Jericho's strong, thick walls crumbled! The Israelites rushed in and conquered the city. (See June 20.)

Page 2
God had given Samson great strength, but Samson did not serve God with it—not until the day he died. By then Samson was a blind prisoner and his captors made fun of him. Samson asked God for strength once more, and he pulled down the Philistine temple pillars with his bare hands. He died in the rubble with God's Philistine enemies. (See June 28.)

Page 3
Esther trusted God enough to risk her life. When she became queen of Persia, she challenged a wicked man named Haman and ended up saving the entire nation of Israel. (See September 15-18.)

Page 4
Samuel grew up in God's temple with Eli the priest. When Samuel heard a voice in the night, he thought Eli was calling. But it was really the Lord. God asked Samuel to serve Him, and Samuel became a great prophet and judge in Israel. (See July 17-18.)

Page 5
All the Israelite soldiers were too scared to battle the Philistines' champion fighter, Goliath. But young David trusted God, and with one zing of his slingshot, he brought that giant crashing to the ground! (See July 24-25.)

Page 6
One day God's prophet Elijah challenged the prophets of the false god Baal to a contest. The god who sent fire from heaven to burn his sacrifice would be declared the true God. Baal's prophets prayed, but nothing happened. Elijah prayed, and an awesome fire fell from heaven! (See August 10-12.)

Page 7
Daniel prayed to God three times a day, even though his enemies got the king to pass a law against it. Daniel was thrown into a den of lions, but God shut the lions' mouths. Daniel came out without a scratch! (See September 6-7.)

Page 8
God wanted Jonah to tell the people of Nineveh to stop sinning and start following Him. Jonah didn't want to go, so he ran away and ended up in the belly of a giant fish. Jonah prayed, and the Lord rescued him. Jonah eventually did what God asked, and Nineveh began to follow God. (See August 14-16.)

The LORD is my shepherd, I shall not be in want.
  He makes me lie down in green pastures,
he leads me beside quiet waters,
    he restores my soul.
He guides me in paths of righteousness
    for his name's sake.
I will fear no evil,
    for you are with me;
your rod and your staff,
    they comfort me.
Surely goodness and love will follow me
    all the days of my life,
and I will dwell in the house of the LORD forever.
Psalm 23:1-3, 4b, 6

READ MORE ABOUT IT: Philippians 4:19

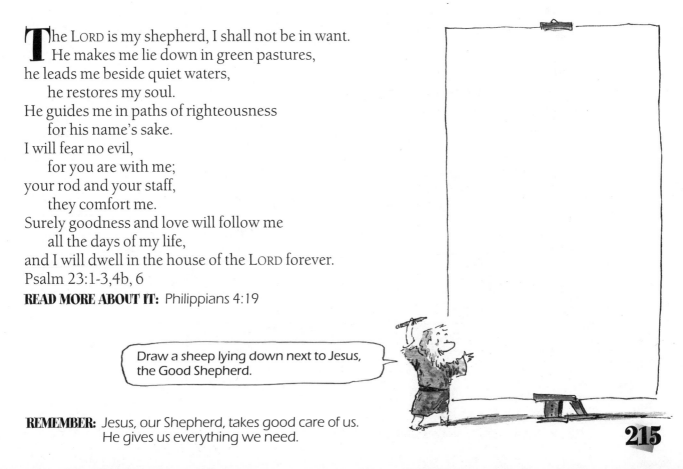

Draw a sheep lying down next to Jesus, the Good Shepherd.

REMEMBER: Jesus, our Shepherd, takes good care of us. He gives us everything we need.

215

Praise the LORD.

Praise God in his sanctuary;
   praise him in his mighty heavens.
Praise him for his acts of power;
   praise him for his surpassing
      greatness.
Praise him with the sounding trumpet,
   praise him with the harp and lyre,
praise him with tambourine and
   dancing,

praise him with the strings
   and flute,
praise him with the clash of cymbals,
   praise him with resounding
      cymbals.
Let everything that has breath praise
   the LORD.

Praise the LORD.
Psalm 150

READ MORE ABOUT IT: *Psalms 33:1-5, 20-22;*
34:1-3

TRY IT!

Do you play an instrument? Play or sing a praise song to God today. If you like to make up songs, make up a tune for Psalm 150—today's reading.

216

REMEMBER: *We can never praise God too much. He loves to hear us praise Him.*

When the time drew near for David to die, he gave a charge to Solomon his son.

"I am about to go the way of all the earth," he said. "So be strong, show yourself a man, and observe what the LORD your God requires: Walk in his ways, and keep his decrees and commands, his laws and requirements, as written in the Law of Moses, so that you may prosper in all you do and wherever you go, and that the LORD may keep his promise to me: 'If your descendants watch how they live, and if they walk faithfully before me with all their heart and soul, you will never fail to have a man on the throne of Israel.'"

Trust in the LORD with all your heart
and lean not on your own understanding;
in all your ways acknowledge him,
and he will make your paths straight.
1 Kings 2:1-4; Proverbs 3:5-6

READ MORE ABOUT IT: Philippians 4:13; John 15:5

MEMORIZE IT!

Trust in the LORD with all your heart and lean not on your own understanding; in all your ways acknowledge him, and he will make your paths straight.
Proverbs 3:5-6

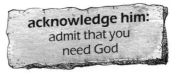

acknowledge him: admit that you need God

Birds need God too!

REMEMBER: Don't try to live for God by yourself. Trust God to help you in everything.

Solomon Asks for Wisdom

At Gibeon the LORD appeared to Solomon during the night in a dream, and God said, "Ask for whatever you want me to give you."

[Solomon answered,] "Now, O LORD my God, you have made your servant king in place of my father David. But I am only a little child and do not know how to carry out my duties. Your servant is here among the people you have chosen, a great people, too numerous to count or number. So give your servant a discerning heart to govern your people and to distinguish between right and wrong. For who is able to govern this great people of yours?"

The LORD was pleased that Solomon had asked for this.
1 Kings 3:5, 7-10

READ MORE ABOUT IT: James 1:5-8

WRITE ABOUT IT: Solomon could have asked God for anything in the world—to be rich or powerful or good looking—but He asked for wisdom. What would you have asked for? Write a note to God here, asking Him for what you think is most important.

218

REMEMBER: Anyone who asks God for wisdom is already learning to be wise.

The Wisdom of Solomon

God gave Solomon wisdom and very great insight, and a breadth of understanding as measureless as the sand on the seashore. Solomon's wisdom was greater than the wisdom of all the men of the East, and greater than all the wisdom of Egypt. He was wiser than any other man.... And his fame spread to all the surrounding nations.

He spoke three thousand proverbs and his songs numbered a thousand and five. He described plant life, from the cedar of Lebanon to the hyssop that grows out of walls. He also taught about animals and birds, reptiles and fish. Men of all nations came to listen to Solomon's wisdom, sent by all the kings of the world, who had heard of his wisdom.
1 Kings 4:29-34

READ MORE ABOUT IT: 1 Chronicles 29:23-25

TALK ABOUT IT!

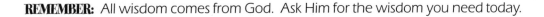

Ask your dad or mom who is the wisest person he or she has ever known. What made that person wise? What were some of that person's wise sayings? How did that person get so wise? Would you like to be known as a wise person? How can you become wise?

REMEMBER: All wisdom comes from God. Ask Him for the wisdom you need today.

Solomon's Wise Sayings

The proverbs of Solomon son of David,
king of Israel:

for attaining wisdom and discipline;
   for understanding words of insight;
for acquiring a disciplined and prudent life,
   doing what is right and just and fair;
for giving prudence to the simple,
   knowledge and discretion to the young—
let the wise listen and add to their learning,
   and let the discerning get guidance—
for understanding proverbs and parables,
   the sayings and riddles of the wise.

The fear of the LORD is the beginning
   of knowledge,
   but fools despise wisdom and discipline.

Proverbs 1:1-7

prudent: careful
the simple: people who are not wise
fear of the Lord: giving God the respect He deserves
discretion: ability to tell good from bad

MEMORIZE IT!

The fear of the LORD is the beginning of knowledge, but fools despise wisdom and discipline.
Proverbs 1:7

I wish I were wiser!

READ MORE ABOUT IT: Luke 11:31

REMEMBER: The book of Proverbs in the Bible is full of wise sayings. You can learn a lot from them.

A Great Temple for Worshiping a Great God

When Solomon had finished building the temple of the LORD and the royal palace, and had achieved all he had desired to do, the LORD appeared to him a second time, as he had appeared to him at Gibeon. The LORD said to him:

"I have heard the prayer and plea you have made before me; I have consecrated this temple, which you have built, by putting my Name there forever. My eyes and my heart will always be there.

"As for you, if you walk before me in integrity of heart and uprightness, as David your father did, and do all I command and observe my decrees and laws, I will establish your royal throne over Israel forever, as I promised David your father when I said, 'You shall never fail to have a man on the throne of Israel.'"

1 Kings 9:1-5

READ MORE ABOUT IT: 1 Kings 5:1-7

Imagine that you, like Solomon, can build a great temple for the Lord. You will probably use only the best lumber and stone. You will hire only the best workers. You won't let anyone mess up anything because you want God to have the very best. Did you know that if you have accepted Christ as your Savior, your life is God's temple? Are you building and decorating your life to bring praise to Him?

REMEMBER: God wants us to bring glory to Him in all we are and do.

It's About Time

There is a time for everything,
and a season for every activity under heaven:
    a time to be born and a time to die,
    a time to plant and a time to uproot,
    a time to kill and a time to heal,
    a time to tear down and a time to build,
    a time to weep and a time to laugh,
    a time to mourn and a time to dance,
    a time to embrace and a time to refrain,
    a time to search and a time to give up,
    a time to keep and a time to throw away,
    a time to be silent and a time to speak,
    a time for war and a time for peace.
Ecclesiastes 3:1-6, 7b, 8b

READ MORE ABOUT IT: Ecclesiastes 3:11

Draw a clock, but in place of the numbers on the face of the clock, write in some of the words from today's reading—like laugh, weep (cry), build, love. Draw in the hands of the clock, pointing to two words you feel like doing today.

REMEMBER: God's wisdom teaches us the proper time for everything.

Not only was the Teacher wise, but also he imparted knowledge to the people. He pondered and searched out and set in order many proverbs. The Teacher searched to find just the right words, and what he wrote was upright and true.

The words of the wise are like goads, their collected sayings like firmly embedded nails—given by one Shepherd. Be warned, my son, of anything in addition to them.

Of making many books there is no end, and much study wearies the body.

Now all has been heard;
    here is the conclusion of
    the matter:
Fear God and keep his
    commandments,
    for this is the whole duty of
    man.
Ecclesiastes 12:9-13

READ MORE ABOUT IT: John 15:14

goad: pointed stick used to make a big animal, like an ox, move

PRAY ABOUT IT: Wise words are like goads or sharp sticks that poke us and remind us to live God's way. What wise words from God have you learned from reading this book? Pray that God will help you obey what you have learned.

REMEMBER: Wise people love God, respect God, and obey God.

In the thirty-eighth year of Asa king of Judah, Ahab son of Omri became king of Israel, and he reigned in Samaria over Israel twenty-two years. Ahab son of Omri did more evil in the eyes of the LORD than any of those before him. He not only considered it trivial to commit the sins of Jeroboam son of Nebat, but he also married Jezebel daughter of Ethbaal king of the Sidonians, and began to serve Baal and worship him. He set up an altar for Baal in the temple of Baal that he built in Samaria. Ahab...did more to provoke the LORD, the God of Israel, to anger than did all the kings of Israel before him.

Now Elijah the Tishbite...said to Ahab, "As the LORD, the God of Israel, lives, whom I serve, there will be neither dew nor rain in the next few years except at my word."
1 Kings 16:29-33; 17:1

READ MORE ABOUT IT: 1 John 4:4-6

TALK ABOUT IT!

Why do you think God was so angry that Ahab was worshiping the false god Baal? (Hint: think about the Ten Commandments. What was the first commandment God gave to His people? And don't forget that Ahab was the king of Israel. Why is that important?) What kinds of things can become false gods to us today?

  REMEMBER: God will not share first place with anyone or anything in our lives.

This is my favorite story!!!

Then the word of the LORD came to Elijah: "Leave here, turn eastward and hide in the Kerith Ravine, east of the Jordan. You will drink from the brook, and I have ordered the ravens to feed you there." So he did what the LORD had told him. The ravens brought him bread and meat in the morning and bread and meat in the evening, and he drank from the brook.

When I shut up the heavens so that there is no rain, ...if my people, who are called by my name, will humble themselves and pray and seek my face and turn from their wicked ways, then will I hear from heaven and will forgive their sin and will heal their land.
1 Kings 17:2-5a, 6; 2 Chronicles 7:13-14

READ MORE ABOUT IT: Psalm 37:25

If ravens were going to deliver lunch to you, what do you think they would bring? Draw it here.

REMEMBER: God will do whatever it takes to give His people what they need.

Contest of the Gods

After a long time, in the third year, the word of the LORD came to Elijah: "Go and present yourself to Ahab, and I will send rain on the land."

When Ahab saw Elijah, he said to him, "Is that you, you troubler of Israel?"

"I have not made trouble for Israel," Elijah replied. "But you and your father's family have. You have abandoned the LORD's commands and have followed the Baals. Now summon the people from all over Israel to meet me on Mount Carmel. And bring the four hundred and fifty prophets of Baal."

So Ahab sent word throughout all Israel and assembled the prophets on Mount Carmel. Elijah went before the people and said, "How long will you waver between two opinions? If the LORD is God, follow him; but if Baal is God, follow him." But the people said nothing.
1 Kings 18:1, 17-19a, 20-21

READ MORE ABOUT IT: 1 Peter 2:21

MEMORIZE IT!

How long will you waver between two opinions? If the LORD is God, follow him.
1 Kings 18:21b

Sometimes you have to make a choice

I know how this story ends. I'll choose God's way.

REMEMBER: You can't follow God and the world at the same time. Make your choice now.

Which God Will Answer?

Then Elijah said to them, "...Get two bulls for us. Let them choose one for themselves, and let them cut it into pieces and put it on the wood but not set fire to it. I will prepare the other bull and put it on the wood but not set fire to it. Then you call on the name of your god, and I will call on the name of the LORD. The god who answers by fire—he is God."

Then all the people said, "What you say is good."

Elijah said to the prophets of Baal, "Choose one of the bulls and prepare it first, since there are so many of you. Call on the name of your god, but do not light the fire." So they took the bull given them and prepared it.

Then they called on the name of Baal from morning till noon. "O Baal, answer us!" they shouted. But there was no response; no one answered.

1 Kings 18:22-26a, b

READ MORE ABOUT IT: Psalm 96:4-6

Imagine that you are one of the prophets of Baal. You have worshiped this god all your life, but he has never done anything good for you. You only know you have to do many good things for your god to keep him from doing bad things to you. What are you thinking when the contest continues for some time and your god doesn't answer?

REMEMBER: There is no other true god but our God, the God of Abraham, Isaac, Jacob—and Elijah.

227

A Fiery Reply

AUGUST 12

slaughtered: killed
prostrate: lying down flat on their stomachs

At the time of sacrifice, the prophet Elijah stepped forward and prayed: "O LORD, God of Abraham, Isaac and Israel, let it be known today that you are God in Israel and that I am your servant and have done all these things at your command. Answer me, O LORD, answer me, so these people will know that you, O LORD, are God."

Then the fire of the LORD fell and burned up the sacrifice, the wood, the stones and the soil, and also licked up the water in the trench.

When all the people saw this, they fell prostrate and cried, "The LORD–he is God! The LORD–he is God!"

Then Elijah commanded them, "Seize the prophets of Baal. Don't let anyone get away!" They seized them, and Elijah had them brought down to the Kishon Valley and slaughtered there. 1 Kings 18:36-37a, 38-40

READ MORE ABOUT IT: Isaiah 45:18-19

WRITE ABOUT IT: In this contest, all God had to do to prove He was God was to send fire from heaven to burn up the sacrifice. Why do you think He made the fire burn up the wood, stones, and soil plus lick up the water in the trench?

_____

_____

REMEMBER: God can do things that we think are impossible.

The Servant Who Saved Her Master's Life

Now Naaman was a commander of the army of the king of Aram.... He was a valiant soldier, but he had leprosy.

Now bands from Aram had gone out and had taken captive a young girl from Israel, and she served Naaman's wife. She said to her mistress, "If only my master would see the prophet who is in Samaria! He would cure him of his leprosy."

So Naaman went with his horses and chariots and stopped at the door of Elisha's house. Elisha sent a messenger to say to him, "Go wash yourself seven times in the Jordan, and your flesh will be restored and you will be cleansed."

But Naaman went away angry.

Naaman's servants...said, "My father, if the prophet had told you to do some great thing, would you not have done it?"

So [Naaman] went down and dipped himself in the Jordan seven times, as the man of God had told him, and his flesh... became clean like that of a young boy. 2 Kings 5:1-3, 9-11a, 13a, 14

leprosy: a skin disease that eats away at a person's flesh

READ MORE ABOUT IT: 2 Kings 5:1-16

TRY IT!

Do you know someone who hasn't accepted Jesus as Savior? In a way, that person is like Naaman. He or she need to be made clean from sin—by Jesus. Today, be like Naaman's servant girl and tell that person where to find help. Explain what Jesus did on the cross and how He offers eternal life to all who believe in Him. (See pages 372-373.)

REMEMBER: God wants us to tell others about Him.

The Prophet Who Ran Away

The word of the LORD came to Jonah son of Amittai: "Go to the great city of Nineveh and preach against it, because its wickedness has come up before me."

But Jonah ran away from the LORD and headed for Tarshish. He went down to Joppa, where he found a ship bound for that port.

Then the LORD sent a great wind on the sea, and such a violent storm arose that the ship threatened to break up.

All the sailors were afraid and each cried out to his own god.

Then the sailors said to each other, "Come, let us cast lots to find out who is responsible for this calamity." They cast lots and the lot fell on Jonah.

"Pick me up and throw me into the sea," [Jonah] replied, "and it will become calm. I know that it is my fault that this great storm has come upon you." Jonah 1:1-3a, 4-5a, 7, 12

READ MORE ABOUT IT: Jonah 1:8-11, 13-16

TALK ABOUT IT!

Ask your dad or mom if he or she ever tried to run away from home and why. Did it work? Did anything funny or scary happen? Sometimes we try to run away from God, too. How? Why? Is it ever too late to turn back?

230

REMEMBER: When we disobey God, the consequences sometimes affect other people.

But the LORD provided a great fish to swallow Jonah, and Jonah was inside the fish three days and three nights.

From inside the fish Jonah prayed...

"In my distress I called to the LORD,
  and he answered me.
You hurled me into the deep,
  into the very heart of the seas,
  and the currents swirled about me.
When my life was ebbing away,
  I remembered you, LORD,
and my prayer rose to you,
to your holy temple.
Those who cling to worthless idols
  forfeit the grace that could be theirs.
But I, with a song of thanksgiving,
  will sacrifice to you.
What I have vowed I will make good.
  Salvation comes from the LORD."

And the LORD commanded the fish, and it vomited Jonah onto dry land.
Jonah 1:17—2:2a, 3a, 7-10

READ MORE ABOUT IT: Jonah 2:3b-6;
1 Chronicles 28:9

PRAY ABOUT IT: Is there something you have promised God you would do that you haven't done? Has God shown you some way He wants you to obey Him, but you want to do things your way? Talk to God today about these things and ask Him to help you do what you know you should.

REMEMBER: God wants willing servants. But if we're not willing, He may have to teach us to be willing.

Nineveh Does an About-Face

Then the word of the LORD came to Jonah a second time: "Go to the great city of Nineveh and proclaim to it the message I give you."

Jonah obeyed the word of the LORD and went to Nineveh. Now Nineveh was a very important city—a visit required three days. On the first day, Jonah started into the city. He proclaimed: "Forty more days and Nineveh will be overturned." The Ninevites believed God. They declared a fast, and all of them, from the greatest to the least, put on sackcloth.

When God saw what they did and how they turned from their evil ways, he had compassion and did not bring upon them the destruction he had threatened.

Jonah 3:1-5, 10

READ MORE ABOUT IT: Jonah 3:7-9

sackcloth: dark, rough-textured clothing people in Bible times wore when they were very sad or sorry for sin

God, save me!

Imagine that you are a young person in Nineveh. People all around you are sinful, and you have followed the crowd. Jonah comes and says God will destroy your whole city in forty days because it is so wicked. How would you react? Would you be willing to do anything to escape God's punishment?

REMEMBER: God never quits caring about us even when we disobey. He is always ready to forgive.

" **A**nd afterward," [the LORD said,]
"I will pour out my Spirit on all people.
Your sons and daughters will prophesy,
    your old men will dream dreams,
    your young men will see visions.
Even on my servants, both men and women,
    I will pour out my Spirit in those days.
I will show wonders in the heavens
    and on the earth,
    blood and fire and billows of smoke.
The sun will be turned to darkness
    and the moon to blood
    before the coming of the great and dreadful
        day of the LORD.
And everyone who calls
    on the name of the LORD will be saved."
Joel 2:28-32a

READ MORE ABOUT IT: Psalm 68:19-20

MEMORIZE IT!

And everyone who calls on the name of the LORD will be saved.
Joel 2:32a

REMEMBER: Many terrible things will happen before the end of the world, but if we're trusting God, He will save us.

233

Amos—Judgment and Hope

AUGUST 18

"**I** hate, I despise your religious feasts.
Even though you bring me...offerings,
I will not accept them.
Away with the noise of your songs!
I will not listen to the music of
your harps.
But let justice roll on like a river,
righteousness like a never-failing
stream!
You have lifted up the shrine of your king,
the pedestal of your idols.

Therefore, I will send you into exile
beyond Damascus," says the LORD.
"The days are coming," declares the LORD,
"when...I will bring back my exiled
people Israel;
they will rebuild the ruined cities and
live in them."
Amos 5:21a, 22a, 23-24, 26a, 27a;
9:13-14a

READ MORE ABOUT IT: Psalm 71:1-5

exile:
being kicked
out of your
country or
land
abhor: hate

WRITE ABOUT IT: God is not pleased when we try to do great things for Him but don't give Him first place in our hearts. He is not pleased when we sing praise songs to Him but don't try to help those who have been treated unfairly. Write down some things you could do to put God first and to help those in need.

_____

_____

REMEMBER: God judges sin, but He never leaves us without hope.

"When Israel was a child, I loved
    him, and out of Egypt I called
        my son.
But the more I called Israel,
    the further they went from me.
They sacrificed to the Baals
    and they burned incense to images.
It was I who taught Ephraim to walk,
    taking them by the arms;
but they did not realize
    it was I who healed them.

I led them with cords of human
    kindness, with ties of love;
I lifted the yoke from their neck
    and bent down to feed them.

Will they not return to Egypt
    and will not Assyria rule over them
    because they refuse to repent?"
Hosea 11:1-5

Ephraim: another way of referring to Israel

READ MORE ABOUT IT: Psalm 103:1-12

TALK ABOUT IT!

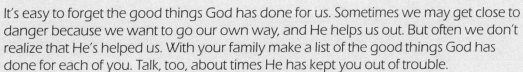

It's easy to forget the good things God has done for us. Sometimes we may get close to danger because we want to go our own way, and He helps us out. But often we don't realize that He's helped us. With your family make a list of the good things God has done for each of you. Talk, too, about times He has kept you out of trouble.

REMEMBER: We need to pay attention to what the Lord is trying to teach us in love.

Isaiah Sees the Lord

In the year that King Uzziah died, I saw the LORD seated on a throne, high and exalted, and the train of his robe filled the temple. Above him were seraphs, each with six wings: With two wings they covered their faces, with two they covered their feet, and with two they were flying. And they were calling to one another:

"Holy, holy, holy is the LORD Almighty;
the whole earth is full of his glory."

At the sound of their voices the doorposts and thresholds shook and the temple was filled with smoke. Isaiah 6:1-4

READ MORE ABOUT IT:
Hebrews 12:1-2

seraphs: angel-like creatures
holy: separated from everything sinful or imperfect

Draw what you think a seraph looked like. Remember that they had six wings—two wings covered their face, two covered their feet, and they used two to fly.

REMEMBER: God is holy, and He wants us to become more and more like Him.

"But you, Bethlehem Ephrathah,
though you are small among
the clans of Judah,
out of you will come for me
one who will be ruler over Israel,
whose origins are from of old,
from ancient times."

Therefore Israel will be abandoned
until the time when she who is in
labor gives birth
and the rest of his brothers return
to join the Israelites.
He will stand and shepherd his flock
in the strength of the LORD,
in the majesty of the name of the
LORD his God.
And they will live securely, for then his
greatness
will reach to the ends of the earth.
And he will be their peace.
Micah 5:2-5a

READ MORE ABOUT IT: Luke 2:1-7

TALK ABOUT IT!

The prophet Micah talked about Jesus bringing peace. How does Jesus' peace make a difference in your life? Does peace simply mean not fighting and not worrying or does it mean more than that?

REMEMBER: God wants us to tell others about the peace they can have by accepting the Lord Jesus Christ.

Good King Hezekiah

Hezekiah...was twenty-five years old when he became king. He did what was right in the eyes of the LORD, just as his father David had done. He removed the high places, smashed the sacred stones and cut down the Asherah poles. He broke into pieces the bronze snake Moses had made, for up to that time the Israelites had been burning incense to it. (It was called Nehushtan.)

Hezekiah trusted in the LORD, the God of Israel. There was no one like him among all the kings of Judah, either before him or after him. He held fast to the LORD and did not cease to follow him; he kept the commands the LORD had given Moses. And the LORD was with him; he was successful in whatever he undertook.
2 Kings 18:1b, 2a, 3-7a

READ MORE ABOUT IT: Proverbs 22:1-6

high places, sacred stones, Asherah poles: places and things people used to worship false gods

PRAY ABOUT IT: God was pleased with King Hezekiah because he obeyed His commandments. Look back at the Ten Commandments section of this book and think about whether you have been obeying each commandment or not. Ask God to forgive you where you have slipped. Then ask Him for His help in obeying so that you, too, can please the Lord.

REMEMBER: God is pleased when we are faithful to Him and encourage others to follow Him.

A Scary Answer to Prayer

In the fourteenth year of King Hezekiah's reign, Sennacherib king of Assyria attacked all the fortified cities of Judah and captured them.

And Hezekiah prayed to the LORD: "O LORD, God of Israel, enthroned between the cherubim, you alone are God over all the kingdoms of the earth. Give ear, O LORD, and hear; open your eyes, O LORD, and see; listen to the words Sennacherib has sent to insult the living God."

Then Isaiah...sent a message to Hezekiah: "This is what the LORD, the God of Israel, says: I have heard your prayer concerning Sennacherib king of Assyria."

That night the angel of the LORD went out and put to death a hundred and eighty-five thousand men in the Assyrian camp.

2 Kings 18:13; 19:15a, 16, 20, 35a

READ MORE ABOUT IT: Isaiah 37:14-20

God is mightier than all His enemies. He is more powerful than anyone or anything. What do you wish He would control for you? Draw it here.

REMEMBER: Whenever we are in a tough situation, we need to turn it over to God.

239

Israel Gets Captured

In the ninth year of Hoshea, the king of Assyria captured Samaria and deported the Israelites to Assyria. He settled them in Halah, in Gozan on the Habor River and in the towns of the Medes.

deported: sent them out of their country

All this took place because the Israelites had sinned against the LORD their God, who had brought them up out of Egypt from under the power of Pharaoh king of Egypt. They worshiped other gods and followed the practices of the nations the LORD had driven out before them, as well as the practices that the kings of Israel had introduced. The Israelites secretly did things against the LORD their God that were not right.

They worshiped idols, though the LORD had said, "You shall not do this." The LORD warned Israel and Judah through all his prophets and seers: "Turn from your evil ways. Observe my commands and decrees."
2 Kings 17:6-9a, 12-13a

READ MORE ABOUT IT:
Ephesians 5:10; Psalm 143:8, 10

Imagine that you are one of the Israelite young people, and you haven't been careful about obeying the Lord. Think of how scary it would be to have to leave your home town and go to Assyria—a land where no one worshiped your God. You have heard how cruel the Assyrians are to those they capture. What would you want to say to God?

REMEMBER: There are sad consequences when we don't obey.

The LORD is a jealous and avenging God;
the LORD takes vengeance and is filled
with wrath.
The LORD takes vengeance on his foes
and maintains his wrath against his
enemies.
The LORD is slow to anger and great in
power; the LORD will not leave the
guilty unpunished.
His way is in the whirlwind and the storm,
and clouds are the dust of his feet.
Who can withstand his indignation?
Who can endure his fierce anger?
His wrath is poured out like fire;
the rocks are shattered before him.
The LORD is good,
a refuge in times of trouble.
He cares for those who trust in him,
but with an overwhelming flood
he will make an end of [Nineveh];
he will pursue his foes into darkness.
Nahum 1:2-3, 6-8

READ MORE ABOUT IT: Romans 12:19-21

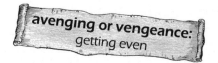

avenging or vengeance:
getting even

WRITE ABOUT IT: Write three words that describe how you feel when others are treating
you unfairly. Then write three words that describe how you feel when God has helped
you in a tough situation.

REMEMBER: We don't have to try to get even. That's God's job.

Zephaniah–God's Joy

Sing, O Daughter of Zion;
shout aloud, O Israel!
Be glad and rejoice with all your heart,
    O Daughter of Jerusalem!
The LORD has taken away your punishment,
    he has turned back your enemy.
The LORD, the King of Israel, is with you;
    never again will you fear any harm.
On that day they will say to Jerusalem,
    "Do not fear, O Zion;
    do not let your hands hang limp.
The LORD your God is with you,
    he is mighty to save.
He will take great delight in you,
    he will quiet you with his love,
    he will rejoice over you with singing."
Zephaniah 3:14-17

READ MORE ABOUT IT: 2 Thessalonians 2:15-17

MEMORIZE IT!

The LORD your God is with you, he is mighty to save. He will take great delight in you, he will quiet you with his love, he will rejoice over you with singing.
Zephaniah 3:17

REMEMBER: God is always with us, and He is always ready to help.

The words of Jeremiah son of Hilkiah.

The word of the LORD came to me, saying,

"Before I formed you in the womb
   I knew you,
      before you were born I set
      you apart;
      I appointed you as a prophet to
      the nations."

"Ah, Sovereign LORD," I said, "I do not know how to speak; I am only a child."

But the LORD said to me, "Do not say, 'I am only a child.' You must go to everyone I send you to and say whatever I command you. Do not be afraid of them, for I am with you and will rescue you," declares the LORD.

Then the LORD reached out his hand and touched my mouth and said to me, "Now, I have put my words in your mouth."
Jeremiah 1:1a, 4-9

READ MORE ABOUT IT: Jeremiah 1:17-19

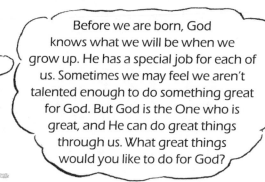

Before we are born, God knows what we will be when we grow up. He has a special job for each of us. Sometimes we may feel we aren't talented enough to do something great for God. But God is the One who is great, and He can do great things through us. What great things would you like to do for God?

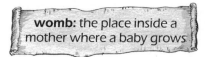

womb: the place inside a mother where a baby grows

REMEMBER: God gives us everything we need for what He wants us to do.

Jeremiah–Stuck in the Mud

Jeremiah...said, "This is what the LORD says: 'Whoever stays in this city will die by the sword, famine or plague, but whoever goes over to the Babylonians will live. He will escape with his life; he will live.' And this is what the LORD says: 'This city will certainly be handed over to the army of the king of Babylon, who will capture it.'"

Then the officials said to the king, "This man should be put to death."

So they took Jeremiah and put him into the cistern of Malkijah, the king's son, which was in the courtyard of the guard. They lowered Jeremiah by ropes into the cistern; it had no water in it, only mud, and Jeremiah sank down into the mud. Jeremiah 38:1b-4a, 6

cistern: a large pit for catching rain water

READ MORE ABOUT IT: James 5:10; 1 Peter 4:12-16, 19

PRAY ABOUT IT: Did you ever get into trouble when you were doing something right? Ask the Lord to help you keep doing what's right even when others misunderstand or get angry or make fun of you.

REMEMBER: Say and do what's right, no matter how others treat you.

But Ebed-Melech, a Cushite, an official in the royal palace, heard that they had put Jeremiah into the cistern. While the king was sitting in the Benjamin Gate, Ebed-Melech went out of the palace and said to him, "My Lord the king, these men have acted wickedly in all they have done to Jeremiah the prophet. They have thrown him into a cistern, where he will starve to death when there is no longer any bread in the city."

Then the king commanded Ebed-Melech the Cushite, "Take thirty men from here with you and lift Jeremiah the prophet out of the cistern before he dies."
Jeremiah 38:7-10

READ MORE ABOUT IT: Psalm 56:3-7

TRY IT!

Design a poster for your room that reminds you where to turn when you're afraid or in trouble. Use Psalm 56:4b for the reminder: "In God I trust; I will not be afraid."

REMEMBER: God knows when you're in trouble, and He will help you.

Babylon Captures Judah

Zedekiah...reigned in Jerusalem eleven years. He did evil in the eyes of the LORD his God and did not humble himself before Jeremiah the prophet, who spoke the word of the LORD.

The LORD...sent word to them through his messengers again and again, because he had pity on his people and on his dwelling place. But they mocked God's messengers... until the wrath of the LORD was aroused against his people and there was no remedy.

God handed all of them over to Nebuchadnezzar. He carried to Babylon all the articles from the temple of God. They set fire to God's temple and broke down the wall of Jerusalem; they burned all the palaces and destroyed everything of value there.

He carried into exile to Babylon the remnant, who escaped from the sword, and they became servants to him...until the kingdom of Persia came to power.
2 Chronicles 36:11-12, 15-16, 17b-18a, 19-20

remnant: those left over

READ MORE ABOUT IT: 2 Kings 20:16-18

TALK ABOUT IT!

Jeremiah the prophet spoke for God, but the people didn't respect him. Do you ever hear anyone talking unkindly about your pastor or other leaders in the church who tell you about God? Have you ever found yourself doing it? Do you think church leaders ever get discouraged? What are some ways we can encourage them?

REMEMBER: God wants us to treat His servants with respect.

How deserted lies the city,
once so full of people!
She who was queen among the
    provinces
    has now become a slave.

Yet this I call to mind
    and therefore I have hope:
Because of the LORD'S great love we are
    not consumed,
    for his compassions never fail.
They are new every morning;

great is your faithfulness.
I say to myself, "The LORD is my
portion;
    therefore I will wait for him."
The LORD is good to those whose hope
    is in him,
    to the one who seeks him;
it is good to wait quietly
    for the salvation of the LORD.
Lamentations 1:1a, c; 3:21-26

READ MORE ABOUT IT: Psalm 137:1-6

WRITE ABOUT IT: The book of Lamentations is a sad song mixed with some happier parts about God's faithfulness and mercy. Sometimes we learn more about God's faithfulness from sad times. What have you learned about God's faithfulness?

_____

_____

REMEMBER: God is faithful. We can count on Him to care for us in the sad times.

God's Revenge on Babylon

The LORD replied:
   "He is arrogant and never at rest...
He gathers to himself all the nations
   and takes captive all the peoples.

Because you have plundered many nations,
   the peoples who are left will plunder you.

Woe to him who builds a city with bloodshed
   and establishes a town by crime!

Yet I will wait patiently for the day of calamity
   to come on the nation invading us.
Though the fig tree does not bud
   and there are no grapes on the vines,
yet I will rejoice in the LORD,
   I will be joyful in God my Savior.

The righteous will live by his faith.
Habakkuk 2:2a, 5, 8a, 12; 3:16c-17a, 18; 2:4b

READ MORE ABOUT IT: Hebrews 10:35-39

MEMORIZE IT!

The righteous will live by his faith.
Habakkuk 2:4b

God, I want to learn to trust you more.

plunder: to take others' possessions by force
calamity: disaster

REMEMBER: You may not see how God is going to work things out, but put your faith in Him. Don't take matters into your own hands.

"The pride of your heart has
   deceived you,
     you who live in the clefts of the rocks
and make your home on the heights,
you who say to yourself,
     "Who can bring me down to
        the ground?"
Though you soar like the eagle
     and make your nest among the stars,
     from there I will bring you down,"
             declares the LORD.

"You should not look down on
     your brother
     in the day of his misfortune.

"The day of the LORD is near
     for all nations.
As you have done, it will be done to you;
     your deeds will return upon your
        own head."
Obadiah 3-4, 12a, 15

READ MORE ABOUT IT: Obadiah 17, 21

**The day of
the LORD:**
the time when
God will make
everything right
forever

PRAY ABOUT IT: Is there something bothering you
that no one seems to be able to make right? Pray
that God will give you the strength you need to
handle it. And trust Him to make everything come
out for His glory in the end.

REMEMBER: We can look forward to a day when God will make everything right.

Ezekiel and the Valley of Bones

The hand of the LORD was upon me, and he brought me out by the Spirit of the LORD and set me in the middle of a valley; it was full of bones.

Then he said to me: "Son of man, these bones are the whole house of Israel. They say, 'Our bones are dried up and our hope is gone.' Therefore...say to them: 'This is what the Sovereign LORD says: O my people, I am going to open your graves and bring you up from them; I will bring you back to the land of Israel. I will put my Spirit in you and you will live, and I will settle you in your own land. Then you will know that I the LORD...have done it,'" Ezekiel 37:1, 11a, b, 12, 14a, b

READ MORE ABOUT IT: Ezekiel 37:2-10

Think of the easel on this page as a comic strip divided into three frames. In the first frame draw a human skull and some bones lying on the ground. In the others show God's progress as He puts the bones together to make a skeleton.

REMEMBER: If God can make a living nation out of dried-up bones, we can trust Him to do anything.

King Belshazzar gave a great banquet for a thousand of his nobles and drank wine with them. While Belshazzar was drinking his wine, he gave orders to bring in the gold and silver goblets that Nebuchadnezzar his father had taken from the temple in Jerusalem. As they drank the wine, they praised the gods of gold and silver, of bronze, iron, wood and stone.

Suddenly the fingers of a human hand appeared and wrote on the plaster of the wall, near the lampstand in the royal palace. The king watched the hand as it wrote. His face turned pale and he was so frightened that his knees knocked together and his legs gave way.

Daniel 5:1-2a, 4-6

READ MORE ABOUT IT: Daniel 5:7-12

Imagine that you are one of the nobles or government officials at the feast with King Belshazzar. Suddenly a hand appears out of nowhere with no body attached, and it starts writing on the wall. Would you (a) faint, (b) get out of there as quickly as you could, or (c) run up to it and try to figure out how it could do that?

REMEMBER: Listen to God so He doesn't have to get your attention the hard way.

Decoding the Message

Then Daniel answered the king, "You did not honor the God who holds in his hand your life and all your ways.

"This is the inscription that was written:

MENE, MENE, TEKEL, PARSIN

"This is what these words mean:

Mene: God has numbered the days of your reign and brought it to an end.
Tekel: You have been weighed on the scales and found wanting.

Peres: Your kingdom is divided and given to the Medes and Persians."
That very night Belshazzar... was slain.
Daniel 5:17a, 23c, 25-28, 30

READ MORE ABOUT IT: Daniel 5:17b-23a; Hebrews 11:6

I'd like to be like Daniel!

TRY IT!

Learn to pronounce the Aramaic words from the hand's message: mene (MEHNAY), tekel (TEHKALE), parsin (PAR-R-RSEEN—roll the R on your tongue like the sound of a motorboat).

252

REMEMBER: God rewards those who follow Him and judges those who refuse to obey.

The administrators...said: "O King Darius, live forever! The royal administrators...have all agreed that the king should issue an edict...that anyone who prays to any god or man during the next thirty days, except to you, O king, shall be thrown into the lions' den." So King Darius put the decree in writing.

Three times a day [Daniel] got down on his knees and prayed giving thanks to his God, just as he had done before.

[The administrators] said to the king, "Daniel...still prays three times a day." When the king heard this he was very distressed.

The king gave the order, and they brought Daniel and threw him into the lions' den. The king said to Daniel, "May your God, whom you serve continually, rescue you!"
Daniel 6:6-7, 9, 10b, 13-14a, 16

edict: command

READ MORE ABOUT IT: Daniel 6:1-5

TALK ABOUT IT!

What would you do if someone made it against the law to pray to God anywhere and at any time? Would you become a secret Christian or would you be courageous and pray where people could see you?

REMEMBER: When we stand up for God, He will give us the strength to face anything others may do to us.

Daniel's Amazing Rescue

At the first light of dawn, the king got up and hurried to the lions' den. When he came near the den, he called to Daniel in an anguished voice, "Daniel, servant of the living God, has your God, whom you serve continually, been able to rescue you from the lions?"

Daniel answered, "O king, live forever! My God sent his angel and he shut the mouths of the lions."

The king was overjoyed.... And when Daniel was lifted from the den, no wound was found on him, because he had trusted in his God.

Then King Darius wrote:

"I issue a decree that...people must fear and reverence the God of Daniel.

"For he is the living God
and he endures forever."
Daniel 6:19-22a, 23, 25a, 26a

READ MORE ABOUT IT: Daniel 6:24, 26-28

WRITE ABOUT IT: Pretend you are the leader of a country and you want to write a decree or order that everyone must follow and serve God. Why do you think they should follow God? Write it here.

_____

_____

REMEMBER: We can't make people love and serve God, but we can show them why we love Him.

254

"This is what Cyrus king of Persia says: "'The LORD, the God of heaven, has given me all the kingdoms of the earth and he has appointed me to build a temple for him at Jerusalem in Judah. Anyone of his people among you—may his God be with him, and let him go up to Jerusalem in Judah and build the temple of the LORD, the God of Israel, the God who is in Jerusalem. And the people of any place where survivors may now be living are to provide him with silver and gold, with goods and livestock, and with freewill offerings for the temple of God in Jerusalem.'"
Ezra 1:2-4

READ MORE ABOUT IT: Ezra 1:5-11

MEMORIZE IT!

Let us not give up meeting together, as some are in the habit of doing, but let us encourage one another.
Hebrews 10:25a

I want to worship God!

REMEMBER: We please God when we get together with others at a special time and place to worship Him.

Haggai—"Rebuild the Temple!"

The word of the LORD came through the prophet Haggai: "Is it a time for you yourselves to be living in your paneled houses, while this house remains a ruin?"

Now this is what the LORD Almighty says: "Give careful thought to your ways. You have planted much, but have harvested little. You eat, but never have enough...You put on clothes, but are not warm. You earn wages, only to put them in a purse with holes in it."

Then Zerubbabel son of Shealtiel, Joshua son of Jehozadak, the high priest, and the whole remnant of the people obeyed the voice of the LORD their God and the message of the prophet Haggai, because the LORD their God had sent him. And the people feared the LORD.
Haggai 1:3-6, 12

READ MORE ABOUT IT: Luke 12:27-34

If you could give something to your church to repair it or make it look nicer, what would you like to give? Draw it here.

REMEMBER: God wants us to take care of the things that belong to Him.

Then the peoples around them set out to discourage the people of Judah and make them afraid to go on building. They hired counselors to work against them and frustrate their plans during the entire reign of Cyrus king of Persia and down to the reign of Darius king of Persia.

Then, because of the decree King Darius had sent, Tattenai, governor of Trans-Euphrates, and Shethar-Bozenai and their associates carried it out with diligence. So the elders of the Jews continued to build and prosper under the preaching of Haggai the prophet and Zechariah, a descendant of Iddo. They finished building the temple according to the command of the God of Israel and the decrees of Cyrus, Darius and Artaxerxes, kings of Persia. Ezra 4:4-5; 6:13-15

READ MORE ABOUT IT: 1 Timothy 4:12

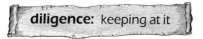

diligence: keeping at it

TALK ABOUT IT!

You don't have to wait until you're older to do things for God. Think of some ways you can use the talents God has given you to serve Him and others this week. Help other family members think of what they can do for God, too.

REMEMBER: When you have a job to do for God, ignore those who try to discourage you.

Next Project–Jerusalem's Walls

The words of Nehemiah son of Hacaliah:

In the month of Kislev in the twentieth year, while I was in the citadel of Susa, Hanani, one of my brothers, came from Judah with some other men, and I questioned them about the Jewish remnant that survived the exile, and also about Jerusalem.

They said to me, "Those who survived the exile and are back in the province are in great trouble and disgrace. The wall of Jerusalem is broken down, and its gates have been burned with fire."

When I heard these things, I sat down and wept. For some days I mourned and fasted and prayed before the God of heaven.
Nehemiah 1:1-4

fasted: didn't eat anything

READ MORE ABOUT IT: Nehemiah 1:5-11

Imagine that you and your family were kidnapped and taken to be slaves in another country. Years later you were allowed to return, but you found that the people who captured you had blown up many of the beautiful buildings and monuments in your city so that you could hardly recognize it. That's how Nehemiah felt when he returned to Jerusalem.

REMEMBER: God cares when we hurt or are disappointed. He wants us to come to Him for comfort.

258

So we rebuilt the wall till all of it reached half its height, for the people worked with all their heart.

But when Sanballat, Tobiah, the Arabs, the Ammonites and the men of Ashdod heard that the repairs to Jerusalem's walls had gone ahead and that the gaps were being closed, they were very angry. They all plotted together to come and fight against Jerusalem and stir up trouble against it. But we prayed to our God and posted a guard day and night to meet this threat.

So the wall was completed...in fifty-two days. When all our enemies heard about this, all the surrounding nations were afraid and lost their self-confidence, because they realized that this work had been done with the help of our God.
Nehemiah 4:6-9; 6:15-16

READ MORE ABOUT IT: Nehemiah 4:16-23

PRAY ABOUT IT: Is there something you need to do that seems impossible? Ask God to help you. Then get busy and work.

REMEMBER: God will help us, but He expects us to do what we can.

A Scripture-Reading Marathon

So on the first day of the seventh month Ezra the priest brought the Law before the assembly, which was made up of men and women and all who were able to understand. He read it aloud from daybreak till noon as he faced the square before the Water Gate in the presence of the men, women and others who could understand. And all the people listened attentively to the Book of the Law.

Ezra opened the book. All the people could see him because he was standing above them; and as he opened it, the people all stood up. Ezra praised the LORD, the great God; and all the people lifted their hands and responded, "Amen! Amen!" Then they bowed down and worshiped the LORD with their faces to the ground. Nehemiah 8:2-3, 5-6

READ MORE ABOUT IT: Nehemiah 8:7-10

TRY IT!

Plan your own Scripture-reading marathon. Decide what portions of Scripture you will read or how long you will keep going. Don't stop reading until you have reached your goal!

REMEMBER: Whenever you read the Bible, listen carefully to what it says. That's how you learn what pleases God.

260

Like newborn babies, crave pure spiritual milk,
so that by it you may grow up in your salvation,
now that you have tasted that the Lord is good.

> Blessed is the man
>   who does not walk in the counsel
>   of the wicked
> or stand in the way of sinners
>   or sit in the seat of mockers.
> But his delight is in the law of the LORD
>   and on his law he meditates day and night.

> When your words came, I ate them;
>   they were my joy and my heart's delight.

1 Peter 2:2; Psalm 1:1-2; Jeremiah 15:16

READ MORE ABOUT IT: Psalm 119:129-130

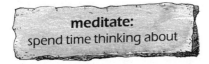

meditate:
spend time thinking about

MEMORIZE IT!

> Like newborn babies,
> crave pure spiritual milk,
> so that by it
> you may grow up
> in your salvation,
> now that you
> have tasted that
> the Lord is good.

1 Peter 2:2

I wish I could read the Bible!

REMEMBER: Keep reading and thinking about God's Word.
That's how you grow as a Christian.

Persia Needs a New Queen

citadel: a protected palace building.
eunuch: palace servant

This is what happened during the time of Xerxes, the Xerxes who ruled over 127 provinces stretching from India to Cush: At that time King Xerxes reigned from his royal throne in the citadel of Susa, and in the third year of his reign he gave a banquet for all his nobles and officials.

On the seventh day, when King Xerxes was in high spirits from wine, he commanded the seven eunuchs who served him...to bring before him Queen Vashti, wearing her royal crown, in order to display her beauty to the people and nobles, for she was lovely to look at. But when the attendants delivered the king's command, Queen Vashti refused to come. Then the king became furious and burned with anger.
Esther 1:1-3a, 10-12

READ MORE ABOUT IT: Esther 1:13-22

WRITE ABOUT IT: Queen Vashti faced a tough decision—obey the drunken king, not knowing what he might do, or disobey and lose her place as queen or possibly be killed. What is the toughest decision you've had to make lately? Write it here. What did you decide?

_____

_____

262

REMEMBER: God sometimes uses unpleasant circumstances to bring about something better.

Now there was in the citadel of Susa a Jew of the tribe of Benjamin, named Mordecai...who had been carried into exile from Jerusalem by Nebuchadnezzar king of Babylon. Mordecai had a cousin named Hadassah, whom he had brought up because she had neither father nor mother. This girl, who was also known as Esther, was lovely in form and features, and Mordecai had taken her as his own daughter when her father and mother died.

Now the king was attracted to Esther more than to any of the other women, and she won his favor and approval.... So he set a royal crown on her head and made her queen instead of Vashti.
Esther 2:5-6a, 7, 17

READ MORE ABOUT IT: Esther 2:18; Philippians 1:6

Draw a beautiful palace for Esther, the new queen of Persia, to live in.

REMEMBER: God is always working in our lives even when we don't realize it.

Haman's Wicked Plot

After these events, King Xerxes honored Haman son of Hammedatha...elevating him and giving him a seat of honor higher than that of all the other nobles. All the royal officials at the king's gate knelt down and paid honor to Haman, for the king had commanded this concerning him. But Mordecai would not kneel down or pay him honor.

When Haman saw that Mordecai would not kneel down or pay him honor, he was enraged. Yet having learned who Mordecai's people were, he scorned the idea of killing only Mordecai. Instead Haman looked for a way to destroy all Mordecai's people, the Jews, throughout the whole kingdom of Xerxes.
Esther 3:1-2, 5-6

READ MORE ABOUT IT: *Esther 3:8-11*

TALK ABOUT IT!

What is the difference between showing respect to others—especially to people older than we are—and refusing to bow down to someone, as Mordecai refused to bow down to Haman? What are some proper ways to show respect?

REMEMBER: God is pleased when we show proper respect, but we are not to treat others as if they are gods.

264

The king and Haman went to dine with Queen Esther, and...the king again asked, "Queen Esther, what is your petition? It will be given you. What is your request? Even up to half the kingdom, it will be granted."

Then Queen Esther answered, "If I have found favor with you, O king, and if it pleases your majesty, grant me my life—this is my petition. And spare my people—this is my request. For I and my people have been sold for destruction and slaughter and annihilation."

King Xerxes asked Queen Esther, "Who is he? Where is the man who has dared to do such a thing?" Esther said, "The adversary and enemy is this vile Haman."

So they hanged Haman on the gallows he had prepared for Mordecai.

Esther 7:1-4a, 5-6a, 10a

READ MORE ABOUT IT: Esther 8:3-11

annihilation: being completely wiped out

Have you ever been scared when you had to act in a play or give a report in front of your class? Imagine that you are Queen Esther, and you know that the king could have you killed if he didn't like what you told him. Why do you think Esther risked her life to tell the king about Haman?

REMEMBER: God used Esther's courage to save the lives of His people, the Jews.

265

Pray for the Peace of Jerusalem

I rejoiced with those who said to me,
    "Let us go to the house of the
        LORD."
Our feet are standing
    in your gates, O Jerusalem.

Pray for the peace of Jerusalem:
    "May those who love you be secure.
May there be peace within your walls
    and security within your citadels."

For the sake of my brothers
    and friends,
    I will say, "Peace be within you."
For the sake of the house of the LORD
    our God,
    I will seek your prosperity.

Psalm 122:1-2, 6-9

READ MORE ABOUT IT: Psalm 122:3-5

PRAY ABOUT IT: Jerusalem is a special city to God. But throughout history, Jerusalem has always been a place of fighting and trouble—as it is today. Pray that God will bring peace to Jerusalem.

266

REMEMBER: Jesus is the One who can bring peace—to us and to all parts of the world.

66 **S**ee, I will send my messenger, who will prepare the way before me. Then suddenly the Lord you are seeking will come to his temple; the messenger of the covenant, whom you desire, will come," says the LORD Almighty.

refiner: person who melts down metal and skims off impurities

But who can endure the day of his coming? Who can stand when he appears? For he will be like a refiner's fire or a launderer's soap. He will sit as a refiner and purifier of silver; he will purify the Levites and refine them like gold and silver. Then the LORD will have men who will bring offerings in righteousness, and the offerings of Judah and Jerusalem will be acceptable to the LORD, as in days gone by, as in former years.
Malachi 3:1-4

READ MORE ABOUT IT: John 1:6-7, 19-23, 29-30

WRITE ABOUT IT: The messenger Malachi was prophesying (telling ahead of time) about John the Baptist—the messenger who told people to turn from their sin because the Savior was coming. God wants us to put away sin. Write down some sin you need God to help you quit doing. (You can write it in a code you've learned or made up.)

REMEMBER: God wants us to be pure for Him.

267

Jesus Is Coming!

And now the LORD says—
"It is too small a thing for you to be my servant
    to restore the tribes of Jacob and bring back
    those of Israel I have kept.
I will also make you a light for the Gentiles,
    that you may bring my salvation to the ends
    of the earth."

For I am honored in the eyes of the LORD
    and my God has been my strength.

But you, Bethlehem Ephrathah,
    though you are small among the clans of Judah,
out of you will come for me
    one who will be ruler over Israel,
whose origins are from of old,
    from ancient times.
Isaiah 49:5a, 6, 5b; Micah 5:2

READ MORE ABOUT IT: Luke 2:1-7

MEMORIZE IT!

Here is a trustworthy
saying that deserves full
acceptance: Christ Jesus
came into the world to
save sinners.
1 Timothy 1:15

Gentiles:
people who aren't Jewish
**whose origins are from of
old, from ancient times:**
Jesus is God, and He existed
before the beginning of time

REMEMBER: God's Word predicted many details of Jesus' coming.
          We can be glad that He came to save us.

Jesus Would Be Son of God, Son of Man

In my vision at night I looked, and there before me was one like a son of man, coming with the clouds of heaven. He approached the Ancient of Days and was led into his presence. He was given authority, glory and sovereign power; all peoples, nations and men of every language worshiped him. His dominion is an everlasting dominion that will not pass away, and his kingdom is one that will never be destroyed.

For to which of the angels did God
   ever say,
"You are my Son;
   today I have become your Father"?

Or again,
   "I will be his Father,
     and he will be my Son"?
Daniel 7:13-14; Hebrews 1:5

Ancient of Days: God

READ MORE ABOUT IT:
Matthew 3:16-17; 18:11

PRAY ABOUT IT: Talk to God and thank Him for sending His Son, the Lord Jesus Christ, to become a man and take our sins away. Thank Him for the eternal life He offers to all who believe in Him. Ask God to help you tell others about Him.

REMEMBER: Jesus is the only one who could take our sins away because He is both God and man.

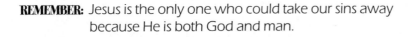

Jesus Christ Is Born

This is how the birth of Jesus Christ came about: His mother Mary was pledged to be married to Joseph, but before they came together, she was found to be with child through the Holy Spirit.

An angel of the Lord appeared to [Joseph] in a dream and said, "Joseph son of David, do not be afraid to take Mary home as your wife, because what is conceived in her is from the Holy Spirit. She will give birth to a son, and you are to give him the name Jesus, because he will save his people from their sins."

All this took place to fulfill what the Lord had said through the prophet: "The virgin will be with child and will give birth to a son, and they will call him Immanuel"—which means, "God with us."   Matthew 1:18, 20b-23

READ MORE ABOUT IT: Isaiah 7:14

If you were going decorate a birthday cake for Jesus, what would it look like? Draw it here.

REMEMBER: Mary was Jesus' mother, but God was Jesus' Father. God worked a miracle when Jesus was born.

Every year [Jesus'] parents went to Jerusalem for the Feast of the Passover. When he was twelve years old, they went up to the Feast, according to the custom. After the Feast was over, while his parents were returning home, the boy Jesus stayed behind in Jerusalem, but they were unaware of it. Thinking he was in their company, they traveled on for a day. Then they began looking for him among their relatives and friends. When they did not find him, they went back to Jerusalem to look for him. After three days they found him in the temple courts, sitting among the teachers, listening to them and asking them questions. Everyone who heard him was amazed at his understanding and his answers. When his parents saw him, they were astonished.

"Why were you searching for me?" he asked. "Didn't you know I had to be in my Father's house?" But they did not understand what he was saying to them. Luke 2:41-48a, 49-50

READ MORE ABOUT IT: Luke 2:51-52

TALK ABOUT IT!

Talk about a time when you or another family member got lost or left behind. What was the person doing just before that? How long did the search last? Do you think Mary and Joseph should have known where to look for Jesus when they discovered He wasn't with them?

REMEMBER: Even when He was a child, Jesus knew that He was here on earth to do His Father's business. So are we.

Jesus' Baptism

It is written in Isaiah the prophet:
"I will send my messenger ahead of you,
who will prepare your way"—
"a voice of one calling in the desert,
'Prepare the way for the Lord,
make straight paths for him.'"

And so John came, baptizing in the desert region and preaching a baptism of repentance for the forgiveness of sins. The whole Judean countryside and all the people of Jerusalem went out to him. Confessing their sins, they were baptized by him in the Jordan River.

At that time Jesus came from Nazareth in Galilee and was baptized by John in the Jordan. As Jesus was coming up out of the water, he saw heaven being torn open and the Spirit descending on him like a dove. And a voice came from heaven: "You are my Son, whom I love; with you I am well pleased."   Mark 1:2-5, 9-11

READ MORE ABOUT IT: Isaiah 40:3

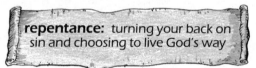

repentance: turning your back on sin and choosing to live God's way

WRITE ABOUT IT: Write here what you would like God to say about the way you serve Him.

_____

REMEMBER: Jesus, God's Son, is the perfect example of how to live if we want to please God.

Then Jesus was led by the Spirit into the desert to be tempted by the devil. After fasting forty days and forty nights, he was hungry. The tempter came to him and said, "If you are the Son of God, tell these stones to become bread."

Jesus answered, "It is written: 'Man does not live on bread alone, but on every word that comes from the mouth of God.'"

Then the devil took him to the holy city and had him stand on the highest point of the temple. "If you are the Son of God," he said, "throw yourself down."

Jesus answered him, "It is also written: 'Do not put the Lord your God to the test.'"

Again, the devil took him to a very high mountain and showed him all the kingdoms of the world and their splendor. "All this I will give you," he said, "if you will bow down and worship me."

attended: took care of

Jesus said to him, "Away from me, Satan! For it is written: 'Worship the Lord your God, and serve him only.'"

Then the devil left him, and angels came and attended him.
Matthew 4:1-6a, 7-11

READ MORE ABOUT IT: Psalm 119:11

TRY IT!

The next time you are tempted to sin, be like Jesus and remind yourself and others of what God has written in the Bible. He wants us to be holy, and He has given us His Word and His Spirit to help us.

REMEMBER: Learn as much Scripture as you can—and use it.

Jesus' First Miracle

On the third day a wedding took place at Cana in Galilee. Jesus' mother was there, and Jesus and his disciples had also been invited to the wedding. When the wine was gone, Jesus' mother said to him, "They have no more wine."

Jesus said to the servants, "Fill the jars with water"; so they filled them to the brim.

Then he told them, "Now draw some out and take it to the master of the banquet."

They did so, and the master of the banquet tasted the water that had been turned into wine. Then he called the bridegroom aside and said, "Everyone brings out the choice wine first and then the cheaper wine after the guests have had too much to drink; but you have saved the best till now."

This, the first of his miraculous signs, Jesus performed at Cana in Galilee. He thus revealed his glory, and his disciples put their faith in him.
John 2:1-3, 7-9a, 9c-11

READ MORE ABOUT IT: John 20:30-31

Imagine that you are one of the servants filling the water jars with ordinary clear water as Jesus said. Then imagine your surprise when you pour some out for the host at the wedding banquet and it's beautiful red wine! Remember, this is the first time you've heard of Jesus. What might you think about Him after this miracle?

REMEMBER: *Jesus could do miracles because He is God.*

Good News and Bad News

"Just as Moses lifted up the snake in the desert, so the Son of Man must be lifted up, that everyone who believes in him may have eternal life.

"For God so loved the world that he gave his one and only Son, that whoever believes in him shall not perish but have eternal life. For God did not send his Son into the world to condemn the world, but to save the world through him. Whoever believes in him is not condemned, but whoever does not believe stands condemned already because he has not believed in the name of God's one and only Son."
John 3:14-18

READ MORE ABOUT IT: Numbers 21:4-9

MEMORIZE IT!

> For God so loved the world that he gave his one and only Son, that whoever believes in him shall not perish but have eternal life. For God did not send his Son into the world to condemn the world, but to save the world through him.
> **John 3:16-17**

REMEMBER: The good news is: God loves us so much that He sent Jesus to die and rise from the dead to save us from our sins. The bad news is: anyone who doesn't believe in Jesus will be cut off from God forever.

275

A Different Kind of Fishermen

As Jesus was walking beside the Sea of Galilee, he saw two brothers, Simon called Peter and his brother Andrew. They were casting a net into the lake, for they were fishermen. "Come, follow me," Jesus said, "and I will make you fishers of men." At once they left their nets and followed him.

Going on from there, he saw two other brothers, James son of Zebedee and his brother John. They were in a boat with their father Zebedee, preparing their nets. Jesus called them, and immediately they left the boat and their father and followed him.

Jesus went throughout Galilee, teaching in their synagogues, preaching the good news of the kingdom, and healing every disease and sickness among the people. Matthew 4:18-23

READ MORE ABOUT IT: Luke 5:1-11

TRY IT!

Would you like to be a fisher of men for Jesus? Think of one person you know who hasn't accepted Jesus as his or her Savior. What "bait" will you use to catch this "fish" for the Lord? Start simply, telling about how good it is to have Jesus in your life. Then you might want to share some of the verses on pages 372-373.

REMEMBER: God doesn't want us to keep the good news of His salvation to ourselves. He wants us to share it.

Sermon on the Mount–Light for the World

You are the light of the world. A city on a hill cannot be hidden. Neither do people light a lamp and put it under a bowl. Instead they put it on its stand, and it gives light to everyone in the house. In the same way, let your light shine before men, that they may see your good deeds and praise your Father in heaven.

For you were once darkness, but now you are light in the Lord. Live as children of light (for the fruit of the light consists in all goodness, righteousness and truth) and find out what pleases the Lord.
Matthew 5:14-16; Ephesians 5:8-10

READ MORE ABOUT IT: Philippians 2:14-15

There are all kinds of lights—lighthouses, street lights, neon lights, flashlights. What others can you think of? What kind of light would you like to be for Jesus? Draw it here.

REMEMBER: God wants us to share the light of His good news with our dark world.

277

Sermon on the Mount—Why Jesus Came

Do not think that I have come to abolish the Law or the Prophets; I have not come to abolish them but to fulfill them. I tell you the truth, until heaven and earth disappear, not the smallest letter, not the least stroke of a pen, will by any means disappear from the Law until everything is accomplished. Anyone who breaks one of the least of these commandments and teaches others to do the same will be called least in the kingdom of heaven, but whoever practices and teaches these commands will be called great in the kingdom of heaven.

abolish the Law or the Prophets: What Jesus taught the people sounded new. But He was explaining what the Bible (the Law and the Prophets) really meant.

Therefore, there is now no condemnation for those who are in Christ Jesus, because through Christ Jesus the law of the Spirit of life set me free from the law of sin and death.
Matthew 5:17-19; Romans 8:1-2

READ MORE ABOUT IT: John 14:20-21

REMEMBER: If we obey what Jesus says, we are doing all that God asks.

Jesus came to set us free!

MEMORIZE IT!

There is now no condemnation for those who are in Christ Jesus, because through Christ Jesus the law of the Spirit of life set me free from the law of sin and death.
Romans 8:1-2

278

Sermon on the Mount–Be Careful What You Say

Again, you have heard that it was said to the people long ago, "Do not break your oath, but keep the oaths you have made to the Lord." But I tell you, Do not swear at all: either by heaven, for it is God's throne; or by the earth, for it is his footstool; or by Jerusalem, for it is the city of the Great King. And do not swear by your head, for you cannot make even one hair white or black. Simply let your "Yes" be "Yes," and your "No," "No"; anything beyond this comes from the evil one.
Matthew 5:33-37

oath:
promise

READ MORE ABOUT IT: Leviticus 19:12; Numbers 30:2

TALK ABOUT IT!

> Do you know people who seem to have to say a swear word or use the Lord's name to let you know they really mean what they're saying? What does God's Word have to say about that? Do you ever find yourself talking like them when you're around them?

REMEMBER: God wants us to keep our promises, but we don't please Him when we swear.

Sermon on the Mount–Love, Not Revenge

Y ou have heard that it was said, "Eye for eye, and tooth for tooth." But I tell you, Do not resist an evil person. If someone strikes you on the right cheek, turn to him the other also. And if someone wants to sue you and take your tunic, let him have your cloak as well. If someone forces you to go one mile, go with him two miles. Give to the one who asks you, and do not turn away from the one who wants to borrow from you.

You have heard that it was said, "Love your neighbor and hate your enemy." But I tell you: Love your enemies and pray for those who persecute you, that you may be sons of your Father in heaven.
Matthew 5:38-45a

READ MORE ABOUT IT: 1 John 4:7-8

PRAY ABOUT IT: Is there someone you consider to be your enemy? Right now, pray for that person to learn about the love of Jesus. It's hard to hang on to angry feelings toward someone you're praying for.

REMEMBER: It's easy to love someone who loves you, but God even wants us to love our enemies.

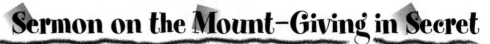

Be careful not to do your "acts of righteousness" before men, to be seen by them. If you do, you will have no reward from your Father in heaven.

So when you give to the needy, do not announce it with trumpets, as the hypocrites do in the synagogues and on the streets, to be honored by men. I tell you the truth, they have received their reward in full. But when you give to the needy, do not let your left hand know what your right hand is doing, so that your giving may be in secret. Then your Father, who sees what is done in secret, will reward you. Matthew 6:1-4

READ MORE ABOUT IT: 2 Corinthians 9:7-8

TRY IT!
Be a secret helper! Do something nice for someone today without that person's finding out who did it.

REMEMBER: Do good things just to please God, not so that others will think you are great.

281

Sermon on the Mount–How to Pray

OCTOBER 5

When you pray, go into your room, close the door and pray to your Father, who is unseen. Then your Father, who sees what is done in secret, will reward you.

This, then, is how you should pray:

"Our Father in heaven,
hallowed be your name,
your kingdom come,
your will be done
   on earth as it is in heaven.
Give us today our daily bread.
Forgive us our debts,
   as we also have forgiven
   our debtors.
And lead us not into temptation,
   but deliver us from the evil one."
Matthew 6:6, 9-13

READ MORE ABOUT IT: 1 Timothy 2:1-4, 8

PRAY ABOUT IT: Today follow Jesus' pattern of things to pray for: tell God how great He is, pray for God's will and for those doing His work, ask for what you need, ask His forgiveness for sin, and ask for help in doing what's right.

REMEMBER: Don't pray the same way all the time, but pray often. God loves to hear from you.

Do not store up for yourselves treasures on earth, where moth and rust destroy, and where thieves break in and steal. But store up for yourselves treasures in heaven, where moth and rust do not destroy, and where thieves do not break in and steal. For where your treasure is, there your heart will be also.

No one can serve two masters. Either he will hate the one and love the other, or he will be devoted to the one and despise the other. You cannot serve both God and Money.

For the love of money is a root of all kinds of evil.
Matthew 6:19-21, 24; 1 Timothy 6:10a

READ MORE ABOUT IT: 1 John 2:15-17

Draw something that you would have a hard time giving away if God asked.

REMEMBER: If getting a lot of money is more important to us than anything, we're serving money not God.

Sermon on the Mount–Why Worry?

Therefore I tell you, do not worry about your life, what you will eat or drink; or about your body, what you will wear. Is not life more important than food, and the body more important than clothes? Look at the birds of the air; they do not sow or reap or store away in barns, and yet your heavenly Father feeds them. Are you not much more valuable than they? Who of you by worrying can add a single hour to his life?

So do not worry, saying, "What shall we eat?" or "What shall we drink?" or "What shall we wear?" For the pagans run after all these things, and your heavenly Father knows that you need them. But seek first his kingdom and his righteousness, and all these things will be given to you as well.
Matthew 6:25-27, 31-33

seek: look for, go after

pagans: people who don't believe in our God

MEMORIZE IT!

But seek first his kingdom and his righteousness, and all these things will be given to you as well.
Matthew 6:33

READ MORE ABOUT IT: Proverbs 12:25; Philippians 4:6-7

REMEMBER: Don't worry about anything. If God is #1, everything else will fall into place.

Do not judge, or you too will be judged. For in the same way you judge others, you will be judged, and with the measure you use, it will be measured to you.

Do not condemn, and you will not be condemned. Forgive, and you will be forgiven. Give, and it will be given to you. A good measure, pressed down, shaken together and running over, will be poured into your lap. For with the measure you use, it will be measured to you.

You, then, why do you judge your brother? Or why do you look down on your brother? For we will all stand before God's judgment seat. Therefore, let us stop passing judgment on one another.
Matthew 7:1-2; Luke 6:37b-38; Romans 14:10, 13a

READ MORE ABOUT IT: James 4:11-12

God's judgment seat: in the future all Christians will be rewarded for how they have served Christ.

WRITE ABOUT IT: Do you tend to judge people according to how they look or what they wear or what they do or don't do? Do you ever think that someone else isn't as good a Christian as you are because they do things that you don't feel right doing? What are one or two of those things?

_____

_____

REMEMBER: God wants us to let Him be the judge.

Sermon on the Mount–Choose Your Path

Enter through the narrow gate. For wide is the gate and broad is the road that leads to destruction, and many enter through it. But small is the gate and narrow the road that leads to life, and only a few find it.

[Jesus said,] "I tell you the truth, whoever hears my word and believes him who sent me has eternal life and will not be condemned; he has crossed from death to life."

Someone asked [Jesus], "Lord, are only a few people going to be saved?"

He said to them, "Make every effort to enter through the narrow door, because many, I tell you, will try to enter and will not be able to. Once the owner of the house gets up and closes the door, you will stand outside knocking and pleading, 'Sir, open the door for us.'

"But he will answer, 'I don't know you.'"
Matthew 7:13-14; John 5:24;
Luke 13:23-25b

READ MORE ABOUT IT: 1 Timothy 2:5-6

TALK ABOUT IT!

If you're not sure if you're going to heaven, ask your mom or dad or a Christian friend to help you make the right choice today. If you have already accepted Christ as your Savior, ask a friend or two if they know whether they are going to heaven or not. Tell them about Jesus—the only way.

REMEMBER: There are only two paths. Which one are you on?

Sermon on the Mount—Two Houses in the Storm

66 "Therefore everyone who hears these words of mine and puts them into practice is like a wise man who built his house on the rock. The rain came down, the streams rose, and the winds blew and beat against that house; yet it did not fall, because it had its foundation on the rock. But everyone who hears these words of mine and does not put them into practice is like a foolish man who built his house on sand. The rain came down, the streams rose, and the winds blew and beat against that house, and it fell with a great crash."

For no one can lay any foundation other than the one already laid, which is Jesus Christ.
Matthew 7:24-27; 1 Corinthians 3:11

READ MORE ABOUT IT: 1 Corinthians 3:10-15

WRITE ABOUT IT: Think of one or two ways Jesus is like the foundation a house is built upon. Write them here.

_____

_____

REMEMBER: If we love Jesus and follow His teachings, our life is built on a solid foundation.

287

"They're Comin' Through the Roof!"

OCTOBER 11

One day as Jesus was teaching, Pharisees and teachers of the law, who had come from every village of Galilee and from Judea and Jerusalem, were sitting there. And the power of the Lord was present for him to heal the sick. Some men came carrying a paralytic on a mat and tried to take him into the house to lay him before Jesus. When they could not find a way to do this because of the crowd, they went up on the roof and lowered him on his mat through the tiles into the middle of the crowd, right in front of Jesus.

When Jesus saw their faith, he said, "Friend, your sins are forgiven."
Luke 5:17-20

READ MORE ABOUT IT: Micah 7:18

paralytic: a person who is paralyzed or can't move

Imagine that you are the paralyzed man. You can't walk up to Jesus to ask for help, so your friends carry you to where He is. But the house is so crowded that you can't get anywhere near. Do you think you would have been afraid to try your friends' plan? Or do you think you would have been willing to try anything if it meant you could walk again?

REMEMBER: Faith is trusting God for whatever we need.

The Pharisees and the teachers of the law began thinking to themselves, "Who is this fellow who speaks blasphemy? Who can forgive sins but God alone?"

Jesus knew what they were thinking and asked, "Why are you thinking these things in your hearts? Which is easier: to say, 'Your sins are forgiven,' or to say, 'Get up and walk'? But that you may know that the Son of Man has authority on earth to forgive sins...." He said to the paralyzed man, "I tell you, get up, take your mat and go home." Immediately he stood up in front of them, took what he had been lying on and went home praising God. Everyone was amazed and gave praise to God.
Luke 5:21-26a

Pharisees: a group of very religious Jews in Jesus' time

READ MORE ABOUT IT: Matthew 4:23-25

PRAY ABOUT IT: Give God praise that He has the power to forgive our sins and to heal people when that is what is best. Confess any sin in your life that you can think of right now. Pray for someone you know who is sick.

REMEMBER: The religious leaders were right. Only God can forgive sins. Jesus is God.

Jesus Brings a Girl Back to Life

OCTOBER 13

synagogue: a place where Jewish people worshiped after the temple was destroyed

A man named Jairus, a ruler of the synagogue, came and fell at Jesus' feet, pleading with him to come to his house because his only daughter, a child of about twelve, was dying.

Someone came from the house of Jairus, the synagogue ruler. "Your daughter is dead," he said. "Don't bother the teacher any more."

Hearing this, Jesus said to Jairus, "Don't be afraid; just believe, and she will be healed."

When he arrived at the house of Jairus... Jesus said, "She is not dead but asleep."

They laughed at him, knowing that she was dead. But he took her by the hand and said, "My child get up!" Her spirit returned, and at once she stood up. Then Jesus told them to give her something to eat.

Luke 8:41-42a, 49b-55

READ MORE ABOUT IT: James 5:13-16

TALK ABOUT IT!

Why do you think that Jesus said the girl wasn't dead but just asleep? Could Jesus, the perfect Son of God, be wrong? Did Jesus not know? Or could He have meant that bringing her back to life would be as easy as waking her from sleep?

REMEMBER: When we pray for those who are sick, we should believe that God can make them well again if that's what is best.

Parables of Jesus—The Farmer and the Seed

While a large crowd was gathering and people were coming to Jesus from town after town, he told this parable: "A farmer went out to sow his seed. As he was scattering the seed, some fell along the path; it was trampled on, and the birds of the air ate it up. Some fell on rock, and when it came up, the plants withered because they had no moisture. Other seed fell among thorns, which grew up with it and choked the plants. Still other seed fell on good soil. It came up and yielded a crop, a hundred times more than was sown."

When he said this, he called out, "He who has ears to hear, let him hear."
Luke 8:4-8

sow: plant
parable: a story from everyday life that teaches spiritual truth

READ MORE ABOUT IT: Psalm 119:130

Divide the easel into four comic frame panels, then draw what happened to the seeds on the four different types of soil.

REMEMBER: God is like a farmer planting the seed of His good news in many places.

Parables of Jesus—Four Kinds of Seed

"This is the meaning of the parable: The seed is the word of God. Those along the path are the ones who hear, and then the devil comes and takes away the word from their hearts, so that they may not believe and be saved. Those on the rock are the ones who receive the word with joy when they hear it, but they have no root. They believe for a while, but in the time of testing they fall away. The seed that fell among thorns stands for those who hear, but as they go on their way they are choked by life's worries, riches and pleasures, and they do not mature. But the seed on good soil stands for those with a noble and good heart, who hear the word, retain it, and by persevering produce a crop."
Luke 8:11-15

READ MORE ABOUT IT: Isaiah 40:8

TRY IT!

Ask permission to plant some seeds like the farmer in the parable. Make a small drainage hole in the bottom of three small yogurt or margarine containers. Fill one with rocks, one with poor soil and lots of weeds, and one with good soil. Plant any kind of seeds in the three containers and throw a few seeds out on the sidewalk or a trampled down path where people walk all the time. Do you get the same results as the farmer in the parable?

REMEMBER: God wants us to help spread the good news, but not everyone will want to follow Christ.

Parables of Jesus—Lost and Found

Now the tax collectors and "sinners" were all gathering around to hear him. But the Pharisees and the teachers of the law muttered, "This man welcomes sinners and eats with them."

Then Jesus told them this parable: "Suppose one of you has a hundred sheep and loses one of them. Does he not leave the ninety-nine in the open country and go after the lost sheep until he finds it? And when he finds it, he joyfully puts it on his shoulders and goes home. Then he calls his friends and neighbors together and says, 'Rejoice with me; I have found my lost sheep.' I tell you that in the same way there will be more rejoicing in heaven over one sinner who repents than over ninety-nine righteous persons who do not need to repent."

Luke 15:1-7

READ MORE ABOUT IT: Luke 15:8-10

MEMORIZE IT!

The Son of Man came to seek and to save what was lost.
Luke 19:10

I found my lamb!

REMEMBER: People have to understand that they are sinners before they want Jesus to save them.

Parables of Jesus–The Boy Who Ran Away from Home

There was a man who had two sons. The younger one said to his father, "Father, give me my share of the estate." So he divided his property between them.

Not long after that, the younger son got together all he had, set off for a distant country and there squandered his wealth in wild living. After he had spent everything, there was a severe famine in that whole country, and he began to be in need. So he went and hired himself out to a citizen of that country, who sent him to his fields to feed pigs. He longed to fill his stomach with the pods that the pigs were eating, but no one gave him anything.

When he came to his senses, he said, "...I will set out and go back to my father and say to him: Father, I have sinned against heaven and against you. I am no longer worthy to be called your son; make me like one of your hired men." So he got up and went to his father.   Luke 15:11-20a

READ MORE ABOUT IT: Isaiah 55:6-7

WRITE ABOUT IT: *Imagine that you are the younger son in the parable. You want to go back home, but your clothes are all tattered, and you smell like pigs. You have no way to get cleaned up. Write here what you're wondering as you head home.*

_____

REMEMBER: Bad choices have bad consequences.

But while he was still a long way off, his father saw him and was filled with compassion for him; he ran to his son, threw his arms around him and kissed him.

The son said to him, "Father, I have sinned against heaven and against you. I am no longer worthy to be called your son."

But the father said to his servants, "Quick! Bring the best robe and put it on him. Put a ring on his finger and sandals on his feet. Bring the fattened calf and kill it. Let's have a feast and celebrate. For this son of mine was dead and is alive again; he was lost and is found." So they began to celebrate.
Luke 15:20b-24

READ MORE ABOUT IT: Matthew 18:12-14

Imagine how you would feel if you were the younger son! The best you had hoped for was to be hired by your father as a servant just so you could eat. What would you say to your father?

REMEMBER: God is like the father in the parable. Even though we sometimes try to go our own way, He's always happy to welcome us back.

Parables of Jesus—The Jealous Brother

Meanwhile, the older son was in the field. When he came near the house, he heard music and dancing. So he called one of the servants and asked him what was going on. "Your brother has come," he replied, "and your father has killed the fattened calf because he has him back safe and sound."

The older brother became angry and refused to go in. "Look! All these years I've been slaving for you and never disobeyed your orders. Yet you never gave me even a young goat so I could celebrate with my friends. But when this son of yours who has squandered your property...comes home, you kill the fattened calf for him!"

"My son," the father said, "you are always with me, and everything I have is yours. But we had to celebrate and be glad, because this brother of yours was dead and is alive again; he was lost and is found."
Luke 15:25-28a, 29b-32

READ MORE ABOUT IT: James 3:13-18

O.K., so I'm jealous!

TALK ABOUT IT!

Talk about a time when you were jealous of a brother, sister, or friend. What does this parable teach us about how to get over jealousy?

296

REMEMBER: Jealousy is as much a sin as running away from God.

When Jesus landed and saw a large crowd, he had compassion on them and healed their sick.

As evening approached, the disciples came to him and said, "...Send the crowds away, so they can go to the villages and buy themselves some food."

Jesus replied, "...You give them something to eat."

"We have here only five loaves of bread and two fish," they answered.

"Bring them here to me," he said. Taking the five loaves and the two fish and looking up to heaven, he gave thanks and broke the loaves. They all ate and were satisfied, and the disciples picked up twelve basketfuls of broken pieces that were left over. The number of those who ate was about five thousand men, besides women and children.

Matthew 14:14, 18, 19b, 20

READ MORE ABOUT IT: Matthew 9:36

> Draw something besides food that you think Jesus could multiply.

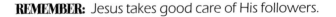

REMEMBER: Jesus takes good care of His followers.

Jesus and the Fierce Storm

One day Jesus said to his disciples, "Let's go over to the other side of the lake." So they got into a boat and set out. As they sailed, he fell asleep. A squall came down on the lake, so that the boat was being swamped, and they were in great danger.

The disciples went and woke him, saying, "Master, Master, we're going to drown!"

He got up and rebuked the wind and the raging waters; the storm subsided, and all was calm. "Where is your faith?" he asked his disciples.

In fear and amazement they asked one another, "Who is this? He commands even the winds and the water, and they obey him."
Luke 8:22-25

READ MORE ABOUT IT: John 1:1-4

PRAY ABOUT IT: Have there been things happening in your life that make you feel scared and upset? Do you sometimes feel as if there's a big storm building up inside you? Pray and ask Jesus to help you be peaceful even if bad things are happening all around you.

REMEMBER: Jesus, the Creator, can calm a terrible storm. There is nothing He can't do.

When Jesus came to the region of Caesarea Philippi, he asked his disciples, "Who do people say the Son of Man is?"

They replied, "Some say John the Baptist; others say Elijah; and still others, Jeremiah or one of the prophets."

"But what about you?" he asked. "Who do you say I am?"

Simon Peter answered, "You are the Christ, the Son of the living God."

Jesus replied, "Blessed are you, Simon son of Jonah, for this was not revealed to you by man, but by my Father in heaven. And I tell you that you are Peter, and on this rock I will build my church, and the gates of Hades will not overcome it."
Matthew 16:13-18

READ MORE ABOUT IT: 1 Peter 3:18

the Christ:
the Messiah, the one God had promised would come and save His people

TRY IT!

Take a survey of people at school, in your neighborhood, or at a mall. Ask people who they think Jesus is: (a) a very good person, (b) a wise teacher, (c) the Son of God who came to save us from our sins, (d) other (have them tell you what they think). Then ask if you can tell them what you believe. Add up the number of people who gave each answer.

REMEMBER: Jesus is not just a good person or wise teacher. He is God who became a man to save us from our sins.

A Dazzling Mountaintop Experience

Jesus took Peter, James and John with him and led them up a high mountain, where they were all alone. There he was transfigured before them. His clothes became dazzling white, whiter than anyone in the world could bleach them. And there appeared before them Elijah and Moses, who were talking with Jesus.

Peter said to Jesus, "Rabbi, it is good for us to be here. Let us put up three shelters—one for you, one for Moses and one for Elijah." (He did not know what to say, they were so frightened.) Then a cloud appeared and enveloped them, and a voice came from the cloud: "This is my Son, whom I love. Listen to him!"
Mark 9:2-7

MEMORIZE IT!

The Word became flesh and made his dwelling among us. We have seen his glory, the glory of the One and Only, who came from the Father, full of grace and truth.
John 1:14

transfigured:
changed

READ MORE ABOUT IT:
Isaiah 48:11

REMEMBER: Jesus is not an ordinary man. He's the Son of God. Listen to Him.

When they came to the crowd, a man approached Jesus and knelt before him. "Lord, have mercy on my son," he said. "He has seizures and is suffering greatly. He often falls into the fire or into the water. I brought him to your disciples, but they could not heal him."

"O unbelieving and perverse generation," Jesus replied, "how long shall I stay with you? How long shall I put up with you? Bring the boy here to me." Jesus rebuked the demon, and it came out of the boy, and he was healed from that moment.

Then the disciples came to Jesus in private and asked, "Why couldn't we drive it out?"

He replied, "Because you have so little faith. I tell you the truth, if you have faith as small as a mustard seed, you can say to this mountain, 'Move from here to there' and it will move. Nothing will be impossible for you."   Matthew 17:14-20

READ MORE ABOUT IT: John 14:12-13

WRITE ABOUT IT: Is there something you need or need to do that seems as impossible as moving a mountain? Write it here. Then ask God to give you the faith to believe He can do it if that's what is best for you.

_____

_____

REMEMBER: Faith is believing that when God says something, He will do it.

Don't Give Up–Keep Praying!

Then [Jesus] said to them, "Suppose one of you has a friend, and he goes to him at midnight and says, 'Friend, lend me three loaves of bread, because a friend of mine on a journey has come to me, and I have nothing to set before him.'

"Then the one inside answers, 'Don't bother me. The door is already locked, and my children are with me in bed. I can't get up and give you anything.' I tell you,... because of the man's boldness he will get up and give him as much as he needs.

"So I say to you: Ask and it will be given to you; seek and you will find; knock and the door will be opened to you. For everyone who asks receives; he who seeks finds; and to him who knocks, the door will be opened." Luke 11:5-10

READ MORE ABOUT IT: Luke 18:1-8

Draw someone or something you have prayed for.

REMEMBER: God wants us to keep asking until He answers.

An argument started among the disciples as to which of them would be the greatest. Jesus, knowing their thoughts, took a little child and had him stand beside him. Then he said to them, "Whoever welcomes this little child in my name welcomes me; and whoever welcomes me welcomes the one who sent me. For he who is least among you all—he is the greatest."

People were bringing little children to Jesus to have him touch them, but the disciples rebuked them. When Jesus saw this, he was indignant. He said to them, "Let the little children come to me, and do not hinder them, for the kingdom of God belongs to such as these. I tell you the truth, anyone who will not receive the kingdom of God like a little child will never enter it." And he took the children in his arms, put his hands on them and blessed them.
Luke 9:46-48; Mark 10:13-16

READ MORE ABOUT IT: Psalm 103:13, 17

Imagine that you are one of the children who had come to see Jesus that day with their parents. You listen to Him tell people to have faith in Him like a little child. Then with a big smile, He reaches over and gives you a big hug. Think of how safe and happy you would feel in Jesus' arms.

REMEMBER: No one is too young or too little or too unimportant for Jesus to love.

What Do You Care About Most?

A certain ruler asked Jesus, "Good teacher, what must I do to inherit eternal life?"

"Why do you call me good?" Jesus answered. "No one is good—except God alone. You know the commandments: 'Do not commit adultery, do not murder, do not steal, do not give false testimony, honor your father and mother.'"

"All these I have kept since I was a boy," he said.

When Jesus heard this, he said to him, "You still lack one thing. Sell everything you have and give to the poor, and you will have treasure in heaven. Then come, follow me."

When he heard this, he became very sad, because he was a man of great wealth.
Luke 18:18-23

READ MORE ABOUT IT: Exodus 20:3

TALK ABOUT IT!

Do you think you could keep all ten of God's commandments perfectly—even for a day—even in your thoughts? The man in this story thought so, but he had fooled himself, hadn't he? Which commandment had he broken if his money was more important to him than God?

304

REMEMBER: Don't let your money or the things you own become more important than God.

Jesus looked at him and said, "How hard it is for the rich to enter the kingdom of God! Indeed, it is easier for a camel to go through the eye of a needle than for a rich man to enter the kingdom of God."

Those who heard this asked, "Who then can be saved?"

Jesus replied, "What is impossible with men is possible with God."

Peter said to him, "We have left all we had to follow you!"

"I tell you the truth," Jesus said to them, "no one who has left home or wife or brothers or parents or children for the sake of the kingdom of God will fail to receive many times as much in this age and, in the age to come, eternal life."
Luke 18:24-30

READ MORE ABOUT IT: Matthew 22:37-40

TRY IT!

Look up camels in an encyclopedia and find out how tall an average camel is. Then, do some figuring. If a needle is about six times longer than its eye (the hole the thread or yarn goes through), how big would the needle have to be for a camel to go through the eye of that needle? (Ask a family member or friend for help if you don't know how to multiply yet.)

REMEMBER: God is pleased when we don't get too attached to things.

Now there was a man...named Nicodemus, a member of the Jewish ruling council. He came to Jesus at night and said, "Rabbi, we know you are a teacher who has come from God. For no one could perform the miraculous signs you are doing if God were not with him."

In reply Jesus declared, "I tell you the truth, no one can see the kingdom of God unless he is born again."

"How can a man be born when he is old?" Nicodemus asked.

[Jesus answered,] "Flesh gives birth to flesh, but the Spirit gives birth to spirit. You should not be surprised at my saying, 'You must be born again.'"
John 3:1-4a, 6-7

READ MORE ABOUT IT: 2 Corinthians 5:17

306

REMEMBER: When we put our trust in Jesus as the Savior for our sins, it's like starting all over again. Now we can live for Him instead of ourselves.

Jesus entered Jericho and was passing through. A man was there by the name of Zacchaeus; he was a chief tax collector and was wealthy. He wanted to see who Jesus was, but being a short man he could not, because of the crowd. So he ran ahead and climbed a sycamore-fig tree to see him, since Jesus was coming that way.

When Jesus reached the spot, he looked up and said to him, "Zacchaeus, come down immediately. I must stay at your house today." So he came down at once and welcomed him gladly.

Zacchaeus stood up and said to the Lord, "Look, Lord! Here and now I give half of my possessions to the poor, and if I have cheated anybody out of anything, I will pay back four times the amount."

Jesus said to him, "Today salvation has come to this house.... For the Son of Man came to seek and to save what was lost."
Luke 19:1-6, 8-10

READ MORE ABOUT IT: Leviticus 6:2-4

PRAY ABOUT IT: Is there someone you have cheated or wronged in some way? Ask God to forgive you and to help you make things right. If at all possible, set things straight today.

REMEMBER: When we make things right, we show that we are truly sorry for what we have done wrong.

Jesus and the Expensive Perfume

OCTOBER 31

While Jesus was in Bethany in the home of a man known as Simon the Leper, a woman came to him with an alabaster jar of very expensive perfume, which she poured on his head as he was reclining at the table.

When the disciples saw this, they were indignant. "Why this waste?" they asked. "This perfume could have been sold at a high price and the money given to the poor."

Aware of this, Jesus said to them, "Why are you bothering this woman?

She has done a beautiful thing to me. The poor you will always have with you, but you will not always have me. When she poured this perfume on my body, she did it to prepare me for burial. I tell you the truth, wherever this gospel is preached throughout the world, what she has done will also be told, in memory of her."
Matthew 26:6-13

READ MORE ABOUT IT: John 12:1-11

alabaster: a beautiful stone that looks something like marble

WRITE ABOUT IT: In Bible times when people died, the body was wrapped in cloths with spices and sweet fragrances tucked inside. Jesus knew He was about to be killed and that those who prepared His body wouldn't have time to get all the spices needed. So this woman's fragrant gift was a special gift of worship. How will you worship the Lord Jesus today? Write it here and then do it.

308

REMEMBER: God is very pleased when we worship Him.

A Donkey Colt for Jesus?

As [Jesus] approached...the hill called the Mount of Olives, he sent two of his disciples, saying to them, "Go to the village ahead of you, and as you enter it, you will find a colt tied there, which no one has ever ridden. Untie it and bring it here. If anyone asks you, 'Why are you untying it?' tell him, 'The Lord needs it.'"

Those who were sent ahead went and found it just as he had told them. As they were untying the colt, its owners asked them, "Why are you untying the colt?"

They replied, "The Lord needs it."

They brought it to Jesus, threw their cloaks on the colt and put Jesus on it. As he went along, people spread their cloaks on the road.   Luke 19:29-36

READ MORE ABOUT IT: John 12:12-19

If you could have chosen a ride into Jerusalem for Jesus, what would it have been (a camel? a chariot? something else?)? Draw it here.

REMEMBER: *Jesus is God. And God knows everything. That's how Jesus knew where His disciples would find a donkey.*

Page 1

An angel of the Lord told some shepherds that the Savior had been born in Bethlehem. When the shepherds got there, they found the baby wrapped in cloths just as the angel had said. One or more of the shepherds may have been about your age. They all praised God for sending our Savior, the Lord Jesus Christ. (See September 23 and December 24.)

Page 2

Jesus welcomed children to be with Him. (See October 26.) If you were with Him and could ask Him any question, what would you ask?

Page 3

One day a girl was very sick, and her father begged Jesus to come and heal her. But by the time they got to the house, the girl was dead. Jesus told the people to believe, and she would be healed. Then He took the girl's hand and spoke to her, and she came back to life! (See October 13.)

Pages 4 and 5

Jesus performed a miracle by feeding over 5,000 people with one little boy's lunch. (See October 20.) If you were going to share your lunch with Jesus, what would you give him? Draw it here.

Page 6

One day a crowd heard that Jesus was coming to Jerusalem. Children and adults ran out and gathered up palm branches. They waved them in the air and cheered as Jesus rode by. (See November 2.)

Page 7

It was a sad day when Jesus was crucified. But when Jesus was nailed to the cross, He took God's punishment for our sin so we could be forgiven. (See April 21 and November 6-7.) It was a sad-happy day when Jesus died. And that's not the end of the story...

Page 8

After three days in the tomb, Jesus came back to life again. He isn't still on the cross. He isn't still in the tomb. Jesus is stronger than death. He came back to life to give us new life through Him. (See April 22-23 and November 8.)

News of His resurrection spread fast, and curious children probably went out to investigate the empty tomb. How do you think they explained the empty tomb to each other?

When [Jesus] came near the place where the road goes down the Mount of Olives, the whole crowd of disciples began joyfully to praise God in loud voices for all the miracles they had seen:

"Blessed is the king who comes in the name of the Lord!"

"Peace in heaven and glory in the highest!"

Some of the Pharisees in the crowd said to Jesus, "Teacher, rebuke your disciples!"

"I tell you," he replied, "if they keep quiet, the stones will cry out."

As he approached Jerusalem and saw the city, he wept over it and said, "If you, even you, had only known on this day what would bring you peace– but now it is hidden from your eyes." Luke 19:37-42

READ MORE ABOUT IT: Psalm 145:21; 148:1-13

WRITE ABOUT IT: If the people hadn't cried out praises to Jesus, He said the rocks would have. Think of what a rock might want to say in praise of Jesus, the Creator. Write it here.

_____

_____

REMEMBER: Keep praising Jesus, the Creator and the One who gives us His peace.

Who Would Betray Jesus?

Then one of the Twelve—the one called Judas Iscariot—went to the chief priests and asked, "What are you willing to give me if I hand [Jesus] over to you?" So they counted out for him thirty silver coins. From then on Judas watched for an opportunity to hand him over.

On the first day of the Feast of Unleavened Bread, the disciples came to Jesus and asked, "Where do you want us to make preparations for you to eat the Passover?"

He replied, "Go into the city to a certain man and tell him, 'The Teacher says: My appointed time is near. I am going to celebrate the Passover with my disciples at your house.'" So the disciples did as Jesus had directed them and prepared the Passover.

When evening came, Jesus was reclining at the table with the Twelve. And while they were eating, he said, "I tell you the truth, one of you will betray me."   Matthew 26:14-21

READ MORE ABOUT IT: Luke 22:1-6

> Imagine that you are Judas, sitting at the dinner table with Jesus and His other friends. You have already decided to turn in Jesus to those who want to kill Him. But you think nobody else knows what you've decided. How do you feel when Jesus says, "One of you will betray me"?

312

REMEMBER: Jesus is pleased when we are friends He can count on.

They went to a place called Gethsemane, and Jesus said to his disciples, "Sit here while I pray." He took Peter, James and John along with him, and he began to be deeply distressed and troubled. "My soul is overwhelmed with sorrow to the point of death," he said to them. "Stay here and keep watch."

Going a little farther, he fell to the ground and prayed that if possible the hour might pass from him. *"Abba,* Father," he said, "everything is possible for you. Take this cup from me. Yet not what I will, but what you will."

Then he returned to his disciples and found them sleeping. "Simon," he said to Peter, "are you asleep? Could you not keep watch for one hour? Watch and pray so that you will not fall into temptation. The spirit is willing, but the body is weak."
Mark 14:32-38

MEMORIZE IT!

Watch and pray
so that you will not
fall into temptation.
The spirit is willing,
but the body is weak.
Mark 14:38

READ MORE ABOUT IT: Colossians 4:2

REMEMBER: We need to pray often that the Lord will help us stay faithful to Him and not give in to temptation.

Judas and Peter Let Jesus Down

NOVEMBER 5

While [Jesus] was still speaking a crowd came up, and the man who was called Judas, one of the Twelve, was leading them. He approached Jesus to kiss him, but Jesus asked him, "Judas, are you betraying the Son of Man with a kiss?"

Then seizing him, they led him away and took him into the house of the high priest. Peter followed at a distance. But when they had kindled a fire in the middle of the courtyard and had sat down together, Peter sat down with them. A servant girl saw him seated there in the firelight. She looked closely at him and said, "This man was with him."

But he denied it. "Woman, I don't know him," he said.
Luke 22:47-48, 54-57

READ MORE ABOUT IT: Mark 14:43-50

TALK ABOUT IT!

Judas betrayed Jesus. Peter denied Him. They both let Him down. What are some ways people can betray Jesus? What if others are saying mean things about Jesus or other Christians? Can you think of other ways? What are some situations in which we might be tempted to deny Jesus as Peter did? What can we do if we get caught up in this?

REMEMBER: Stand up for Jesus and other Christians, no matter what people say or do.

The chief priests and the whole Sanhedrin were looking for evidence against Jesus so that they could put him to death, but they did not find any. Many testified falsely against him, but their statements did not agree.

Again the high priest asked him, "Are you the Christ, the Son of the Blessed One?"

"I am," said Jesus. "And you will see the Son of Man sitting at the right hand of the Mighty One and coming on the clouds of heaven."

The high priest tore his clothes. "Why do we need any more witnesses?" he asked. "You have heard the blasphemy. What do you think?"

They all condemned him as worthy of death. Then some began to spit at him; they blindfolded him, struck him with their fists, and said, "Prophesy!" And the guards took him and beat him.   Mark 14:55-56, 61b-65

READ MORE ABOUT IT: 1 Samuel 12:24

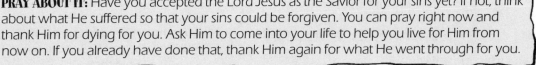

PRAY ABOUT IT: Have you accepted the Lord Jesus as the Savior for your sins yet? If not, think about what He suffered so that your sins could be forgiven. You can pray right now and thank Him for dying for you. Ask Him to come into your life to help you live for Him from now on. If you already have done that, thank Him again for what He went through for you.

REMEMBER: If you believe that Jesus died to take away your sins, He will give you eternal life in heaven with Him someday.

315

Today They Crucify Him!

When they came to the place called the Skull, there they crucified Jesus, along with the criminals—one on his right, the other on his left. Jesus said, "Father, forgive them, for they do not know what they are doing." And they divided up his clothes by casting lots.

It was now about the sixth hour, and darkness came over the whole land until the ninth hour, for the sun stopped shining.

Jesus called out with a loud voice, "Father, into your hands I commit my spirit." When he had said this, he breathed his last.

At that moment the curtain of the temple was torn in two from top to bottom. The earth shook and the rocks split.

When the centurion and those with him who were guarding Jesus saw the earthquake and all that had happened, they were terrified, and exclaimed, "Surely he was the Son of God!"

Luke 23:33-34, 44-45a, 46; Matthew 27:51, 54

READ MORE ABOUT IT: Psalm 22

Imagine that you are sitting with the crowd, watching Jesus hang on the cross. Most people don't understand what it's all about, but you do. How do you feel? You know Jesus has to die to pay the penalty for all our sins. But it hurts you so much to watch Him suffer. Tell Jesus how you feel about what He did for you.

REMEMBER: Jesus took the punishment for the sins of the whole world. Jesus died for you.

When the Sabbath was over, Mary Magdalene, Mary the mother of James, and Salome bought spices so that they might go to anoint Jesus' body. Very early on the first day of the week, just after sunrise, they were on their way to the tomb and they asked each other, "Who will roll the stone away from the entrance of the tomb?"

But when they looked up, they saw that the stone, which was very large, had been rolled away. As they entered the tomb, they saw a young man dressed in a white robe sitting on the right side, and they were alarmed.

"Don't be alarmed," he said. "You are looking for Jesus the Nazarene, who was crucified. He has risen! He is not here. See the place where they laid him. But go, tell his disciples and Peter." Mark 16:1-7a

READ MORE ABOUT IT: John 20:1-9

Draw what you think the angel or messenger looked like.

REMEMBER: Because Jesus died but came alive again, He can give new life to all who believe in Him.

The Disciples See Their Master Again

On the evening of that first day of the week, when the disciples were together, with the doors locked for fear of the Jews, Jesus came and stood among them and said, "Peace be with you!" After he said this, he showed them his hands and side. The disciples were overjoyed when they saw the Lord.

Again Jesus said, "Peace be with you! As the Father has sent me, I am sending you."

Jesus did many other miraculous signs in the presence of his disciples, which are not recorded in this book. But these are written that you may believe that Jesus is the Christ, the Son of God, and that by believing you may have life in his name.
John 20:19-21, 30-31

READ MORE ABOUT IT: 1 Corinthians 15:3-8

TRY IT!

Today tell someone you know about Jesus—the one who died for our sins, came back to life, and showed himself to over 500 people to prove that He really was alive! It's exciting, isn't it?

REMEMBER: Jesus is alive! And He is working in your life if you have accepted Him as your Savior.

The eleven disciples went to Galilee, to the mountain where Jesus had told them to go. When they saw him, they worshiped him; but some doubted. Then Jesus came to them and said, "All authority in heaven and on earth has been given to me. Therefore go and make disciples of all nations, baptizing them in the name of the Father and of the Son and of the Holy Spirit, and teaching them to obey everything I have commanded you. And surely I am with you always, to the very end of the age."

You will receive power when the Holy Spirit comes on you; and you will be my witnesses in Jerusalem, and in all Judea and Samaria, and to the ends of the earth.
Matthew 28:16-20; Acts 1:8

READ MORE ABOUT IT: 1 Corinthians 15:58; Philemon 6

REMEMBER: Our assignment is to tell others about Jesus.

MEMORIZE IT!

> Therefore go and make disciples of all nations, baptizing them in the name of the Father and of the Son and of the Holy Spirit, and teaching them to obey everything I have commanded you. And surely I am with you always, to the very end of the age.
> **Matthew 28:19-20**

319

Jesus Is Taken Up into Heaven

"This is what is written: The Christ will suffer and rise from the dead on the third day, and repentance and forgiveness of sins will be preached in his name to all nations, beginning at Jerusalem," [Jesus told them]. "You are witnesses of these things. I am going to send you what my Father has promised; but stay in the city until you have been clothed with power from on high."

When he had led them out to the vicinity of Bethany, he lifted up his hands and blessed them. While he was blessing them, he left them and was taken up into heaven. Then they worshiped him and returned to Jerusalem with great joy. And they stayed continually at the temple, praising God.

Luke 24:46-53

READ MORE ABOUT IT: Acts 1:1-11

PRAY ABOUT IT: Jesus' disciples worshiped Him after He went back to heaven. Talk to God today and tell Him how great He is to have sent Jesus to us.

REMEMBER: Jesus returned to heaven to be with God the Father. But Jesus is coming again for us someday.

When the day of Pentecost came, the believers were all together in one place. Suddenly a sound like the blowing of a violent wind came from heaven and filled the whole house where they were sitting. They saw what seemed to be tongues of fire that separated and came to rest on each of them. All of them were filled with the Holy Spirit and began to speak in other tongues as the Spirit enabled them.

Now there were staying in Jerusalem God-fearing Jews from every nation under heaven. When they heard this sound, a crowd came together in bewilderment, because each one heard them speaking in his own language. Amazed and perplexed, they asked one another, "What does this mean?"

Some, however, made fun of them and said, "They have had too much wine." Acts 2:1-6, 12-13

READ MORE ABOUT IT: John 14:15-27

WRITE ABOUT IT: Jesus gave the gift of the Holy Spirit to His followers to comfort them, to help them learn more about Jesus, and to give them the strength to do great things for God. What would you like to do for God that you couldn't do without the Holy Spirit?

_____

_____

REMEMBER: Jesus gives His Holy Spirit to those who have trusted in Him as their Savior.

321

"What's Happening Here?"

Then Peter stood up with the Eleven, raised his voice and addressed the crowd: "Fellow Jews and all of you who live in Jerusalem, let me explain this to you; listen carefully to what I say. These men are not drunk, as you suppose. It's only nine in the morning! No, this is what was spoken by the prophet Joel:

"'In the last days, God says,
I will pour out my Spirit on all people.
Your sons and daughters will prophesy,
your young men will see visions,
your old men will dream dreams.
Even on my servants,
both men and women,
I will pour out my Spirit
in those days,
and they will prophesy.
And everyone who calls
on the name of the Lord
will be saved.'" Acts 2:14-18, 21

Imagine that you are in the crowd that day. You hear the strange sounds. Then above the noise you hear someone preaching about Jesus. You have studied the Scripture all your life, so you know the prophecy Peter quotes. Now it's happening. Don't you think you would want to follow Jesus, too?

READ MORE ABOUT IT: Joel 2:28-29

REMEMBER: The prophet Joel predicted the coming of the Holy Spirit who came to live in those who follow Jesus.

"Men of Israel, listen to this: Jesus of Nazareth was a man accredited by God to you by miracles, wonders and signs, which God did among you through him, as you yourselves know. This man was handed over to you by God's set purpose and foreknowledge; and you, with the help of wicked men, put him to death by nailing him to the cross. But God raised him from the dead, freeing him from the agony of death, because it was impossible for death to keep its hold on him.

"Therefore let all Israel be assured of this: God has made this Jesus, whom you crucified, both Lord and Christ."

When the people heard this, they were cut to the heart and said to Peter and the other apostles, "Brothers, what shall we do?"

Peter replied, "Repent and be baptized, every one of you, in the name of Jesus Christ for the forgiveness of your sins. And you will receive the gift of the Holy Spirit."
Acts 2:22-24, 36-38

READ MORE ABOUT IT: Romans 10:9-13

TALK ABOUT IT!

The word Lord means the master or the one who's in charge. What does it mean for Jesus to be Lord in our lives? How does it affect how we make choices? How does it affect how we act and what we say?

REMEMBER: Jesus wants to be our Lord.

The Crippled Beggar

One day Peter and John were going up to the temple at the time of prayer—at three in the afternoon. Now a man crippled from birth was being carried to the temple gate called Beautiful, where he was put every day to beg from those going into the temple courts. When he saw Peter and John about to enter, he asked them for money. Peter looked straight at him, as did John. Then Peter said, "Look at us!" So the man gave them his attention, expecting to get something from them.

Then Peter said, "Silver or gold I do not have, but what I have I give you. In the name of Jesus Christ of Nazareth, walk." Taking him by the right hand, he helped him up, and instantly the man's feet and ankles became strong. He jumped to his feet and began to walk. Then he went with them into the temple courts, walking and jumping, and praising God.
Acts 3:1-8

READ MORE ABOUT IT: Acts 3:9-16

WRITE ABOUT IT: God gave Peter and some of Jesus' other followers the ability to heal people as Jesus did. If you had been crippled from the time you were born and Jesus healed you, what is the first thing you would do now that you could walk? Write it here.

REMEMBER: God wants us to help people and tell them about Jesus.

"We Can't Stop Talking About Jesus!"

When [the rulers, elders and teachers of the law] saw the courage of Peter and John and realized that they were unschooled, ordinary men, they were astonished and they took note that these men had been with Jesus. "What are we going to do with these men?" they asked. "Everybody living in Jerusalem knows they have done an outstanding miracle, and we cannot deny it. But to stop this thing from spreading any further among the people, we must warn these men to speak no longer to anyone in this name."

Then they called them in again and commanded them not to speak or teach at all in the name of Jesus. But Peter and John replied, "Judge for yourselves whether it is right in God's sight to obey you rather than God. For we cannot help speaking about what we have seen and heard."

Acts 4:13, 16-20

READ MORE ABOUT IT: Jeremiah 20:9

REMEMBER: When people want you to do things that go against the teaching of the Bible, choose to obey God rather than people.

MEMORIZE IT!

You will receive power when the Holy Spirit comes on you; and you will be my witnesses in Jerusalem, and in all Judea and Samaria, and to the ends of the earth. **Acts 1:8**

325

Peter's Fantastic Escape

King Herod arrested some who belonged to the church, intending to persecute them.

So Peter was kept in prison, but the church was earnestly praying to God for him.

Peter was sleeping between two soldiers, bound with two chains. Suddenly an angel of the Lord appeared.... "Quick, get up!" he said, and the chains fell off Peter's wrists. Peter followed him out of the prison. They passed the first and second guards and came to the iron gate leading to the city. It opened for them by itself, and they went through it. When they had walked the length of one street, suddenly the angel left him.

Then Peter...said, "Now I know without a doubt that the Lord sent his angel and rescued me."
Acts 12:1b, 5, 6b, 7a, c, 9a, 10-11a

READ MORE ABOUT IT: Acts 12:1-4

Do you ever wish an angel would rescue you? Draw something you would like to be rescued from.

REMEMBER: God is all-powerful. Nothing is impossible for Him.

When [Peter's rescue] had dawned on him, he went to the house...where many people had gathered and were praying. Peter knocked at the outer entrance, and a servant girl named Rhoda came to answer the door. When she recognized Peter's voice, she was so overjoyed she ran back without opening it and exclaimed, "Peter is at the door!"

"You're out of your mind," they told her. When she kept insisting that it was so, they said, "It must be his angel."

But Peter kept on knocking, and when they opened the door and saw him, they were astonished. Peter motioned with his hand for them to be quiet and described how the Lord had brought him out of prison.
Acts 12:12-18

READ MORE ABOUT IT: James 5:13, 16

PRAY ABOUT IT: Did you ever pray about something that seemed impossible, and then when God did answer you could hardly believe it? Who do you know that is in trouble and needs God's help? Pray for that person today, and ask God to rescue that person as He rescued Peter. Then don't be surprised when God answers.

REMEMBER: God does answer prayer.

A Blinding Light from Heaven

Meanwhile, Saul was...breathing out murderous threats against the Lord's disciples. He went to the high priest and asked him for letters to the synagogues in Damascus, so that if he found any there who belonged to the Way, whether men or women, he might take them as prisoners to Jerusalem. As he neared Damascus on his journey, suddenly a light from heaven flashed around him. He fell to the ground and heard a voice say to him, "Saul, Saul, why do you persecute me?"

"Who are you, Lord?" Saul asked.

"I am Jesus, whom you are persecuting," he replied. "Now get up and go into the city, and you will be told what you must do."

Saul got up from the ground, but when he opened his eyes he could see nothing. For three days he was blind, and did not eat or drink anything. Acts 9:1-6, 8a, 9

Imagine that you are Saul. You love God so much that when you hear about this Jesus who seems to be starting up a new religion, you want to get rid of anyone who joins Him. How do you feel when all these scary things start happening? Does Jesus get your attention? Do you think you will want to follow Jesus now, or will you be afraid?

READ MORE ABOUT IT: Acts 26:1-23

REMEMBER: Saul's life changed so much that he even changed his name—to Paul. God can turn a person's whole life around.

In Damascus there was a disciple named Ananias. The Lord called to him in a vision, "Ananias!"

"Yes, Lord," he answered.

The Lord told him, "Go to the house of Judas on Straight Street and ask for a man from Tarsus named Saul, for he is praying. In a vision he has seen a man named Ananias come and place his hands on him to restore his sight."

Then Ananias went to the house and entered it. Placing his hands on Saul, he said, "Brother Saul, the Lord—Jesus, who appeared to you on the road as you were coming here—has sent me so that you may see again and be filled with the Holy Spirit." Immediately, something like scales fell from Saul's eyes, and he could see again. He got up and was baptized, and after taking some food, he regained his strength.

Saul spent several days with the disciples in Damascus. At once he began to preach in the synagogues that Jesus is the Son of God.
Acts 9:10-12, 17-20

READ MORE ABOUT IT: 1 Corinthians 15:1-8

TALK ABOUT IT!

Who is the last person you would think might become a follower of the Lord Jesus Christ? Are you willing to pray for him or her to come to know Christ? Can you find a friend or family member who will help you pray?

REMEMBER: God can save the most unlikely people.

The First Missionaries

In the church at Antioch there were prophets and teachers: Barnabas, Simeon called Niger, Lucius of Cyrene, Manaen (who had been brought up with Herod the tetrarch) and Saul [Paul]. While they were worshiping the Lord and fasting, the Holy Spirit said, "Set apart for me Barnabas and Saul for the work to which I have called them." So after they had fasted and prayed, they placed their hands on them and sent them off.

The two of them, sent on their way by the Holy Spirit, went down to Seleucia and sailed from there to Cyprus. When they arrived at Salamis, they proclaimed the word of God in the Jewish synagogues. John was with them as their helper.   Acts 13:1-5

READ MORE ABOUT IT: Acts 13:26-33

Think of a country where many people still need to hear the good news of Jesus' salvation. Find an encyclopedia or atlas and copy the shape of that country here.

330

REMEMBER: We can all be missionaries right where we live now.

In Lystra there sat a man crippled in his feet, who was lame from birth and had never walked. He listened to Paul as he was speaking. Paul looked directly at him, saw that he had faith to be healed and called out, "Stand up on your feet!" At that, the man jumped up and began to walk.

Then some Jews came from Antioch and Iconium and won the crowd over. They stoned Paul and dragged him outside the city, thinking he was dead.

But...he got up and went back into the city. The next day he and Barnabas left for Derbe.

They preached the good news in that city and won a large number of disciples. Then they returned to Lystra, Iconium and Antioch, strengthening the disciples and encouraging them to remain true to the faith. "We must go through many hardships to enter the kingdom of God," they said.   Acts 14:8-10, 19-22

READ MORE ABOUT IT: Acts 14:26-28

stoned: threw big rocks at him, trying to kill him

WRITE ABOUT IT: Has anyone ever done anything mean to you because you were talking about Jesus? If so, how did you react? If not, what do you think you would do? Write about it here.

_____

_____

REMEMBER: Some people may not like it when you stand up for God, but spread His good news anyway.

Jailhouse Earthquake

NOVEMBER 23

After [Paul and Silas] had been severely flogged, they were thrown into prison, and the jailer was commanded to guard them carefully.

About midnight Paul and Silas were praying and singing hymns to God, and the other prisoners were listening to them. Suddenly there was such a violent earthquake that the foundations of the prison were shaken. At once all the prison doors flew open, and everybody's chains came loose. The jailer...drew his sword and was about to kill himself because he thought the prisoners had escaped. But Paul shouted, "Don't harm yourself! We are all here!"

The jailer...fell trembling before Paul and Silas. He then brought them out and asked, "Sirs, what must I do to be saved?"

They replied, "Believe in the Lord Jesus, and you will be saved—you and your household."
Acts 16:22-23, 25-31

READ MORE ABOUT IT: Acts 16:32-34

MEMORIZE IT!

Believe in the Lord Jesus, and you will be saved—you and your household.
Acts 16:31

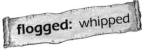
flogged: whipped

REMEMBER: The only way to be saved from your sins is to believe that Jesus died to take your punishment and came back to life to give you eternal life. Pass it on!

Give Thanks—For God's Care

Come, let us sing for joy to the LORD;
   let us shout aloud to the Rock of
      our salvation.
Let us come before him with
      thanksgiving
   and extol him with music
      and song.

For the LORD is the great God,
   the great King above all gods.
In his hand are the depths of the earth,
   and the mountain peaks belong
      to him.

The sea is his, for he made it,
   and his hands formed the dry land.

Come, let us bow down in worship,
   let us kneel before the LORD
      our Maker;
for he is our God
   and we are the people of
      his pasture,
   the flock under his care.
Psalm 95:1-7a

READ MORE ABOUT IT: Psalm 8

TRY IT!

Take out a sheet of paper and list all the things you can think of that God does to care for you every minute of every day. Think of everything it takes to keep your body working. List all the things He has made for you to enjoy. Keep adding to your list over the next few days and see how many things you can think of.

REMEMBER: Give thanks to God because He is powerful, but also because He is very loving.

Give Thanks—For God's Goodness

bestow: give

Give thanks to the LORD,
for he is good;
his love endures forever.
Let the redeemed of the LORD say this.

How great is your goodness,
which you have stored up for those
who fear you,
which you bestow in the sight of men
on those who take refuge in you.

Let them give thanks to the LORD for
his unfailing love

and his wonderful deeds for men,
for he satisfies the thirsty
and fills the hungry with good
things.
Psalms 107:1-2a; 31:19; 107:8-9

READ MORE ABOUT IT: Psalm 119:68

God takes care of birds too!

TALK ABOUT IT!

Talk with your family about the good gifts God has given you—a home where you feel safe? food to eat? the Bible? friends? grandparents? a pet to play with? toys? In what other ways is God good to you? Add these things to your list. How long is it now? Tape additional sheets of paper to the bottom of the first one if you need more room.

REMEMBER: Give thanks to God for all His goodness to you.

Shout for joy to the LORD, all the earth.
Worship the LORD with gladness;
   come before him with joyful songs.
Know that the LORD is God.
   It is he who made us, and we are his;
   we are his people, the sheep of his pasture.

Enter his gates with thanksgiving
   and his courts with praise;
   give thanks to him and praise his name.
For the LORD is good and his love endures forever;
   his faithfulness continues through all
generations.

Be joyful always; pray continually; give thanks
in all circumstances, for this is God's will for
you in Christ Jesus.
Psalm 100, 1 Thessalonians 5:16-18

READ MORE ABOUT IT: Psalm 34:1-3

REMEMBER: Never stop giving thanks to God.

Imagine that you see a girl drowning in a river. You jump in and pull her to shore. She has no family, so you take her into your home, buy her some clothes, and give her anything else she needs for the rest of her life. How would you feel if she never thanked you for anything you did for her? Do you think God feels that way about us sometimes?

Give Thanks—For God's Love and Peace

Give thanks to the LORD,
for he is good.
His love endures forever.
Give thanks to the God of gods.
His love endures forever.
Give thanks to the LORD of lords:
His love endures forever.

Whoever is wise, let him heed
these things
and consider the great love
of the LORD.

Great peace have they who love
your law,
and nothing can make
them stumble.

I will lie down and sleep in peace,
for you alone, O LORD,
make me dwell in safety.
Psalms 136:1-3; 107:43; 119:165; 4:8

READ MORE ABOUT IT: Psalm 101:1

dwell: live

PRAY ABOUT IT: Today, start going through your list of all the things God gives you and does for you, and thank Him for a few of those things every day. How long is your list now? Keep adding when you think of something.

336   **REMEMBER:** In everything you do, give thanks to God.

At once I was in the Spirit, and there before me was a throne in heaven with someone sitting on it.
A rainbow, resembling an emerald, encircled the throne.
In the center, around the throne, were four living creatures, and they were covered with eyes, in front and in back. Day and night they never stop saying:

> "Holy, holy, holy
> is the Lord God Almighty,
> who was, and is, and is to come."

The twenty-four elders fall down before him who sits on the throne and worship him who lives for ever and ever...and say:

"You are worthy, our Lord and God,
   to receive glory and honor and power,
Revelation 4:2, 3b, 6b, 8b, 10-11

READ MORE ABOUT IT: Revelation 4:4-6a

Imagine what these eye-covered creatures looked like, and draw one of them near God's throne. Don't forget the rainbow!

REMEMBER: Keep thanking God for all the many things, big and small, that He does for you.

Since, then, you have been raised with Christ, set your hearts on things above, where Christ is seated at the right hand of God.

Let the peace of Christ rule in your hearts, since as members of one body you were called to peace. And be thankful. Let the word of Christ dwell in you richly as you teach and admonish one another with all wisdom, and as you sing psalms, hymns and spiritual songs with gratitude in your hearts to God. And whatever you do, whether in word or deed, do it all in the name of the Lord Jesus, giving thanks to God the Father through him. Colossians 3:1-2, 15-17

READ MORE ABOUT IT: Ephesians 5:15-20

MEMORIZE IT!

And whatever you do, whether in word or deed, do it all in the name of the Lord Jesus, giving thanks to God the Father through him. **Colossians 3:17**

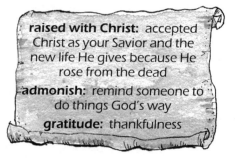

raised with Christ: accepted Christ as your Savior and the new life He gives because He rose from the dead

admonish: remind someone to do things God's way

gratitude: thankfulness

REMEMBER: We can bring glory to God in everything we do if we are thankful for all He has done for us.

There are different kinds of gifts, but the same Spirit. There are different kinds of service, but the same Lord. There are different kinds of working, but the same God works all of them in all men.

Now to each one the manifestation of the Spirit is given for the common good. All these are the work of one and the same Spirit, and he gives them to each one, just as he determines.

The body is a unit, though it is made up of many parts; and though all its parts are many, they form one body. So it is with Christ. For we were all baptized by one Spirit into one body—whether Jews or Greeks, slave or free—and we were all given the one Spirit to drink.
1 Corinthians 12:4-7, 11-13

READ MORE ABOUT IT: Romans 12:1-2, 5-8

TALK ABOUT IT!

Sometimes it is difficult for us to see our own special abilities. Talk to various members in your family about what kinds of talents or abilities they think God has given you. Ask them to suggest ways to use those gifts for Him.

REMEMBER: God gives special abilities to every person who trusts in Him. He wants us to use them to serve Him and to help others.

Now we know that if the earthly tent we live in is destroyed, we have a building from God, an eternal house in heaven, not built by human hands.
Therefore we are always confident and know that as long as we are at home in the body we are away from the Lord. We live by faith, not by sight. We are confident, I say, and would prefer to be away from the body and at home with the Lord. So we make it our goal to please him, whether we are at home in the body or away from it. For we must all appear before the judgment seat of Christ, that each one may receive what is due him for the things done while in the body, whether good or bad.
2 Corinthians 5:1, 6-10

READ MORE ABOUT IT: Philippians 1:20-26; 3:20-21

WRITE ABOUT IT: If we're trusting in Jesus, we don't have to be afraid of dying. Jesus is getting a new home ready for us in heaven. What are you looking forward to most in heaven? Write it here.

_____

_____

REMEMBER: We can know we are going to heaven if we've trusted in the Lord Jesus Christ as the Savior for our sin.

What You Plant Is What You Get

Do not be deceived: God cannot be mocked. A man reaps what he sows. The one who sows to please his sinful nature, from that nature will reap destruction; the one who sows to please the Spirit, from the Spirit will reap eternal life. Let us not become weary in doing good, for at the proper time we will reap a harvest if we do not give up. Therefore, as we have opportunity, let us do good to all people, especially to those who belong to the family of believers.

And God is able to make all grace abound to you, so that in all things at all times, having all that you need, you will abound in every good work.
Galatians 6:7-10; 2 Corinthians 9:8

READ MORE ABOUT IT: 2 Corinthians 9:6-15

PRAY ABOUT IT: Pray that the Lord will help you to do good things for others even when it's not easy. Ask Him to help you see things that need to be done. Ask Him to help you do them for the right reason—to please Him—not so that others will praise you.

REMEMBER: Never give up doing good things for God and others. The Lord will reward you for everything you do for Him.

341

Adopted!

Praise be to the God and Father of our Lord Jesus Christ, who has blessed us in the heavenly realms with every spiritual blessing in Christ. For he chose us in him before the creation of the world to be holy and blameless in his sight. In love he predestined us to be adopted as his sons through Jesus Christ, in accordance with his pleasure and will—to the praise of his glorious grace, which he has freely given us in the One he loves. In him we have redemption through his blood, the forgiveness of sins, in accordance with the riches of God's grace that he lavished on us with all wisdom and understanding.
Ephesians 1:3-8

READ MORE ABOUT IT:
John 1:10-13

Imagine that you are the Creator, and you want the people you've created to know how much you love them. You can't stand their sin, so you send your Son, Jesus, to die in their place. Then you tell them you'll adopt them into your family if they will put their trust in your Son. How will you feel when some people ignore your loving offer? How will you feel when some accept it?

REMEMBER: When we believe in Jesus, God adopts each one of us as His child.

Finally, be strong in the Lord and in his mighty power. Put on the full armor of God so that you can take your stand against the devil's schemes.

Stand firm then, with the belt of truth buckled around your waist, with the breastplate of righteousness in place, and with your feet fitted with the readiness that comes from the gospel of peace. In addition to all this, take up the shield of faith, with which you can extinguish all the flaming arrows of the evil one. Take the helmet of salvation and the sword of the Spirit, which is the word of God.

With this in mind, be alert and always keep on praying for all the saints.
Ephesians 6:10-11, 14-17, 18b

READ MORE ABOUT IT: Ephesians 6:12-13

> Draw yourself wearing the armor God wants you to put on. Put your name or initials on the shield.

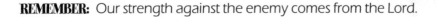

REMEMBER: Our strength against the enemy comes from the Lord.

What's Humility?

DECEMBER 5

selfish ambition and vain conceit: trying to make yourself look better than somebody else

humility: not proud

Do nothing out of selfish ambition or vain conceit, but in humility consider others better than yourselves. Each of you should look not only to your own interests, but also to the interests of others.

Your attitude should be the same as that of Christ Jesus:

Who, being in very nature God,
did not consider equality with
God something to be grasped,
but made himself nothing,
taking the very nature
of a servant,

being made in human likeness.
And being found in appearance
as a man,
he humbled himself
and became obedient to death—
even death on a cross!
Therefore God exalted him to the
highest place
and gave him the name that is
above every name.

Philippians 2:3-9

READ MORE ABOUT IT: 1 Peter 5:5-6;
Proverbs 27:2;
Micah 6:8

PRAY ABOUT IT: Pray that God will help you be a servant to others today without trying to get praise or compliments for yourself.

344

REMEMBER: We please God when we are willing to serve.

I want to know Christ and the power of his resurrection and the fellowship of sharing in his sufferings, becoming like him in his death, and so, somehow, to attain to the resurrection from the dead.

Not that I have already obtained all this, or have already been made perfect, but I press on to take hold of that for which Christ Jesus took hold of me. Brothers, I do not consider myself yet to have taken hold of it. But one thing I do: Forgetting what is behind and straining toward what is ahead, I press on toward the goal to win the prize for which God has called me heavenward in Christ Jesus.
Philippians 3:10-14

READ MORE ABOUT IT: Hebrews 12:1-3; Galatians 2:20

MEMORIZE IT!

Forgetting what is behind and straining toward what is ahead, I press on toward the goal to win the prize for which God has called me heavenward in Christ Jesus.
Philippians 3:13b-14

I'm moving toward the goal.

Where are you going?

REMEMBER: Get to know Jesus by reading the Bible.

Jesus Christ Is #1

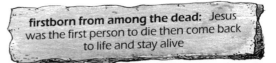

firstborn from among the dead: Jesus was the first person to die then come back to life and stay alive

Christ is the image of the invisible God, the firstborn over all creation. For by him all things were created: things in heaven and on earth, visible and invisible, whether thrones or powers or rulers or authorities; all things were created by him and for him. He is before all things, and in him all things hold together. And he is the head of the body, the church; he is the beginning and the firstborn from among the dead, so that in everything he might have the supremacy.

Once you were alienated from God and were enemies in your minds because of your evil behavior. But now he has reconciled you by Christ's physical body through death to present you holy in his sight, without blemish and free from accusation. Colossians 1:15-18, 21-22

READ MORE ABOUT IT: Hebrews 1:1-4

TALK ABOUT IT!

What are some ways we can be sure to make Jesus #1 in our lives? What might He have to compete with?

REMEMBER: Jesus deserves first place in our lives. And He doesn't want to share that position with anything or anyone. He is God.

We believe that Jesus died and rose again and so we believe that God will bring with Jesus those who have fallen asleep in him. According to the Lord's own word, we tell you that we who are still alive, who are left till the coming of the Lord, will certainly not precede those who have fallen asleep. For the Lord himself will come down from heaven, with a loud command, with the voice of the archangel and with the trumpet call of God, and the dead in Christ will rise first. After that, we who are still alive and are left will be caught up together with them in the clouds to meet the Lord in the air. And so we will be with the Lord forever. Therefore encourage each other with these words. 1 Thessalonians 4:14-18

fallen asleep in him: died physically but their spirits are with Jesus in heaven

archangel: a chief angel with special responsibilities

READ MORE ABOUT IT: 1 Thessalonians 5:1-6

WRITE ABOUT IT: What would you like Jesus to find you doing when He comes back? Write about it here.

_____

_____

REMEMBER: Jesus is coming soon. And He will take all those who believe in Him back to heaven with Him.

347

Good Work

We were not idle when we were with you, nor did we eat anyone's food without paying for it. On the contrary, we worked night and day, laboring and toiling so that we would not be a burden to any of you. We did this, not because we do not have the right to such help, but in order to make ourselves a model for you to follow. For even when we were with you, we gave you this rule: "If a man will not work, he shall not eat."

We hear that some among you are idle. They are not busy; they are busybodies. Such people we command and urge in the Lord Jesus Christ to settle down and earn the bread they eat. And as for you, brothers, never tire of doing what is right.
2 Thessalonians 3:7b-13

READ MORE ABOUT IT: 1 Thessalonians 4:11-12

TRY IT!

Do you have chores or responsibilities around the house? Do them cheerfully today without having to be reminded. Surprise your mom or dad and even do a little extra. Tell God you want to do it all for Him.

348

REMEMBER: Work cheerfully. It's another way we can serve God.

But godliness with contentment is great gain. For we brought nothing into the world, and we can take nothing out of it. But if we have food and clothing, we will be content with that. People who want to get rich fall into temptation and a trap and into many foolish and harmful desires that plunge men into ruin and destruction. For the love of money is a root of all kinds of evil. Some people, eager for money, have wandered from the faith and pierced themselves with many griefs.

Command those who are rich in this present world not to be arrogant nor to put their hope in wealth, which is so uncertain, but to put their hope in God, who richly provides us with everything for our enjoyment.
1 Timothy 6:6-10, 17

READ MORE ABOUT IT: Proverbs 11:24-26

Draw a way you would use your money for God if you were rich.

REMEMBER: If everything we have comes from God, shouldn't we be happy with what He gives us?

How the Scriptures Help Us

But mark this: There will be terrible times in the last days. People will be lovers of themselves, lovers of money, boastful, proud, abusive, disobedient to their parents, ungrateful, unholy, without love, unforgiving, slanderous, without self-control, brutal, not lovers of the good, treacherous, rash, conceited, lovers of pleasure rather than lovers of God—having a form of godliness but denying its power. Have nothing to do with them.

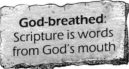

God-breathed: Scripture is words from God's mouth

But as for you, continue in what you have learned.... The holy Scriptures...are able to make you wise for salvation through faith in Christ Jesus. All Scripture is God-breathed and is useful for teaching, rebuking, correcting and training in righteousness, so that the man of God may be thoroughly equipped for every good work. 2 Timothy 3:1-5, 14-17

READ MORE ABOUT IT: Isaiah 40:8; Psalm 119:33-37

MEMORIZE IT!

All Scripture is God-breathed and is useful for teaching, rebuking, correcting and training in righteousness, so that the man of God may be thoroughly equipped for every good work.
2 Timothy 3:16-17

REMEMBER: All of Scripture has something to teach us. So keep reading the Bible.

Jesus Knows How It Feels

Therefore, since we have a great high priest who has gone through the heavens, Jesus the Son of God, let us hold firmly to the faith we profess. For we do not have a high priest who is unable to sympathize with our weaknesses, but we have one who has been tempted in every way, just as we are— yet was without sin. Let us then approach the throne of grace with confidence, so that we may receive mercy and find grace to help us in our time of need.

Because he himself suffered when he was tempted, he is able to help those who are being tempted.
Hebrews 4:14-16; 2:18

READ MORE ABOUT IT: Hebrews 5:7-9

WRITE ABOUT IT: In Bible times the high priest was the person who could offer sacrifices for sin in the temple. Jesus became our perfect once-for-all sacrifice for sin. When He came to live here on earth, He experienced everything we experience as humans—even Satan's temptation. When we're feeling sad or scared or happy or troubled, we can talk to a friend who has felt that same way—Jesus. Write about something in your life that you're glad Jesus understands.

REMEMBER: We can talk with Jesus about our troubles because He knows how we feel.

Faith Heroes

Now faith is being sure of what we hope for and certain of what we do not see. This is what the ancients were commended for.

By faith we understand that the universe was formed at God's command, so that what is seen was not made out of what was visible.

By faith Abel offered God a better sacrifice than Cain did. By faith he was commended as a righteous man, when God spoke well of his offerings. And by faith he still speaks, even though he is dead.

By faith Enoch was taken from this life, so that he did not experience death; he could not be found, because God had taken him away. For before he was taken, he was commended as one who pleased God. And without faith it is impossible to please God, because anyone who comes to him must believe that he exists and that he rewards those who earnestly seek him. Hebrews 11:1-6

commended: praised

READ MORE ABOUT IT: Hebrews 11:7-10

TALK ABOUT IT!

Do you need faith to believe in things you can see or touch or only things you can't? In your life, what kinds of things do you need faith for? to believe that God created the world? to believe that God will help you out of a tough situation? to trust that God knows what He's doing when nothing is going right? How can you strengthen your faith?

352 **REMEMBER:** Faith is believing that God keeps His promises.

By faith Abraham, when God tested him, offered Isaac as a sacrifice. He who had received the promises was about to sacrifice his one and only son, even though God had said to him, "It is through Isaac that your offspring will be reckoned." Abraham reasoned that God could raise the dead.

By faith Moses, when he had grown up, refused to be known as the son of Pharaoh's daughter. He chose to be mistreated along with the people of God rather than to enjoy the pleasures of sin for a short time. He regarded disgrace for the sake of Christ as of greater value than the treasures of Egypt, because he was looking ahead to his reward.

By faith the walls of Jericho fell, after the people had marched around them for seven days.
Hebrews 11:17-19a, 24-26, 30

READ MORE ABOUT IT: Hebrews 11:4-38

Go ahead, ask me something

TRY IT!

Read through the READ MORE ABOUT IT passage and decide who your favorite faith hero is. Then pretend you're a newspaper reporter, and make up some questions you would like to ask that person in an interview.

REMEMBER: We can trust God. He always keeps His promises. But sometimes we have to wait.

When Life Gets Tough

Consider it pure joy, my brothers, whenever you face trials of many kinds, because you know that the testing of your faith develops perseverance. Perseverance must finish its work so that you may be mature and complete, not lacking anything. If any of you lacks wisdom, he should ask God, who gives generously to all without finding fault, and it will be given to him. But when he asks, he must believe and not doubt, because he who doubts is like a wave of the sea, blown and tossed by the wind. That man should not think he will receive anything from the Lord; he is a double-minded man, unstable in all he does.

Blessed is the man who perseveres under trial, because when he has stood the test, he will receive the crown of life that God has promised to those who love him.
James 1:2-8, 12

READ MORE ABOUT IT: Romans 5:1-3

PRAY ABOUT IT: Are you going through some trials or tough times right now? Talk to God about them. Remember, He understands and wants to help. Don't rely on your own wisdom to solve your problems. Ask God to help you know what is best. If your life is going well right now, pray for someone you know who has problems.

REMEMBER: When things get tough, ask God for wisdom and help.

Not many of you should presume to be teachers, my brothers, because you know that we who teach will be judged more strictly. We all stumble in many ways. If anyone is never at fault in what he says, he is a perfect man, able to keep his whole body in check.

All kinds of animals, birds, reptiles and creatures of the sea are being tamed and have been tamed by man, but no man can tame the tongue. It is a restless evil, full of deadly poison.

With the tongue we praise our Lord and Father, and with it we curse men, who have been made in God's likeness. Out of the same mouth come praise and cursing. My brothers, this should not be.
James 3:1-2, 7-10

READ MORE ABOUT IT: Proverbs 10:19-20; 26:28

MEMORIZE IT!

Keep your tongue from evil and your lips from speaking lies.
Psalm 34:13

You'd better watch your language, buster!

REMEMBER: Your tongue can be a powerful weapon. Use it for good.

Everything Will Be All Right

new birth: believing in Jesus is like being born all over again—only this time spiritually

Praise be to the God and Father of our Lord Jesus Christ! In his great mercy he has given us new birth into a living hope through the resurrection of Jesus Christ from the dead, and into an inheritance that can never perish, spoil or fade—kept in heaven for you, who through faith are shielded by God's power until the coming of the salvation that is ready to be revealed in the last time.

In this you greatly rejoice, though now for a little while you may have had to suffer grief in all kinds of trials. These have come so that your faith—of greater worth than gold, which perishes even though refined by fire—may be proved genuine and may result in praise, glory and honor when Jesus Christ is revealed.
1 Peter 1:3-7

READ MORE ABOUT IT:
1 Peter 1:8-19; Colossians 1:3-6

Imagine that you have a rich elderly aunt. When she dies, you find out that she left you one million dollars! Her will says that some of that money must pay for your college education, and some for a small weekly allowance. The rest you get when you're 21 years old. That's a little bit like our spiritual inheritance—except we'll get the biggest part of it when we get to heaven instead of when we turn 21.

REMEMBER: Our salvation from sin is more valuable than money. And no one can ever take it away.

My dear children, I write this to you so that you will not sin. But if anybody does sin, we have one who speaks to the Father in our defense— Jesus Christ, the Righteous One. He is the atoning sacrifice for our sins, and not only for ours but also for the sins of the whole world.

We know that we have come to know him if we obey his commands. The man who says, "I know him," but does not do what he commands is a liar, and the truth is not in him. But if anyone obeys his word, God's love is truly made complete in him. This is how we know we are in him: Whoever claims to live in him must walk as Jesus did.
1 John 2:1-6

READ MORE ABOUT IT: 1 John 1:9

TALK ABOUT IT!

Once we accept Jesus as our Savior from sin, God does not punish us for those sins. Jesus already took our punishment. But God does want us to admit when we have sinned, to tell Him we're sorry. Why do you think He wants us to do that? When is the best time to confess your sins? Is there something you need to confess right now?

REMEMBER: When we confess our sins and ask Jesus for forgiveness, God does not punish us for those sins. Jesus has paid for them. But He wants us to confess them.

Love Your Heavenly Father

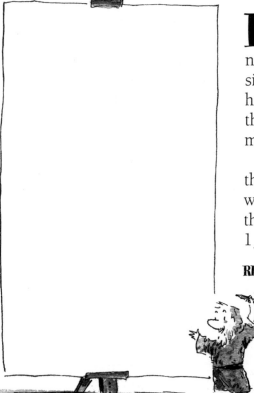

Do not love the world or anything in the world. If anyone loves the world, the love of the Father is not in him. For everything in the world—the cravings of sinful man, the lust of his eyes and the boasting of what he has and does—comes not from the Father but from the world. The world and its desires pass away, but the man who does the will of God lives forever.

How great is the love the Father has lavished on us, that we should be called children of God! And that is what we are! The reason the world does not know us is that it did not know him.
1 John 2:15-17; 3:1

READ MORE ABOUT IT: 1 John 5:1-5

lust:
evil desires

Draw something you might be tempted to love more than God.

REMEMBER: Nobody loves us more than God loves us. So don't waste your time on things that don't matter.

358

Many deceivers, who do not acknowledge Jesus Christ as coming in the flesh, have gone out into the world. Any such person is the deceiver and the antichrist. Watch out that you do not lose what you have worked for, but that you may be rewarded fully. Anyone who runs ahead and does not continue in the teaching of Christ does not have God; whoever continues in the teaching has both the Father and the Son. If anyone comes to you and does not bring this teaching, do not take him into your house or welcome him. Anyone who welcomes him shares in his wicked work.   2 John 7-11

deceiver: someone who tries to get you to believe something that's not true

antichrist: someone who pretends to be Christ or as great as Christ

READ MORE ABOUT IT: Acts 17:11

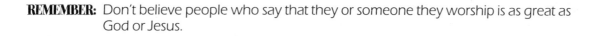

WRITE ABOUT IT: If someone started teaching you something about God that didn't sound right, what would be the best way to find out if it's true? (Hint: read the READ MORE ABOUT IT for today)

_____

_____

REMEMBER: Don't believe people who say that they or someone they worship is as great as God or Jesus.

Faith Muscle Building

Dear friends, although I was very eager to write to you about the salvation we share, I felt I had to write and urge you to contend for the faith that was once for all entrusted to the saints. For certain men whose condemnation was written about long ago have secretly slipped in among you. They are godless men, who change the grace of our God into a license for immorality and deny Jesus Christ our only Sovereign and Lord.

But you, dear friends, build yourselves up in your most holy faith and pray in the Holy Spirit. Keep yourselves in God's love as you wait for the mercy of our Lord Jesus Christ to bring you to eternal life.

Jude 3-4, 20-21

contend for the faith: stand up for what you believe about Jesus

READ MORE ABOUT IT: 1 Timothy 6:11-12

MEMORIZE IT!

Grow in the grace and knowledge of our Lord and Savior Jesus Christ. To him be glory both now and forever! Amen.
2 Peter 3:18

REMEMBER: Read the Bible and pay attention to those who will help you grow stronger in your faith.

"**B**lessed is she who has believed that what the Lord has said to her will be accomplished!"
And Mary said:

> "My soul glorifies the Lord
>   and my spirit rejoices in God my Savior,
> for he has been mindful
>   of the humble state of his servant.
> From now on all generations will call me blessed,
>   for the Mighty One has done great things for me—
>   holy is his name.
> His mercy extends to those who fear him,
>   from generation to generation."

Luke 1:45-50

READ MORE ABOUT IT: Luke 2:39-44, 51-56

Imagine that you are Mary or Joseph or one of the other people in the Christmas story. Imagine how excited you would be that you could be a part of what God was doing! For hundreds of years God's people had been looking forward to this One who would rescue them. And now it was happening!

REMEMBER: *Praise God for sending Jesus into the world to save us.*

Jesus—The Savior

The people walking in darkness
have seen a great light;
For to us a child is born,
to us a son is given,
and the government
will be upon his shoulders.
And he will be called
Wonderful Counselor, Mighty God,
Everlasting Father, Prince of Peace.
Of the increase of his government and
peace there will be no end.
He will reign on David's throne
and over his kingdom,

establishing and upholding it
with justice and righteousness
from that time on and forever.
The zeal of the LORD Almighty
will accomplish this.
Isaiah 9:2a, 6-7

READ MORE ABOUT IT: Luke 2:25-33

TALK ABOUT IT!

Talk about what our world would be like today if Jesus had never come. For example, the Red Cross and most hospitals were originally set up by Christians. Jesus taught us how to love and help one another. What else can you think of that we wouldn't have today if Jesus had not come?

REMEMBER: Jesus brings us wisdom, strength, peace, eternal life, and much more.

Jesus' Birthday

So Joseph also went up...to Bethlehem the town of David, because he belonged to the house and line of David. He went there to register with Mary, who was pledged to be married to him and was expecting a child. While they were there, the time came for the baby to be born, and she gave birth to her firstborn, a son. She wrapped him in cloths and placed him in a manger, because there was no room for them in the inn.

And there were shepherds living out in the fields nearby, keeping watch over their flocks at night. An angel of the Lord appeared to them, and the glory of the Lord shone around them, and they were terrified. But the angel said to them, "Do not be afraid. I bring you good news of great joy that will be for all the people. Today in the town of David a Savior has been born to you; he is Christ the Lord."   Luke 2:4-11

READ MORE ABOUT IT: Luke 2:12-20

TRY IT!

Jesus said that if we do kind things for others, it is as though we are doing them for Him. As a birthday present to Jesus, buy or collect some canned goods for a local food shelf, or do some other kind thing for those who are less fortunate than you. Get some friends to work together with you. It's more fun that way.

REMEMBER: Celebrate! Jesus came to save us.

After Jesus was born in Bethlehem in Judea, during the time of King Herod, Magi from the east came to Jerusalem and asked, "Where is the one who has been born king of the Jews? We saw his star in the east and have come to worship him."

Then Herod...sent them to Bethlehem.

After they had heard the king, they went on their way, and the star they had seen in the east went ahead of them until it stopped over the place where the child was. When they saw the star, they were overjoyed. On coming to the house, they saw the child with his mother Mary, and they bowed down and worshiped him. Then they opened their treasures and presented him with gifts of gold and of incense and of myrrh.
Matthew 2:1-2, 7-8a, 9-11

READ MORE ABOUT IT: 2 Corinthians 9:15; Romans 2:10-11

PRAY ABOUT IT: Christmas is usually an exciting day full of activity and fun. But before you go to bed tonight be sure to thank God for sending His Son into the world to save us from our sin so that we could live with Him in heaven some day. That's the greatest gift anyone could ever receive.

REMEMBER: Jesus is the greatest gift of all.

Jesus...looked toward heaven and prayed:

"I pray also for those who will believe in me through [the disciples'] message, that all of them may be one, Father, just as you are in me and I am in you.

"May they be brought to complete unity to let the world know that you sent me and have loved them even as you have loved me.

"Father, I want those you have given me to be with me where I am, and to see my glory, the glory you have given me because you loved me before the creation of the world.

"Righteous Father, I have made you known to them, and will continue to make you known in order that the love you have for me may be in them."
John 17:1a, 20b-21a, 23b-25a, 26a, b

READ MORE ABOUT IT: Psalm 133:1

TRY IT!

The Bible calls Jesus' followers brothers and sisters in Christ. And Jesus wants us to get along with one another. Is there another Christian who has hurt you or made you angry by something he or she said or did? Be the one to straighten things out—even if you think it's the other person's fault. Jesus will be pleased.

REMEMBER: Jesus want us to get along with other Christians.

God's Promise–New Heaven, New Earth

"**B**ehold, I will create
new heavens and a new earth.
The former things will not be remembered,
    nor will they come to mind.
For I will create Jerusalem to be a delight
    and its people a joy.
I will rejoice over Jerusalem
    and take delight in my people;
the sound of weeping and of crying
    will be heard in it no more.

The wolf and the lamb will feed together,
    and the lion will eat straw like the ox,
        but dust will be the serpent's food.
They will neither harm nor destroy
    on all my holy mountain," says the LORD.
Isaiah 65:17, 18b-19, 25

READ MORE ABOUT IT: Revelation 21:1, 4

Draw something that you think will be better in
the new heaven and new earth.

REMEMBER: Everything will be perfect in the new heaven and the
new earth.

The Glory Returns to Jerusalem

Then the man brought me to the gate facing east, and I saw the glory of the God of Israel coming from the east. His voice was like the roar of rushing waters, and the land was radiant with his glory. The glory of the Lord entered the temple through the gate facing east. Then the Spirit lifted me up and brought me into the inner court, and the glory of the Lord filled the temple.

While the man was standing beside me, I heard someone speaking to me from inside the temple. He said: "Son of man, this is the place of my throne and the place for the soles of my feet. This is where I will live among the Israelites forever."
Ezekiel 43:1-2, 4-7a

READ MORE ABOUT IT: Revelation 21:1, 3, 5

Imagine what it will be like to live in a perfect world with the Almighty God in charge. Imagine being able to see God with your eyes anytime you want to. Imagine being able to hear His voice with your ears. Imagine being able to talk to Him face-to-face!

REMEMBER: When God sets up His new kingdom, He will live with His people forever.

Judgment Day

I saw a great white throne and him who was seated on it. Earth and sky fled from his presence, and there was no place for them. And I saw the dead, great and small, standing before the throne, and books were opened. Another book was opened, which is the book of life. The dead were judged according to what they had done as recorded in the books. The sea gave up the dead that were in it, and death and Hades gave up the dead that were in them, and each person was judged according to what he had done. Then death and Hades were thrown into the lake of fire. The lake of fire is the second death. If anyone's name was not found written in the book of life, he was thrown into the lake of fire. Revelation 20:11-15

READ MORE ABOUT IT: Daniel 12:1-3

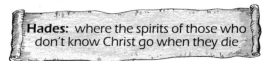

Hades: where the spirits of those who don't know Christ go when they die

TALK ABOUT IT!

Talk about what's happening here. Who do you think is sitting on the throne? What do you think the Book of Life is? (Hint: read John 5:24.) Where are those who are in the Book of Life? What is the lake of fire? Who will go there? Doesn't all this make you want to tell everyone you know about Jesus?

REMEMBER: People who do not believe in Jesus will be punished forever.

Then I saw a new heaven and a new earth, for the first heaven and the first earth had passed away, and there was no longer any sea. I saw the Holy City, the new Jerusalem, coming down out of heaven from God.

It shone with the glory of God, and its brilliance was like that of a very precious jewel.

The great street of the city was of pure gold, like transparent glass.

The city does not need the sun or the moon to shine on it, for the glory of God gives it light. On no day will its gates ever be shut, for there will be no night there. Nothing impure will ever enter it.

[God] will wipe every tear from their eyes. There will be no more death or mourning or crying or pain, for the old order of things has passed away. Revelation 21:1-2a, 11a, 21b, 23a, 25, 27a, 4

READ MORE ABOUT IT: 1 John 5:10-13

PRAY ABOUT IT: If you still haven't put your trust in Christ as your Savior from sin, wouldn't you like to do that right now? (See pages 372-373 for help.) If you already have, pray for friends of yours who won't get to spend eternity with Jesus if they don't trust in Him. And don't forget to thank Jesus again for all He has done for you. Tell Him you can't wait to see Him.

REMEMBER: Heaven is only for those who have accepted Christ's death on the cross as the payment for their sin.

Jesus Is Coming Soon!

DECEMBER **31**

"**B**ehold, I am coming soon! Blessed is he who keeps the words of the prophecy in this book.

"Behold, I am coming soon! My reward is with me, and I will give to everyone according to what he has done. I am the Alpha and the Omega, the First and the Last, the Beginning and the End."

The Spirit and the bride say, "Come!" And let him who hears say, "Come!" Whoever is thirsty, let him come; and whoever wishes, let him take the free gift of the water of life.

He who testifies to these things says, "Yes, I am coming soon."

Amen. Come, Lord Jesus.

The grace of the Lord Jesus be with God's people. Amen.
Revelation 22:7, 12-13, 17, 20-21

READ MORE ABOUT IT: Revelation 1:1-3

Alpha and Omega: the first and last letters in the Greek alphabet

the bride: another name for all those who have trusted Jesus to be their Savior

REMEMBER: Get excited! Jesus is coming again!

God's Plan of Salvation

1. GOD LOVES US

God loves us, and He knows we need Him to make our lives complete.

"For God so loved the world that he gave his one and only Son, that whoever believes in him shall not perish but have eternal life." John 3:16

2. WE ARE ALL SINNERS

No one in this world has ever been completely perfect except Jesus. We all do things that are wrong.

"For all have sinned and fall short of the glory of God." Romans 3:23

3. SIN COMES BETWEEN US AND GOD

"For the wages of sin is death..." Romans 6:23a

4. BUT GOD OFFERS US ETERNAL LIFE AS A GIFT

The Lord Jesus Christ came to this earth to give up His life to pay for our sin. Then He came back to life again to give us new life—eternal life.

"...but the gift of God is eternal life in Christ Jesus our Lord." Romans 6:23b

"It is by grace you have been saved, through faith—and this is not from yourselves, it is the gift of God—not by works, so that no one can boast." Ephesians 2:8-9

"I tell you the truth, whoever hears my word and believes him who sent me has eternal life and will not be condemned; he has crossed over from death to life." John 5:24

5. JESUS IS THE ONLY WAY TO HEAVEN

"Jesus answered, 'I am the way and the truth and the life. No one comes to the Father except through me.'" John 14:6

6. IF WE ACCEPT HIM, WE BECOME GOD'S CHILDREN

To accept or receive Him means we admit that we need someone to take away our sin, and we trust Jesus to do that for us. Jesus was both God and man. He had no sin of His own, so by dying for us, He could pay the death penalty we deserved for our sins.

"We all, like sheep, have gone astray, each of us has turned to his own way; and the LORD has laid on him the iniquity [sin] of us all." Isaiah 53:6

"To all who received him, to those who believed in his name, he gave the right to become children of God." John 1:12

7. WE CAN BE SURE WE HAVE ETERNAL LIFE

"I write these things to you who believe in the name of the Son of God so that you may know that you have eternal life." 1 John 5:13

"In my Father's house are many rooms; if it were not so, I would have told you. I am going there to prepare a place for you. And...I will come back and take you to be with me that you also may be where I am." John 14:2-3

8. DON'T LET SIN COME BETWEEN YOU AND GOD ANYMORE

Confess sin whenever you become aware of it.

"If we confess our sins, he is faithful and just and will forgive us our sins and purify us from all unrighteousness." 1 John 1:9

9. PASS ON THE GOOD NEWS

"That if you confess with your mouth, 'Jesus is Lord,' and believe in your heart that God raised him from the dead, you will be saved. For it is with your heart that you believe and are justified, and it is with your mouth that you confess and are saved." Romans 10:9-10

[Jesus said,] "Therefore go and make disciples of all nations, baptizing them in the name of the Father and of the Son and of the Holy Spirit; and teaching them to obey everything I have commanded you. And surely I will be with you always, to the very end of the age." Matthew 28:20

373

Glossary

Abba: the word for father or daddy in the Aramaic language

abhor: hate

abounding: overflowing

acknowledge Him: admit that you need God

admonish: remind someone to do things God's way

afflicted: hurting, troubled

alabaster: a beautiful stone that looks something like marble

alienate: turn away or make enemies of

Ancient of Days: God

anguish: pain, suffering

anoint: to dedicate someone to God by pouring special oil on that person

antichrist: someone who pretends to be Christ or as great as Christ

archangel: a chief angel with special responsibilities

ascend: go up

Asherah poles: wooden objects used in the worship of the false goddess Asherah (the "Lady of the Sea"), probably carved with her image

attended: took care of

avenge: get even, pay someone back for an evil deed

bestow: give

bear with each other: to be patient and not get angry if people do not do things your way

birthright: when a father died, the son with the birthright (usually the oldest) got the most possessions and became the leader of the family

blasphemy: claiming to be God

bride of Christ: all those who have

trusted in Jesus as their Savior are known together as the bride of Christ

calamity: disaster

Christ: the Messiah, the one God had promised would come and save His people

church: in the Bible, the church is made up of all those who have accepted Jesus Christ as the Savior for their sins

cistern: a large pit for catching rain water

citadel: a protected palace building

clean animals: animals that God allowed Jewish people to eat and to sacrifice

consume: destroy, use up, eat up

contempt: much disrespect

contend for the faith: stand up for what you believe about Jesus

covet: to want something someone else has

compassion: deep concern for people who are hurting or needy

deceiver: someone who tries to get you to believe something that's not true

deport: to send someone out of the country

despise: to hate or be mean to someone

diligence: keeping at it

discretion: ability to tell good from bad

dwell: live

edict: command

enmity: extreme hatred

Ephraim: one of Joseph's sons, also another way of referring to Israel

esteem: think highly of

eunuch: palace servant

exile: being kicked out of your country or land

expanse: wide open space

asleep in Christ: when a person is physically dead but that person's spirit is with Jesus in heaven

fat of rams: the sheep offered in sacrifice

to God

fear the Lord: give God the respect He deserves

firstborn from among the dead: Jesus, the first person to die then come back to life and stay alive

flog: whip

foreknowledge: knowing something before it happens

forsake: to turn a person's back on someone

futile: useless

galled him: irritated him

garland: a ring of flowers or leaves

gathered to their fathers: died

generation: people about the same age (Your parents belong to a different generation than you do. The children you may have someday will belong to the next generation)

goad: pointed stick used to make a big animal, such as an ox, move

God-breathed: Scripture is words from God's mouth

gratitude: thankfulness

grievances: things people do that bother others or make them angry

Hades: where the spirits of those who don't know Christ go when they die

harden your heart: ignore or refuse to listen to God

heed: pay attention (to what God wants)

high places: places where people worshiped false gods

holy: set apart to be and do what's right

humbly: the opposite of proudly

humility: not being proud, having the spirit of a servant

hyssop: a bushy, sweet-smelling plant that grew everywhere in Bible lands

ill-gotten gain: money or anything else people get illegally or unfairly

indignant: angry because something is unfair or not right

infirmities: weaknesses or flaws

iniquity: sin

integrity: determination to do what's right

kinsman-redeemer: a relative who would marry and take care of a widow

laden: loaded down

lame: unable to use arms or legs

last days: the time just before Jesus comes again

Levites: the people who took care of the Jewish place of worship

leprosy: a skin disease that eats away at a person's flesh

lust: evil desires

man of standing: a well-respected, important person in the community

manna: special bread God provided for Israel in the desert

meditate: spend time thinking about something

meditation: what a person thinks about

medium: someone who claims to be able to talk to dead people's spirits

Nazirites: people who promised in unusual ways to be set apart for God's service (one way was not to cut their hair)

new birth: believing in Jesus is like being born all over again—only this time spiritually

oath: promise, also sometimes used to mean swearing

oppress: treat cruelly

Passover: celebration of the time God delivered the Israelites from Egypt

parable: a story from everyday life that teaches spiritual truth

paralytic: a person who is paralyzed or can't move

Pentecost: a Jewish festival celebrated fifty days after Passover

persevere: to keep going no matter how rough the circumstances

Pharisees: a group of very religious Jews in Jesus' time

plunder: to take the possessions of others by force, or the things taken by force

precepts: laws or commandments

prophecy: the message of a prophet, often a prediction of things that will happen in the future

prophesy: to announce something important, often something that will happen in the future

prostrate: lying down flat on the stomach

prudent: careful or cautious

raised with Christ: having accepted Christ as Savior and accepting the new life He gives because He rose from the dead

recount: tell again

refiner: person who melts down metal and skims off impurities

repentance: turning a person's back on sin and choosing to live God's way

restitution: making things right

righteous: being fair and doing what's right

ruddy: having a healthy, reddish complexion

ruthless: cruel, showing no mercy

sackcloth: dark, rough-textured clothing people in Bible times wore when they were sorry for sin or were very sad

seek: look for, go after

seraphs: angel-like creatures

shrewd: clever

shun: avoid, stay away from

the simple: those who are not wise

slaughtered: killed

sovereign: a ruler, one who doesn't have

to take orders from anyone else

sow: to plant

steadfast: settled, faithful, unmovable

stiff-necked: stubborn

stone: to throw big rocks at someone, trying to kill

supremacy: first place, above everything else

sustain: to support

synagogue: a place where Jewish people worshiped after the temple was destroyed

thwarted: stopped

transfigured: changed

transgressions: sins

unclean animals: animals that God had forbidden Jewish people to eat or sacrifice

vengeance: getting even, paying back someone for an evil deed

venomous: poisonous

vow: a promise

womb: the place inside a mother where a baby grows

yearn: to want something very much